Praise for David Parker and *Slam Dun*

"I have personally benefited from Dave Parker's Slam Dunk technique, landing the job of my dreams in sustainable tech during an economic crisis. And now, he's opened up his secrets to the world! Don't miss your chance to learn from his remarkable wisdom."

DANA JENNINGS, Former Senior Project Manager, Global Sustainability, LinkedIn

"Dave Parker's book is a phenomenal tool that condenses the otherwise daunting task of a job search and packages it in a simple step-by-step process that is manageable and extremely effective. A 'must have' for all job seekers."

JAIME DIETENHOFER, President and Cofounder, Figueroa Mountain Brewing Co.

"Dave Parker is unmatched in his insights into navigating the stressful world of job seeking. He knows his stuff when it comes to helping job seekers secure their dream jobs. *Slam Dunk Job Search* is more than just a book of advice—it's a tried-and-true program that unlocks the hiring black box."

ERIN WILLIAMSON, Manager, Energy & Sustainability Strategy, Edison Energy

"While there have been many books written about finding the perfect job, few share the same level of empathy, motivation, and drive to propel the reader to take the necessary steps to proceed in confidence. I have no doubt that everyone will learn something valuable from Dave Parker's *Slam Dunk Job Search* book."

JOSH LEVINE, Senior Vice President, Wealth Management Company

"Dave Parker's guidance has been so influential to me and my career. The takeaways from his workshops, especially his *spot-on* interviewing tips, have helped me through two job searches that led to career-defining roles."

LOUISA MCGUIRK, Senior Manager Sustainable Procurement, Salesforce

"Dave Parker's use of powerful imagery, combined with actionable and tried-and-true tactics, makes *Slam Dunk Job Search* not just a reference, but a powerful tool that will be indispensable to anyone navigating the job search process."

JENNIFER DUBUISSON, Senior Director, Government and Public Affairs, Global Consumer Products Company

"*Slam Dunk Job Search* encapsulates the passion Dave Parker has for helping people find the best possible career—a meaningful career, and not just a job. His practical and comprehensive guide is just as effective for recent graduates as it is for experienced professionals seeking a mid-career change. Read Dave's book and see how you can land your ideal job and advance within your career."

JOTA SHOHTOKU, President, Asia Pacific-Global Insurance
and Reinsurance Solutions Company

"As a graduate student, Dave Parker's advice helped me land internships with four tech companies—ranging from small startups to large public companies—one of which turned into full-time employment. I wouldn't be at my dream job today without his career advice!"

MATT PANOPIO, Technical Product Manager, Energy & Carbon, Amazon

"Dave made me feel SO confident going into interviews. For one of my interviews, the hiring manager even said, 'Let's hire her!' after I gave an answer to one of the questions. I learned from the best! I am so glad to see his wealth of knowledge finally being made available to the public with the release of his first book *Slam Dunk Job Search*."

ALISAN THEODOSSIOU, Senior Communications Manager, California Trout

"*Slam Dunk Job Search* is a remarkable book! It outlines a step-by-step process to help you get the job you want and deserve. I would have landed my dream job much faster if I would have known about Dave Parker's six steps early in my career."

OWEN BARRETT, Founder & President, Rayven

"In *Slam Dunk Job Search*, Dave Parker breaks down the daunting task of finding (and landing) your dream job into a systematic, logical, doable process. Dave knows how to help you elevate your confidence, identify targets, and put your best self out there. I wouldn't have had the amazing experiences I've had in my career without Dave!"

ANNE MIDDLETON, Executive Director, ECOLIFE Conservation

"*Slam Dunk Job Search* takes job seekers out of their heads and into the real world, focusing on what it truly takes to win—a step that hurried job seekers often overlook. Dave Parker's book is an essential read for job seekers facing steep competition in a highly competitive job market."

LACRISSA DAVIS, Vice President and Chief Financial Officer, Rincon Consultants Inc.

"Dave Parker helped me land a great Fortune 500 job out of graduate school that has set me on a career path of growth and leadership. Almost 20 years later, I still lean on Dave's guidance and approach."

JOHN ONDERDONK, Associate Vice President, Facilities Management, Science and Engineering Institute

"Anyone who has had the good fortune of having Dave Parker as their career coach knows that his advice is good advice. Read this book, apply what you learn, and see the magic of Dave Parker."

MICHELLE GRAFF, Policy Analyst, United States Federal Government

"Speaking with Dave Parker has always led to pivotal moments in my career. He delivers the same level of insight, consideration, and generous enthusiasm in this book that he brings to every coaching session, leaving the reader excited to get in the game."

ELEANOR JOHNSTONE, Senior Project Manager, Gladstein Neandross & Associates

"Whereas most job search books leave you saying 'OK, that's great, but how?' Dave brings a refreshing measure of intentionality as he systematically guides the reader through proactive and proven strategies for an engaging, rewarding, and ultimately successful job search."

ANDREW BILICH, Data and Projects Manager, EarthSpark International

"I have no doubt that Dave Parker's *Slam Dunk Job Search* book will change how you approach your job search, turning what is an otherwise grueling experience into one that is both fun and incredibly effective!"

KAVITHA NAMBIAR, Senior Compliance Manager, Fortune 50 MNC Conglomerate

"I had the privilege of having Dave Parker personally help me land a job right out of grad school at a Fortune 500 company. Dave's insights will empower you to take the first steps on your new journey and prepare you for every stage of the process."

BRYAN HENSON, Founder and CEO, Bevyhouse

"The knowledge and insights shared in Dave Parker's *Slam Dunk Job Search* book will provide valuable guidance to anyone in search of an ideal job. It is an incredibly useful book filled with innovative and effective tips."

DR. ELISSA FOSTER, Former Head of Product Environmental Impact, Patagonia

"Dave Parker's career coaching helped me land my dream job! Now, he's assembled his innovative and practical tactics into an easy to understand approach that demystifies the job search process. *Slam Dunk Job Search* will give you the clarity and confidence you need to be competitive in any job market!"

LINDSAY BASS, Senior Management Analyst, City of Santa Cruz

"Dave Parker has personally guided me with a masterful hand through multiple career transitions and salary negotiations. *Slam Dunk Job Search* canonizes Dave's wisdom and gives you an approachable, tactical, and impactful guidebook for landing your dream job."

KELLEN KLEIN, Executive Director, Citizens4Community

"Before working with Dave, I never knew where to start with my job search. I was often left feeling frustrated and unmotivated. Dave's 6-Step Slam Dunk Job Search Process has completely shifted how I pursue jobs. In *Slam Dunk Job Search*, you'll not only learn how to efficiently and effectively make yourself stand out in the job market, but you'll also enjoy sharing your skills with others."

LILLIAN MIRVISS, Director, Government Affairs, Nonprofit Energy Advisory Services Organization

"Dave Parker's thoughtful, expert guidance was invaluable to me in successfully landing a job in a tough job market. If you're job-hunting and want the edge, I'd highly recommend buying *Slam Dunk Job Search*."

LENA MOFFITT, Executive Director, Evergreen Action

"Dave Parker's guidance helped me identify, negotiate, and secure a dream job offer that launched my career. He genuinely cares about helping job seekers succeed at their highest potential, as evidenced by the thoughtful, clear, and practical steps laid out in his book."

CAROLINE HOLMES, Senior Manager, Fortune 500 Retail Company

"Dave Parker is an expert in every aspect of the job search process, from developing connections to sealing the deal. I wouldn't be where I am today without his guidance. Everyone can learn something valuable from Dave, and I'm so glad he's sharing his toolkit with the world!"

ALIANA LUNGO-SHAPIRO, Manager, Financial Planning & Analysis, Colburn School

"It's great to see Dave Parker's 25+ years of job search tactics consolidated into one comprehensive book and multi-faceted approach for today's marketplace. Read it, use it, be confident, and the opportunities are limitless."

IAN ADAM, Principal, Fuscoe Engineering Inc.

"As a career changer at age 30, I followed Dave's step-by-step process and ended up with three job offers from three highly desirable organizations. I can't thank him enough for all of his help, and you will too after you have read this book and followed Dave's advice."

STACY KATZ, Project Director, WSP

"If you want to know how to stand out and land your ideal job, follow every step outlined in Dave's *Slam Dunk Job Search* book!"

JASON PEERY, Resident Managing Director, Executive Vice President, Aon

"Dave's proven strategies, techniques, and useful tips will allow you to stand head and shoulders above the competition."

ALLISON TURNER, Public Outreach Director, ManTech International Corporation

"Dave Parker's *Slam Dunk Job Search* is a new 'must-read' for job seekers everywhere who want to differentiate themselves from the crowd."

JILL MATTESON, Founder and President, EcoStrategies

"Following Dave's ideas, now outlined in this book, gave me a solid process to focus on that put me on a path to success. Don't wait to read Dave's book. The 6-Step Slam Dunk Job Search Process can make a difference in your career as well."

CHRIS MINTON, Vice President, Larry Walker Associates

"I used Dave Parker's job search process to shift my mindset and efficiently identify and successfully land an ideal position that more clearly aligned with my career goals. I am truly grateful for the Slam Dunk Process, and you will be too if you want to land your ideal job!"

DR. JILL RICHARDSON, Director of Students Affairs, Top 40 US News University

"Dave Parker's methodology works—read this book, do the work, and make your ideal job search a slam dunk!"

JESSICA SAGER, AICP, Manager of Land Development, Fortune 500 Automobile Manufacturer

"Dave Parker's mentorship has been invaluable in my career journey. His guidance helped me nurture connections and open doors that allowed me to land a position at my dream company and quickly rise through the ranks. His steps are a must follow for anyone looking to stand out during the job search process."

CASEY GARRETT, Program Manager, Strategic Philanthropy, Fortune 50 Media and Entertainment Company

"I have never worked with anyone as passionate about helping people with their job search as Dave Parker. His insight, expertise, and years of experience make this book a must-read job search guide!"

MARILYN KEYS, Senior HR Business Partner, Fortune 50 Company

"Dave Parker effectively distills the knowledge he has built during his decades-long career into six simple steps to help anyone land their dream job. The energy and expertise he brings to the job search is unparalleled—and his approach will be a true asset to those who read this book."

LISA CAMPBELL, Client Director, Context Group

SLAM DUNK JOB SEARCH

DAVID ALLEN PARKER JR.

SLAM DUNK
JOB SEARCH

—— LEAVE NOTHING TO CHANCE ——

6 Steps to Landing
Your Ideal Job in Any Market

Beyond
Competitive

Published by Beyond Competitive LLC
Goleta, California
beyondcompetitive.com

For press inquiries or other information, please contact info@beyondcompetitive.com.

Library of Congress Cataloguing-in-Publication Data has been applied for.

ISBN: 979-8-9865451-0-3 (paperback)
ISBN: 979-8-9865451-1-0 (ebook)

First Edition
Printed in the United States of America

Lead editor: Mara Eller
Copy editor: Brian Baker
Developmental editor: Kelly Lydick
Indexer: Heather Pendley
Interior designer: George Stevens
Illustrator: Hazel Clegg

To all the people who want to share their unique talents and passions with the world.

In loving memory of my parents,
Gay and David Parker.

Table of Contents

A Note to the Job Seeker

D o you jump up and down with excitement each time you begin a job search? If you don't, you aren't alone. Most people believe the job search process is time-consuming, out of their control, and full of uncertainty, unfairness, and rejection.

While this book may not entice you to put the job search process at the top of your list of favorite activities, it will help you understand the true purpose of every job search and make the process much more engaging, rewarding, and even inspiring, for both you and your potential employers. It will also reduce anxiety about uncertainty, unfairness, rejection, and lack of control by taking you through a process that will help you stand out, seal the deal, and land your ideal job.

I wrote this book because I know what it feels like when you are unable to land your ideal job and don't know how to stand out and close the deal. It feels awful!

Early in my career, I didn't grab interviewers' attention and inspire them to remember me, and I didn't know how to make my ideal job search a slam dunk. I was following the same job search advice that most people were following, and I was trying to do everything the way I'd been told was the "right" way. I didn't know I could break the script and be creative, different, and inspiring. If I had, I would have made the process much more engaging for myself and the people around me, and I would have been more successful in landing my ideal jobs early in my career.

I had to learn to navigate the job search process successfully on my own, and when I finally cracked the job search code, I made a commitment to help more job seekers land their ideal jobs. I began my career development path working as a recruiter for a Fortune 50 company and soon began running a university career development program for one of the top environmental science and management schools in the world. With more than 25 years of experience helping thousands of job seekers land jobs in all types of markets and industries, I decided to pull my key steps, tools, and tactics into one book to help job seekers take control of the search process and elevate their careers to the next level.

The term "slam dunk" surfaced organically years ago as I was helping job candidates prepare for the interview stage. I found myself asking them what they were going to do to make the interview a slam dunk—regardless of whom they were competing against. I wanted job seekers to be proactive and come up with ways that would all but guarantee they would move on to the next interview or land the job offer. I didn't want them to leave anything to chance.

In basketball, a slam dunk is when a player jumps through the air and slams the ball down through the hoop. While it's an extremely successful technique, anyone who has watched or played basketball knows that not all slam dunk attempts work. The job search process is no different. No one can guarantee your ideal job search will be a success. But you *can* follow a process that will considerably elevate your job search performance above your competitors.

Through the years, the slam dunk name and mindset expanded to all stages of the job search process: How will you all but guarantee you move on from one stage to the next? As I thought about the job search process and observed what was holding people back, I developed the 6-Step Slam Dunk Job Search Process to help job seekers elevate their performance and compete effectively for their ideal jobs.

I can't wait to share with you what I wish I had known early in my career. You are about to begin a journey that will guide you through all the steps you need to stand out and become the job candidate employers can't wait to hire.

Here's to your best job search ever!

David Allen Parker Jr.

Do you want
to know
how to
elevate your
job search
performance
above your
competitors to
seal the deal
and land your
ideal job?

Introduction

THE 6-STEP SLAM DUNK JOB SEARCH PROCESS

Some people want it to happen, some wish it would happen, and others make it happen.[1]

—MICHAEL JORDAN

ongratulations! You have committed to a Slam Dunk Job Search. The 6-Step Slam Dunk Job Search Process outlined in this book will provide you with all the steps, tools, and tactics you need to help you seal the deal and make your ideal job search a slam dunk.

No longer do you need to remain unemployed, working in a job you dislike, unsure about how to conduct a successful job search, or concerned about pivoting from one job or industry to another. Whether you are a student getting ready to graduate, a professional interested in making a career change, or a seasoned employee focused on landing a higher-level job, the 6-Step Slam Dunk Job Search Process will help you get from where you are to where you want to be.

Reaching your destination isn't difficult, but it may require you to shift your thinking and start to see the job search process in a new way. Let's begin by looking at a championship basketball game.

I was fortunate to watch an exciting club championship basketball game between two powerhouse teams: Golden Pacific and Rising Tsunami. Golden Pacific led for most of the game, and they were ahead 43 to 28 at one point. By the fourth quarter, the Rising Tsunami players had mounted an impressive comeback, and with only nine seconds left in the game, they took a 68 to 66 lead over Golden Pacific when one of the players made a quick move around his defender and went up for a spectacular slam dunk. It was a wow moment. The game could have gone either way, but in the end, the Rising Tsunami team won by two points with a combination of solid play across the board and one memorable moment toward the end of the game.

What stuck in my mind was the image of the Golden Pacific team watching the Rising Tsunami players line up with big smiles as they posed behind the championship banner and a five-foot-tall trophy. A dozen photographers were capturing the moment. Unlike the Rising Tsunami team, the Golden Pacific players were now out of the public eye. It was over, they had lost, and they slowly retreated to the bench to collect their gear and head to the locker room with little to no fanfare.

Here is the message I got from this scene that I want you to think about as you turn the pages of this book, pursue your ideal job, and strive to realize your career aspirations:

Make sure you are number one!

Golden Pacific was good. They weren't just good—they were great. They only lost by two points, and they led for most of the game. They technically did almost everything right. They committed the time and made the sacrifices, but they still went home empty-handed. They didn't close the deal and win the championship, and they weren't able to pose in front of all the photographers with the championship banner and trophy. They could only watch.

The difference between first and second place came down to one memorable moment—a slam dunk by one of the players. Both teams played well along the way, but the Rising Tsunami players rose to the occasion and separated themselves from their competitors to win the game. They weren't just great—they were remarkable.

The same happens when people compete for jobs. They either get the job or they don't. There are few gray areas when it comes to job offers, and the outcome often comes down to one or two memorable moments combined with a lot of little moments done well along the way.

The stakes are high when you're searching for a new job. If you land an ideal job, your life changes:

- You get to work in a job you enjoy.
- You don't have to look for jobs in the near future.
- You probably have more stability in your life.
- You get to meet a new group of people and possibly develop new friendships.
- You get a paycheck or a larger paycheck.
- You probably get a benefits package.
- Your self-esteem could increase.
- Your credibility and status elevate.
- You may enter a job or career that will last for the next 20 to 30 years.

If you're reading this book, you probably already know that landing a job you enjoy can have a positive impact on your life. The question is, how do you make sure *you* are number one? How do you make your ideal job search a slam dunk? Answer: You follow a process that leaves nothing to chance.

To develop an effective job search process, I listened to the concerns of job seekers, observed how they were conducting their job searches, reflected on my own job search experience, and pulled in all my recruiting and hiring experience. Themes developed. It became very apparent that many job seekers didn't have critical elements in place to conduct an effective job search:

- They didn't have a simple, proven job search process to take them from start to finish.
- They weren't motivated to conduct the type of job search needed to land their ideal jobs.
- They weren't thinking the right way throughout the process.
- They weren't prepared to begin an effective job search.
- They didn't know how to get in the door at their target organizations and tap into the hidden job market.
- They weren't committed to conducting a competitive job search across the board.
- They didn't have the right strategies in place to wow employers, close the deal, and land their ideal jobs.

To help job seekers function well within each of these areas, I developed the 6-Step Slam Dunk Job Search Process. The six steps take job seekers from A to Z, elevate their job search performance above their competitors, and help them seal the deal and land their ideal jobs. Here are the six steps:

Step 1: Career Design
Establish a motivating destination and reverse engineer your ideal career path.

Step 2: Success Mindset
Understand the job search playing field and start to think the right way.

Step 3: Market Ready
Prepare to compete effectively for your ideal job.

Step 4: Relationship Team
Form long-lasting professional relationships, seek advice, become more marketable, connect with decision makers, and open the door to your target organizations.

Step 5: Competitive Commitment
Conduct a quality job search from start to finish by excelling at the basics across the board.

Step 6: Slam Dunk
Implement tactics to help you stand out and seal the deal.

The 6-Step Slam Dunk Job Search Process capitalizes on little moments to get big results. It will help you elevate your job search performance across the board and magnify your performance during key moments. Unlike most job search books that focus on the fundamentals, this book goes beyond the basics with specific steps and tactics that will help you rise above your competitors.

Throughout this book, I condense more than 30 years of experience in recruiting, human resources, career development, corporate training, management, and consulting to bring you a job search process that will help you view things differently, think differently—and most importantly—do things differently.

I have hired hundreds of employees as a recruiter at a Fortune 50 company, and, as a career coach, I have helped thousands of job seekers land rewarding positions in all types of companies, sectors, and job markets. I have viewed the job search process from all sides, including the job candidate side, and I am excited to bring you something new, something different—something that will help you successfully navigate the often frustrating, tedious, and dreaded job search process. I think you will find the journey rewarding, effective, and maybe even inspiring when you have the right steps in place to guide you through your job search and ultimately get you the job you desire and deserve.

Do you want to wake up in the morning inspired to work hard on your job search and land a job that allows you to unlock your full potential?

Step 1

CAREER DESIGN

*A vision is not just a picture of what could be; it is an appeal
to our better selves, a call to become something more.*[1]

—ROSABETH MOSS KANTER

What happens when you decide to take a vacation and you identify a meaningful dream destination? You get excited about your trip and you start to create a plan to get to where you want to go. Having a meaningful destination is just as important for a job search as it is for a vacation.

When job seekers don't have a vision of what they want and haven't identified where to begin, they often struggle to elevate their job search performance and compete effectively for jobs. Sometimes we need to step back before we can move forward. The Career Design step was created to ensure you take some time to think about what is important to you and what you really want to do. It will help you begin your ideal job search with a meaningful destination in mind. The clearer you are about your career aspirations, and the more you understand the "why" behind what you want to do, the more motivated you will be during each job search and throughout your career.

Your goal in the Career Design step is to identify your ideal career path, starting with where you want to end up and working backward to determine where you should begin—either right now or whenever you start a new job search. It all starts with a meaningful career vision.

Chapter 1

DEFINE YOUR DESTINATION

The following conversation between Alice and the Cheshire cat in Lewis Carroll's *Alice's Adventures in Wonderland* is a good illustration of why you should have a general idea of where you are headed before you take off on your journey:

> "Would you tell me, please, which way I ought to go from here?"
>
> "That depends a good deal on where you want to get to," said the Cat.
>
> "I don't much care where—" said Alice.
>
> "Then it doesn't matter which way you go," said the Cat.
>
> "—so long as I get *somewhere*," Alice added as an explanation.
>
> "Oh, you're sure to do that," said the Cat, "if you only walk long enough."[1]

Without a vision of where you want to go and an idea of how to get there, you will have a hard time deciding which path to take each time you come to a fork in the road. You will probably find yourself meandering through your career with little meaning, purpose, direction, or heart. You will also have a difficult time getting the help you need if you don't know where you want to go.

I remember when a talented, 25-year-old job seeker named Angela came to me one day and asked, "How can I be strategic when I don't know what I want to do?"[2] The answer is that you can't. When job seekers spend too little time figuring out who they want to be, where they want to go, and whom they want to help, it's no surprise when they're not motivated to put in the time to conduct a successful job search. It is much easier to be proactive, decisive, and motivated when you know your destination and are excited to get there.

Develop Your Career Vision

To avoid conducting an unfocused and general job search, spend some time coming up with a career destination that is important to you. The more meaningful the destination, the more motivated you will be to find a way to get there. If you can't get specific with your destination (career vision) right now, start with a broad career vision statement that reflects some interest or inspiration. Here are some examples:

- Work in a field of interest (e.g., work in the finance field).
- Help a particular group of people (e.g., assist veterans and their families).
- Use a skill you have acquired or were gifted (e.g., entertain people in some way).
- Work for a specific company or within a particular industry (e.g., work for an outdoor apparel company).
- Help solve one of life's pressing problems (e.g., address global food security and safety issues).
- Work in a desirable location or setting (e.g., land a job in Hawaii).
- Strive for a particular benefit (e.g., work in a company that provides flexibility).

If you start with a broad vision, you will often become more focused as you move through your career. It may even take you a few jobs before you come up with a more specific career vision statement and begin to get focused on exactly where you want to go. As you have probably noticed, career paths are rarely linear. Your goal is to take a step in a meaningful direction and then look for clues that help you see the next right step to get closer to who you want to be and what you want to do.

Although you will continue to work toward your career vision, always remember that every job (ideal and less ideal) you have held throughout your career will allow you to bring something special and unique to your future jobs. The minute you see value in everything you do and have done, the easier it will be to move toward what you want without feeling like you need to have everything figured out from the very beginning. There is more than one path to get to your ultimate career destination, and all the experiences along the way, no matter how inconsequential they may seem at the time, will help you get to where you want to go and perform well along the way.

Your Career Masterpiece Ps

As you move through your career, use six Career Masterpiece Ps (CMPs) to refine your vision and develop a more specific and motivating career vision statement. For any job, you want to think about

1. **Passion:** The type of work you are passionate about or interested in doing.
2. **Purpose:** The type of work in which you will have a significant and meaningful impact on the world through the people you help or the causes you support.
3. **Potential:** The type of work in which you can apply your relevant knowledge, education, skills, experience, and unique talents.
4. **Priorities:** The type of work that reflects what is important to you in your career and life (e.g., career satisfaction, financial compensation, work-life balance, travel opportunities, or a combination of factors).
5. **Personality:** The type of work that allows you to be around people you enjoy and be yourself without feeling like you must be someone you are not.
6. **Place:** The type of work in which you are in one of your preferred geographic locations and working in one of your target organizations.

The first three Ps—passion, purpose, and potential—are focused on what you have to share with the world, while the last three Ps—priorities, personality, and place—are mainly focused on your comfort and satisfaction within your career. Your first goal is to figure out what you are passionate about doing, whom you want to help, and what talents and gifts you want to share with the world. You will then use your priorities, personality, and desired place to help you figure out how to bring the six CMPs together to realize your career aspirations.

Here are some examples of more refined career vision statements that incorporate all or most of the CMPs:

- Work at a wealth management firm in Las Cruces, New Mexico, to help retirees manage their money effectively so they can live the lives they desire throughout their retirement.
- Become the head of sustainability for a large manufacturing company headquartered in the Boston area and turn it into one of the greenest and most efficient manufacturing operations in the industry.
- Run a small, alternative health clinic in the San Francisco Bay Area using a unique combination of medical and customer service experience to help people maintain wellness and live happy and productive lives.
- Work for a nonprofit organization in Chicago making documentary videos and films that move people to act against urban violence.

> ## What is so powerful and meaningful that you would be willing to persevere no matter how difficult it is?

The more you refine your career vision and incorporate the CMPs, the more motivated you will be to make your vision a reality, and the more decisive you will be each time you come to a fork in your career path.

Your Why

Once you have a career vision in place, identify the "why" behind what you want to do. A meaningful why will keep you motivated throughout your entire career. As Dean Graziosi, *New York Times* best-selling author and entrepreneur, points out, "The issue with most people is that they simply don't go deep enough into their hearts and souls to find out the truth about why they want what they want. And without a depth of purpose, you can't push through your most challenging times."[3] The question is, how do you figure out your why? What is so powerful and meaningful that you would be willing to persevere no matter how difficult it is? As Austrian neurologist and psychologist Viktor Frankl said, "Those who have a 'why' to live, can bear with almost any 'how.'"[4]

To develop a deeper awareness of your why, use the 7 Levels Deep Exercise created by consultant Joe Stump.[5] Start with your career vision and then ask yourself why seven times. Begin with the following question: "Why is my vision important to me?" From there, dig down six more layers by asking why for each of your responses ("Why is _____ important to me?"). By peeling back the layers, you will uncover the truth about the why behind what you want to do.

Now is the time to dig deep and discover what really motivates you. What is the real meaning behind what you want? The more you are aware of why something is important to you, the more motivated you will be to follow through on the how and get to where you want to go. When you have a vision of where you are headed and understand the meaning behind what you want, your mind will automatically start to focus on what is important to you, and your eyes will be wide open to opportunities and resources that will help you move toward your destination.

Identify Your Ideal Job

With a meaningful career vision in place, you can now reach out to people working in jobs that closely align with your vision. Your goal is to reverse engineer a career path from where you ultimately want to end up back to where you will begin. You want to accelerate your learning curve and identify the specific job you will pursue at this time. Why try to figure everything out yourself when others have already paved the way? Ask the people you contact to recommend the best career path to reach your ultimate destination. Ideally, you will talk to three to five people who currently work in jobs that closely align with your career vision.

By reaching out to people, you will start to build a relationship team within your chosen field, identify potential career paths to reach your ultimate destination, uncover the best job(s) to pursue now (your ideal job), and start to determine what credentials are most important for your career path. Here are some questions you may ask when you seek advice:

- What career path did you take to get into your position?
- Was that the best path or would you recommend better ways to reach this level?
- Given my background, what would you recommend as the best first job for this career path?
- What companies would you suggest I pursue to land these types of jobs?
- What skills are essential for landing jobs in this field and doing well in them?

- Are there any other credentials I should acquire, including certifications, skills, education, training, or experience?
- Are there any conferences I should try to attend?
- What are the best professional associations to join to meet key people in this industry?
- What will help me stand out in this field?
- Is there anyone else you would recommend I talk to about this type of career?
- Are there any other companies I should explore?
- Where do you see the field going in the next two to three years?

Although you will get valuable advice, you don't need to follow anyone's recommended career path. You are unique, and your path could be very different. If you think you have a better way to reach your destination and bring your unique talents to market, go for it. More than anything, the conversations you have through these relationship-building sessions will help you think differently and will start to develop a relationship team within your chosen field.

Your Target Organizations and Contacts

Once you have identified your ideal job (the job you will pursue now), locate the organizations where you would like to work and where you want to put your credentials and unique talents to use. Compile a list of your target organizations and make sure you include small and medium-sized companies. Smaller companies account for nearly two-thirds of all new jobs, so they shouldn't be ignored.[6] Additionally, advancement can often accelerate within smaller, emerging companies.

With your target organizations in place, identify a contact for each—a person you will reach out to for advice on the best ways to pursue opportunities in the organization and the field. This approach will further expand your relationship team and start to get you in the door at your desired organizations.

Before you read on, be sure you have a career vision in place (specific or broad), a career path in mind, an ideal job identified, target organizations listed, and contacts assigned to each target company—as many contacts as possible. If you aren't quite there yet with what job you plan to pursue, spend a little more time figuring out your destination and your desired career path.

Don't skip any of these exercises. The sooner you establish a career vision and understand the why behind what you want to do, the sooner you will get on your desired career path and land your ideal job. Good things will happen when you follow each step of the process and take action.

Your Action

No career vision, motivational book, career activity or exercise, inspiring quote, TED Talk, or success video will result in anything if you don't act. Your thoughts and actions must work in tandem if you plan to land your ideal job and make your career vision a reality.

The first action is the hardest to take because people are set in their ways, and it is difficult to break old patterns. Fear often makes people resist change and revert to what is most comfortable for them, especially when they rely on old ways of thinking. Keep the following paraphrased story in mind each time you resist taking the steps that will help you realize your career aspirations.

> An old man was teaching his grandson about life. "A fight is going on inside me," he said to the boy. "It is a terrible fight and it is between two wolves. One is evil—he is anger, envy, regret, greed, arrogance, self-pity, guilt, resentment, inferiority, lies, fear, superiority, and resistance." He continued, "The other is good—he is joy, peace, love, hope, serenity, humility, kindness, empathy, generosity, truth, compassion, courage, and faith. The same fight is going on inside you—and inside every other person, too."
>
> The grandson thought about it for a minute and then asked his grandfather, "Which wolf will win?"
>
> The old man replied simply, "The one you feed."[7]

When you can control your mind and feed it the right thoughts, you will have all the power you need to move forward and get what you want. Don't let the bad wolf hold you back with fear and doubt. When you limit yourself, you become limited. When you expand yourself and your thoughts, you become limitless. Feed yourself with confidence, motivation, and courage. Don't let anyone or anything stop you from moving toward your desired destination. This is your journey, no one else's, and the world needs what you have to offer. Never let others take that away from you.

Having a limitless mindset is important because you never want to look back on your life and say, "I should have listened to my heart and gone after what was important and meaningful to me." Failing to become your true self will not only haunt you at the end of your life but will steal joy throughout your life.

If you don't find some way to release your talents and do what you love in either your professional or personal life, your body will keep reminding you of this untapped potential and service. Although you may be able to suppress your feelings and desires, your true self will always exist below the surface. Instead of resisting it, your job is to identify it and then release it so you can be the best version of yourself and make the world a better place through your unique qualities and talents. You don't want to feel like you have left any untapped potential in the tank at the end of your life. You want to empty the tank so you feel good about yourself and your impact.

> You never want to look back on your life and say, "I should have listened to my heart and gone after what was important and meaningful to me."

Your Chosen Path

Your passion and what you believe in are always important. Don't compare yourself to others as you move along your unique career path. We all move at a different pace, and what is right for someone else isn't necessarily right for you.

Continue to remind yourself that there are no wrong career decisions or paths as long as you come up with a meaningful career vision, understand the why behind what you want to do, and keep your eyes open for the clues that lead you closer to what is important to you. Now that you are more focused on your destination and understand why you are motivated to get there, you can put a solid foundation in place to help you get from where you are to where you want to be.

Do you want to understand the job search playing field, think the right way, and be able to handle anything that comes your direction?

Step 2

SUCCESS MINDSET

You must learn a new way to think before you can master a new way to be.[1]

—MARIANNE WILLIAMSON

During the 2017 NCAA men's basketball tournament (March Madness), a 14-year-old *Sports Illustrated for Kids* reporter by the name of Max Bonnstetter asked the University of South Carolina coach, Frank Martin, if he thought attitude or technique was most important after his team beat Baylor to advance to the Elite Eight. Here was the coach's response: "Attitude comes first. We gotta have guys that are gonna believe in our mission, that are gonna believe in what we want to do. Once they believe, then we can teach them the technique. It all starts with our mindset, and we've got guys that are completely bought into what we do."[2]

You must have the right perspective, attitude, and beliefs in place to navigate the job search process effectively and land your ideal job. The right mindset sets the stage for everything that follows, and it is a critical step for achieving your greatest career aspirations.

The Success Mindset step will reset your thinking so you can understand the job search playing field and approach the job search process the right way. You are on a mission to become the job candidate employers can't wait to hire, and the Success Mindset step will help prepare you for this journey.

Chapter 2

REFRAME YOUR JOB SEARCH

Wouldn't it be nice if you could go into a store and select whatever job you wanted right off the shelf? Unfortunately, as we all know, a high percentage of job searches aren't that simple. In most cases, job seekers must go through a long search process and compete with many qualified candidates before finally landing a job. Additionally, positions aren't sitting on store shelves right in front of us. Studies have shown that as many as 80 percent of jobs exist in the hidden job market and are never advertised or posted.[1]

> Studies have shown that as many as 80 percent of jobs exist in the hidden job market and are never advertised or posted.

The good news is that your job search doesn't need to feel long and arduous. By developing the right mindset and modifying your approach, you will start to see value in everything you do during your search and shift from focusing on what is urgent to what is important.

Embracing the following 12 new perspectives will get you started as you reframe your job search.

1. **Instead of dreading your job search, embrace the process and cherish everything it has to offer.**

   Your job search gives you an opportunity to establish a solid foundation for your entire career or reset an existing foundation. Your search isn't about one job search; it's about all your job searches.

   Your job search is about

   - Slowing down, reflecting on your career, and developing meaningful goals.
   - Building a relationship team that can help you throughout your entire career.
   - Identifying your strengths, weaknesses, likes, and dislikes.
   - Improving your technical and nontechnical skills so you can function well during your job search and throughout your career.
   - Understanding the ins and outs of your field as they relate to your job search, overall job performance, and career advancement.
   - Identifying employers' needs and showing how you can help them reach their goals and overcome their challenges.
   - Seeing the value of everything you have done and then determining how your past experiences fit into the present and future.
   - Finding ways to make any process or task enjoyable for yourself and others.
   - Exhibiting your work so employers can start to gravitate toward you.
   - Learning more about yourself and getting closer to reflecting your true self within your career.

   Rather than dreading this time, embrace each job search and take full advantage of it to advance your entire career. Laying a solid foundation now will make future job searches and career moves much easier.

2. **Instead of thinking that all job searches work the same way, understand that every search is different.**

   No matter what you hear, remind yourself that the way job candidates are evaluated isn't the same from company to company. While the general job search process (job search script) is similar, there are still many gray areas where you will need to use your best judgment based on your audience. There is no one best way to approach your search.

Here is how the job search playing field really functions:

- There are no perfect cover letters or résumés.
- Every document review process is different.
- Every interview is unique.
- All employers come with their own special needs and desires.
- Many hiring managers bring their own biases to the process and have their own theories on how to evaluate and hire the best candidates.
- Most people you know will have different opinions about how you should conduct your job search.
- Most interviewers aren't trained on how to conduct effective interviews.
- Many employers don't know how to hire the best candidates.

The bottom line is that you need to remember that nothing is set in stone during your job search. There isn't one approach or strategy that will work well for all people, at all times, and during all situations. If there were, there would probably only be a handful of job search books on the market rather than the thousands of books that currently exist.

Even when this book highlights a particular approach, use your best judgment for each situation and go with what feels right, especially if you have inside information that points you in a different direction. You can always break the rules when you have a better way of doing something and addressing employers' needs.

3. Instead of focusing on the results, focus on the process.

Most job seekers focus too much on the outcome and don't put enough emphasis on what it takes to get the desired results. While you do want to begin with a destination (start with the end in mind), you will get frustrated and put too much pressure on yourself if you focus on the results. You never have full control over the outcome, but you do have control over the process you follow. When you follow a process that works and take one step at a time, you often get what you want in the end, and you don't need to worry about the score along the way.

4. **Instead of wishing and waiting to be hired, think of your job search as a business with you as CEO.**

    You own your job search, and you can run the business however you want. You are selling the value you bring to the marketplace, and you can

    - Find ways to increase your value even during the job search process.
    - Impress employers with your potential value.
    - Tell employers why the value you can provide is better and different.
    - Share a story about the value you can offer.
    - Demonstrate your value.
    - Share what others say about your value.
    - Test your value in various markets.
    - Implement effective strategies to get employers to purchase your value.
    - Thank employers for hiring you for your potential value.

    While you can never force employers to want the value you offer, you can put the right strategies in place to get employers to gravitate toward you because you offer something that is important to them. Embrace this time when you are empowered to accomplish your career goals and get what you want.

5. **Instead of procrastinating during your job search, look for ways to make the job search process engaging and inspiring for you and employers.**

    The job search process can be quite intimidating, but there are ways to make the process more enjoyable. You can make it more engaging and inspiring by

    - Identifying accomplishments you are excited to share with the employer and finding interesting ways to present them.

- Being creative and different in a tactful way (e.g., riding a skateboard to an interview you have with an eco-friendly and hip company or sending a PowerPoint résumé along with a standard résumé).
- Impressing the employer through your extraordinary customer service and above-and-beyond approach.
- Telling engaging stories and sharing your impressive accomplishments and credentials.
- Connecting the dots by matching up your credentials to the required qualifications and pulling everything together for the employer.
- Impressing the employer with all of your preparation.
- Sharing a portfolio of your most impressive work.
- Using testimonials or evaluations to make your point and wow the employer.
- Helping solve the employer's problems by recommending changes or improvement strategies.
- Connecting with the hiring committee members by sharing something you have in common with them based on your LinkedIn research.
- Taking a calculated risk and seeing what happens (e.g., recommending changes to a program or initiative, incorporating a unique story, or sending a video thank-you message after an interview).
- Bringing a relevant report or paper you wrote and sharing it with the hiring committee members during an interview to see how they react.
- Creating something for the employer that demonstrates your skills.
- Designing a visually appealing, professional, and targeted website for employers to see.
- Writing down motivating job search goals that will inspire you to excel. (People who write down their goals are 42 percent more likely to achieve them![2])

When you are engaged in the process and inspired to share information with an employer, your energy and enthusiasm will be contagious and will help set you apart.

6. **Instead of despising a competitive job search, appreciate the benefits of competing with other candidates.**

    When you compete with others, you raise your game and become a better person and a more productive future employee. Yes, the job search process can be stressful, but this type of stress can be good because it forces you to grow.

    During a competitive job search, look for ways to market yourself better, differentiate yourself, expand your skills, connect with others, and stand out. Having a job drop into your lap doesn't force you to get better and improve. Instead of looking to make the process easier, look for ways to make yourself better.[3] Competition will help you get better, especially if you are focused on making sure you are the top candidate.

7. **Instead of feeling uncomfortable about promoting yourself, always remember that you are doing potential employers a service by convincing them that you are the right person for the job.**

    If you have chosen your ideal job carefully, then you know you can excel in the position, and you will be doing employers a disservice if you don't show them why you are the best person for the job. Don't let employers down by allowing them to hire someone who can't do the job as well as you can.

    When you know you need to show employers why you are the best candidate and future employee, you will focus your attention on helping the employer get what they want. You! Your confidence will soar, and you will find creative ways to make it happen.

8. **Instead of thinking that you either need to stand out or fit in, seek to stand out *and* fit in during your job search.**

    Employers want employees who will fit in with the company values, core competencies, and professional standards. But they also want people who will bring something different to the department and the team. The better companies want a diverse group of people who can work well together. Look for ways to fit in, but don't forget to find ways to show employers the unique talent, value, and diversity you will bring to the job. If you can find the right balance between standing out and fitting in, you will often seal the deal and land the job. The Slam Dunk Guiding Principles described in chapter 3 will help you stand out and fit in at the same time.

9. **Instead of thinking that everything will go smoothly during the job search process, understand that most job searches have tailwinds, headwinds, and even side winds.**

If you think the job search process and your career will be smooth sailing all the time with the wind at your back, you will be in for a big surprise and disappointment. The winds have been put in place for a reason. Your goal is to uncover the lesson that each wind current brings.

The tailwinds let you know what it feels like to be in the zone, and they give you the motivation to keep moving forward. In contrast, the headwinds force you to slow down, assess your situation and progress, and make sure you are on the right track and approaching everything in a productive manner. They will also force you to be creative and open your eyes to new opportunities and new ways to realize your career aspirations. While tailwinds give you a push and headwinds slow you down, side winds are life's expected and unexpected twists and turns: a newborn, health issues, aging parents, a partner's career change, and so on. They can force you off your desired course—your ideal job search—but the twists and turns open your eyes to new perspectives, build character as you're forced to adapt, and make you a more well-rounded person. You may be surprised how those experiences will end up proving valuable later on.

An inspiring and meaningful career vision will pull you back on track and keep you moving forward no matter where you are on your journey and no matter which way the wind is blowing. Spend time understanding what each wind current means, and then see the value that each adds to your job search and career.

10. **Instead of thinking that your job search is all about you, understand that your job search is about the hiring manager and the job you will do for the manager, department, company, and ultimately, the company's clients.**

Your task is to make employers' jobs easier by helping them tackle their challenges and reach their goals. When you are focused on employers' needs, interested in helping them, and intent on developing a long-term relationship no matter what happens, you will approach your job search very differently. You will

- Read job announcements thoroughly to determine what employers really need.
- Use a word cloud generator to unearth the most relevant skills within each job announcement and the language used to describe the skills.
- Seek to collect additional inside information—by talking to customers, current employees, and past employees—that will allow you to understand employers' needs even more.
- Look for ways to show employers how you can address their needs better than anyone.
- Research all the hiring committee members on LinkedIn to see if you have anything in common with them.
- Be creative and make the hiring process different, interesting, and engaging for employers.
- Ask questions during the interview that help you uncover what is truly important to each employer.
- Send a thank-you note after each interview. (Unless otherwise stated, thank-you notes and messages refer to thank-you "email" messages in this book.)

Your job search is bigger than you. Once you have the job offer in hand, the power will shift in your direction, and you can begin to focus more on your needs. But before you receive the offer, your attention should be focused on understanding employers' needs and showing them how you can address their needs better than anyone else.

11. **Instead of thinking that "job search" means searching and applying for jobs online, think of your job search as a process where you connect with decision makers, seek advice, develop relationships, and tap into people's emotions.**

Eliminate the phrase "applying for jobs" from your vocabulary. Focus instead on "pursuing connections and opportunities." Reframe the process by thinking about CARE—Connections, Advice, Relationships, and Emotions—rather than focusing on "apply" and "jobs." When you think of your job search as using CARE to pursue connections and opportunities, you start to focus on developing relationships that will uncover both hidden and advertised positions.

What do you think is the easiest way to connect with key decision makers (people who can hire you or advocate your hire)? You approach them for targeted advice or show how you can help them. Most people are willing to share advice or hear how you can assist them, but not many are eager to hand you a job or go to bat for you before they know you. If the door opens for "advice requests" or "offers to help" but closes for "job requests," what approach do you think you should use? What approach do you think leads to long-term relationships, and what approach do you think leads to jobs?

Jack Daly has it right: "When you care more about the customer than the sale, you will sell more than anyone else."

The candidates who often receive the offers are those who first developed a connection with the hiring committee members and showed the members they cared about them, the business, and the company. The candidates understood the hiring committee members' desires and tapped into their emotions. International sales expert Jack Daly has it right: "When you care more about the customer than the sale, you will sell more than anyone else."[4]

12. **Instead of thinking that you need to have every detail of your ideal career figured out, understand that everything you do adds value as long as you continue to look for the clues along the way that get you closer to who you want to be and what you want to do.**

Your job is to find the hidden gems within you and within everything you do and have done and then put them to use in an important way. The more you can observe yourself in action and uncover your abilities, desires, passions, and values, the closer you will get to understanding and fulfilling your grand career aspirations and, ultimately, reflecting your true self within your career and life.

See the Long Game

When you frame the job search process differently, you will start to understand your job search's true purpose: to learn more about yourself and your field and start to establish a solid foundation for your entire career. And when you understand that it's about the long game, you will be more open to doing things differently.

Now that you are starting to reframe the way you view your job search, you will use the six principles described in the next chapter to guide you through the process so you can handle anything that comes your way.

Chapter 3

FOLLOW THE SLAM DUNK GUIDING PRINCIPLES

Many job seekers don't have anything to guide their decision-making throughout the job search process, and they don't have anything to help them handle all the unexpected moments that come with each job search. To help you move through the 6-Step Slam Dunk Job Search Process, you will use six Slam Dunk Guiding Principles (Figure A) to help you get into tight spots (competitive jobs) and out of difficult situations (unexpected moments and challenges).

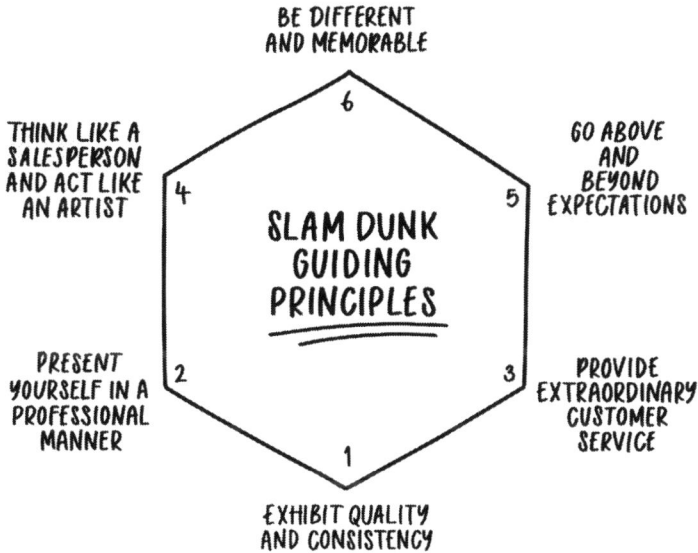

Figure A: Slam Dunk Guiding Principles

These principles will help you stand out at each stage of the job search process, wow employers, and excel in your career. And you will do this in a way that involves minimal risk. Why? Because most employers will value these principles, and most job seekers will not follow them. The principles will allow you to stand out and fit in at the same time. Your goal is to get the most return with the least amount of risk, and the Slam Dunk Guiding Principles will help you accomplish this goal.

The Slam Dunk Guiding Principles also help you handle all the unexpected moments that come your way. During each job search, you will need to make on-the-spot decisions that could determine your fate. While job seekers may prepare well for 80 to 90 percent of what they encounter, the unexpected 10 to 20 percent often makes or breaks them. More employers are throwing in assessments and unique questions to see how candidates respond when tested and put in unfamiliar and challenging situations. Without the right mindset, you may have a hard time navigating these unstructured and unanticipated moments that can either cause you to fall behind your competitors or allow you to pull ahead.

Let's now take a close look at each guiding principle.

Guiding Principle 1: Exhibit Quality and Consistency

Why do you think so many companies pour thousands of dollars into quality improvement programs? Consistently delivering a quality product or service and meeting or exceeding expectations are vital to them and their customers. Quality and consistency impact the bottom line. As a result, they are the cornerstones to a successful job search and a productive career. They are what separate excellent job applicants from mediocre applicants, superstar employees from average employees, and successful companies from struggling companies. When you are focused on quality and consistency, you are taking a long-term view of a business, career, brand, and life, showing you care about your customers, the people around you, your reputation, and the impact you will have on the world.

The job search process can be painfully tedious, but the job seekers who conduct a quality job search from beginning to end and maintain consistency throughout are those who often get the jobs.

Exhibit Quality

Quality is an essential guiding principle because, based on years of hiring and placement experience, I believe it can elevate you above 90 to 100 percent of your competitors from the start. The job candidates who conduct a quality search across the board are the candidates who often stand out in the end.

Everything you do needs to display quality. You are in the job search process to impress employers. If you don't meet or exceed the employer's expectations, you will be eliminated from the hiring process and won't get the job offer. Commit to producing quality work by making sure you meet all deadlines, your materials and correspondence are error-free and professional, and your LinkedIn profile and professional career website are well laid out, visually appealing, and engaging.

Producing quality work in all areas may sound exhausting, but it isn't if you frame the process differently. Take a longer view of the process and understand why putting in the time now is important for your career and the people you serve. Hard work in the short-term often makes life much easier in the long-term. Everything you do during your job search should focus on building your relationship team, establishing your brand, putting a solid career infrastructure in place (professional career website, LinkedIn profile, and other relevant platforms), and improving work-related skills. When you believe you are putting a long-term foundation in place, you will view the process very differently, and you will do things differently to set yourself up well for both the present and the future.

Exhibit Consistency

In his book *Motivation*, Brian Tracy recommends interviewing job candidates in three different physical spaces within or outside the organization.[1] He believes you may see a different side of a candidate in a new area and under different conditions. What Tracy is looking for is consistency. Who is the real person behind the job candidate facade? What we do consistently is who we really are. Employers want to know what they're getting when they bring in new employees. Consistency is essential to a business, and it is essential during the job search process.

Dealing with inconsistent people is frustrating. Think about driving your car on the freeway behind someone who drives slowly for 20 seconds, and then speeds up for 10 seconds, and then slows down for 15 seconds, and then speeds up again. This inconsistency is maddening and exhausting. You must be on constant alert, and you don't know what the person will do next. The same frustration exists when you manage inconsistent employees. Nothing seems to flow smoothly, and you are always wondering what will come next: good or poor performance? friendly or unfriendly attitude? excellent or poor customer service? Most supervisors find it challenging to manage these types of employees. Inconsistency isn't good for business or for overall department morale.

Try this exercise: Visualize yourself dressing the top half of your body in business attire (a nice blouse with a blazer or a white shirt, tie, and sport coat) and the bottom half in casual attire (shorts, white socks, and tennis shoes). Now imagine going into a bathroom that has a mirror above the vanity so all you can see is the upper half of your body. How do you look? You look professional and impressive. Now, visualize yourself getting in front of a full-length mirror and looking at yourself. You don't look professional or impressive anymore, do you? You look quite ridiculous because the top half of you isn't consistent with the bottom half, and the impact is significant, especially when you looked so impressive at the start.

The clothing example may seem extreme, but it isn't that far-fetched. What if a job seeker wears a professional suit and then has a wrinkled shirt or puts on too much cologne or perfume? What if a candidate dresses professionally but then has a flimsy handshake and doesn't look the hiring manager in the eyes? In each of these situations, one part stands out in a negative way, and the employer may have doubts about the candidate. Make sure everything works well together.

Employers will immediately pick up on inconsistencies, and they are always on the lookout for warning signs. When they sense a disparity in quality of work, attitude, customer service, or anything else during the hiring process, they will move on to other candidates.

Consistency is exhibited in four main ways during the job search process:

1. Performing well at each stage of the process.
2. Following through on what you say you will do.
3. Backing up what you say about yourself in all areas of your life.
4. Being consistent with how you treat people.

Let's take a closer look at these four main ways to exhibit consistency throughout your job search.

1. **Perform well at each stage of the process.**

    You can learn a lot about marketing yourself by talking to real estate agents. If homebuyers see something wrong in a house, they will assume other parts of the home will lack quality as well, and they will start to look for all the flaws. The job search process works the same way. If employers believe quality is lacking somewhere along the line, they will assume this problem exists in other areas, too. And, unfortunately, they don't have much time to test this assumption. Instead, they will move you to the rejection stack and focus on stronger candidates who exhibit quality across the board. Even if they decide to keep you around a little longer, they will put on their "flaw" filter and look for anything else that confirms their negative observations.

    Job seekers often perform well in a few areas of the job search process but then struggle in other areas. A job applicant's résumé looks good, but the cover letter is weak. Written documents are strong, but the candidate's interview skills leave something to be desired. The candidate does everything well during the interview but doesn't send a thank-you note or follow-up message afterward. When there is inconsistency, the weak part will often stand out, especially if the weakness is significant and it comes after the candidate has exhibited a strength. Expectations are high, and then the weakness highlights the contrast between good and bad.

    Of course, if you make a strong first impression, employers will often overlook minor hiccups. This is the power of the halo effect, in which an employer's positive impression of someone from the start can unconsciously cause the employer to see all the good in a candidate and overlook some minor inconsistencies and errors along the way.

    However, if the contrast between good and bad is significant, the inconsistency will stand out even more. For example, I worked with a 26-year-old job seeker from Miami, Florida, named Carol who had strong cover letters and résumés.[2] She was getting interviews but wasn't getting second interviews and wasn't receiving job offers. She was struggling because she had strong writing skills and an impressive marketing mindset but was uncomfortable talking to people one-on-one. And, of course, this came across the minute she walked through the door. The awkwardness was also more apparent because it was in such contrast to her written documents. When Carol met with interviewers, they were expecting a completely different person. The significant contrast made it difficult for her to move along in the process and get job offers. Carol needed to work on her social skills before she could do well during the job search process and on the job, particularly since she was pursuing jobs that valued strong interpersonal communication skills. She had to overcome or minimize her weakness in order to present herself in a consistent manner and land her ideal job. The good news is that she was aware of the issue and was seeking help from a career coach.

Inconsistency will put doubts in the hiring manager's mind. It can be the one piece of information the employer uses to decide between top candidates, especially when employers are hypersensitive to anything that will allow them to make a quick decision with limited information. By performing well across the board, you won't give employers that easy out.

2. Follow through on what you say you will do.

If you say you are going to send a document, attend an interview, complete an assessment, or call the employer by a particular time, do each of these at the expected level of quality (or higher) and within the expected and promised time frame. Consistency really comes down to integrity—doing what you say you will do all the time. Very few employers will hire job candidates if they feel they lack integrity and can't trust them. Instead, generate trust by following through on every commitment you make.

3. Back up what you say about yourself in all areas of your life.

When you say you behave a certain way but don't exhibit the same behavior in other areas of your job search, this shows inconsistency. You must show consistency by demonstrating that you "walk the talk" and don't just "talk the talk."

If you say you can work independently yet you tend to contact the employer numerous times for information you could have found through other means, the employer will question your ability to work independently and be resourceful. The employer will also see you as a high-maintenance candidate and future employee. If this is the case, you will probably be rejected because employers know that past or current behavior is often a predictor of future behavior. If you are seen a certain way in the interview, employers will visualize you that way as a potential employee of the company. You never want to leave the employer with any doubt. You want them to visualize you excelling in the job.

If you say you are professional in your marketing documents, not only do you need to be professional during the interview by being prepared and focused, you also need to make sure all the other areas of your life show you in this light. For instance, your Facebook and Instagram pages need to be professional (no inappropriate photos or content), as well as all your email correspondence (friendly, thoughtfully laid out, error-free, targeted, clear, and effective). Being professional also means you have a customer-focused greeting on your voicemail system, use an appropriate email address, and have a professional signature line that includes your phone number.

If you can make the little things the big things during your job search, you will often get what you want in the end.

If you indicate you have strong communication skills, back this statement up with strong marketing materials and promotional platforms (cover letter, résumé, email correspondence, LinkedIn profile, professional career website, and thank-you notes). When I was a recruiter, I received a cover letter from a highly qualified applicant who stated that he had excellent communication skills. Unfortunately, he spelled the word "excellent" with an "a" (excellant). Needless to say, the applicant wasn't invited in for an interview.

During the job search process, you are in the business of details,[3] and attention to detail is part of the price of admission to your ideal job. Follow artist Andy Warhol's advice: "You need to let the little things that would ordinarily bore you suddenly thrill you."[4] If you can make the little things the big things during your job search, you will often get what you want in the end.

4. **Be consistent with how you treat people.**

Recruiters know that job candidates can elevate their game during a formal one-hour interview. However, job candidates' true personalities often come out when they don't think employers are evaluating them. Treating the receptionist and parking attendant differently than the hiring manager and CEO isn't being consistent. While you don't need to ask the same questions or say precisely the same things, you should be friendly, professional, respectful, and polite to everyone. When I was a recruiter, I would ask the receptionist and anyone else who met the job candidate what the person was like and how the person treated them. It was from these peripheral engagements that I often learned the most about job candidates.

If you follow the Golden Rule and treat everyone how you would like to be treated, you will consistently treat people the right way. You will also have an easier time expanding your relationship team because people will gravitate toward you and want to interact with you.

Care About Quality and Consistency

The Quality and Consistency Guiding Principle is the most important principle; it is foundational for the other principles, and that is why it is placed at the bottom of the hexagon (Figure A). If you want to stand out, be a notch above your competitors, and impress the employer, you need to care about quality and consistency. Make sure the employer sees you as a highly polished professional who behaves in a consistent manner and is focused and ready to step in and do top-quality work on time all the time. If the employer sees you in this light, you will most likely move on in the process. Make quality and consistency your core foundational guiding principle.

Guiding Principle 2: Present Yourself in a Professional Manner

Will employers feel like they can trust you in any situation to present yourself in a professional manner? If not, you will probably not get the job offer. Employers can teach new hires technical skills, but they have a hard time teaching people how to present themselves the right way in a variety of situations. Employers want low-maintenance employees who consistently behave in a competent, reliable, respectful, and polished manner.

Don't take this principle lightly. If employers sense you can't or won't be professional in all settings by what you say, what you wear, or how you act, they will move on and hire someone else. For example, during one recruitment when I was looking to hire someone to manage a training and development program, I had two excellent applicants. While both had strong technical skills, one was a little uncomfortable and awkward on the interpersonal side—not in all cases, but in a few. Since I needed someone who was professional in all situations, I ended up hiring the person I knew would excel in the position from day one and whom I would feel comfortable putting in any situation. I hired the person who had both technical and nontechnical skills, and I never had to worry about her performance. She excelled on the job just like she did during the interview process.

Part of being professional is also having a positive attitude. This is critical during the job search process because frustration and stress can easily creep into your documents, interviews, and correspondence. No matter what is happening with your job search and life, remain positive, pleasant, respectful, and courteous when you are in front of employers. Your documents and correspondence should also reflect a pleasant and confident tone. Always remind yourself of what you are really selling: a relationship. Most employers would rather hire a person with a great attitude and fewer skills than a highly skilled person with a bad attitude. People hire people; they don't hire résumés and credentials. Your goal is to have a great attitude *and* a great skill set.

A professional and positive attitude is important in the hiring process because it's important in the workplace, particularly when professional standards have been put in place by companies to help employees better serve customers and function more effectively as a team. Nontechnical or "soft" skills help employees work effectively and seamlessly with other people.

A study conducted by Wonderlic found that 93 percent of employers indicated that soft skills are "essential" or are a "very important" factor when making hiring decisions.[5] The results of a National Association of Colleges and Employers survey found that employers ranked leadership skills and the ability to work on a team as more important than problem-solving, analytical, or quantitative skills.[6] And a study by LinkedIn showed that 59 percent of US hiring managers believe it is difficult to find job candidates with soft skills.[7] The same LinkedIn study found that employers consider the following to be the most important soft skills: "communication, organization, teamwork, punctuality, critical thinking, social skills, creativity, interpersonal communication, adaptability, and friendly personality."

> You can't afford to neglect the soft skills that will advance your job search and career.

The majority of these can be summed up as skills that help you present yourself in a professional manner.

You can't afford to neglect the soft skills that will advance your job search and career. Many interview evaluation forms contain a list of 80 to 90 percent soft skills and only 10 to 20 percent technical skills, which shouldn't surprise you given the study results mentioned above.

Professional standards will vary depending on the position, department, company, field, and industry. Your goal is to know as much as you can about what is required and desired by each company and field and what drives the company culture. With more information in hand, you can determine how well you align with what is required, assess how much you want to work at the organization, and decide what you want to communicate to the employer through all your promotional platforms. With limited inside information, you should assume most employers want job candidates who

- Meet or exceed all deadlines.
- Arrive early to meetings.
- Exhibit excellent communication skills, including strong listening skills.
- Know the company's or the department's needs and show how they can address the needs.
- Submit clean, error-free, and well-designed documents.
- Dress appropriately for the audience and the setting.
- Exhibit superb follow-through and follow-up skills.
- Prepare thoroughly for important meetings.
- Showcase their ability to work well on teams.
- Exhibit emotional intelligence (the ability to understand and manage one's own emotions and the emotions of others) and show they can function well in any situation.
- Are flexible and adaptable.
- Greet people with a pleasant tone.
- Look people in the eyes and smile.
- Shake hands firmly.
- Display good manners.
- Exhibit a consistent brand (consistent goals, interests, standards, and priorities).
- Are excited but also relaxed (can be "themselves").
- Exhibit consistently courteous behavior (e.g., treating people well, being on time, listening closely, and phrasing remarks in a positive way).
- Thank people for their help.

These soft skills—the emotional intelligence, interpersonal skills, attitude, teamwork, collaboration, and work ethic—are hard to teach. They take time to develop, and employers know it. Employers also know they may never get new hires to develop these skills. As a result, they tend to hire candidates who they know already have important job-related soft skills and will present themselves professionally in any situation.

If you think you may be weak in one or more of these areas, seek help from a job search or career coach. If you lack key job search skills and have a hard time with one or more of the Slam Dunk Guiding Principles, you probably lack essential "on the job" skills as well. Your job search is all about performing well in your career and making a significant and positive impact on the world. You don't want to land your ideal job and then struggle in your new role, as these deficiencies will surface more in the workplace over a longer period. Get help now. The training or assistance you receive will not only help your job search but also your job performance and long-term career advancement.

To locate people who can help you, conduct a Google search to identify potential career and job search coaches, reach out to your university career center for help, tap into online resources like The Muse and Career Contessa to access professional career services, and ask around for referrals. You can also access online professional development resources through platforms like Coursera, LinkedIn Learning, and Udemy.

Guiding Principle 3: Provide Extraordinary Customer Service

The subtitle for the third guiding principle, Provide Extraordinary Customer Service, should be "keep the vacuum cleaner in the back room until the customers are gone." How many times have you been in a store at the end of the day and an employee starts vacuuming or closing parts of the store during operating hours? Is this excellent customer service? Absolutely not, and it sends the following messages:

- We don't care about the customer's shopping experience.
- We are frugal and can't afford to hire enough staff or pay employees to work longer.
- We don't know our customers' needs and buying experience desires.
- We don't want to give our customers our full attention and would rather leave work sooner.
- We don't know how to approach the job in a professional manner.
- We don't have strong customer service values throughout the organization.
- We care more about ourselves than the customers.
- We don't enjoy our jobs and want to leave work as quickly as possible.

Are you surprised that a vacuum cleaner is capable of communicating so much? Well, you can send the same types of messages at each stage of the job search process if you don't treat employers like customers. Remember, you're marketing yourself and your credentials during the job search process, so the employer is quite literally your customer. Here are some ways you could send negative messages:

- You aren't very accommodating when scheduling an interview.
- You ask too many questions that are irrelevant or could be answered through your own research.
- You are demanding and challenging to get along with during the process.
- You don't respond quickly to phone calls or email messages.
- You talk too much and fail to demonstrate active listening skills.
- You aren't friendly and pleasant to interact with throughout the process.
- You don't follow directions.
- You aren't focused on the employer's needs and wants.
- You are more interested in what you will get out of the job and less focused on how you can help the employer.
- You haven't done your research on the company.
- You demand parking assistance or reimbursement for local travel.
- You don't meet deadlines.
- You come across as a know-it-all.
- You wait for employers to make all the moves.
- You communicate in an informal or unprofessional manner.

As you can imagine, this list could go on and on. With customer service, you are always "on," and you must strive to provide extraordinary service until the customers are gone.

Employers will be impressed when you are focused on their needs, have a genuine interest in working for the company, and have a long-term commitment to the field. As a recruiter, I can't tell you how many times candidates failed to answer the following question adequately: "What are your career goals?" While I did get some good responses (and I probably hired those candidates), I would often have them tell me exactly what an employer doesn't want to hear: goals unrelated to the job, company, or field. Candidates, for example, would say they planned to go back to graduate school in six months to a year. One hiring manager in Seattle, Washington, recently told me that she asked a job candidate to share his career goals, and he said he wanted to be a journalist.[8] There is nothing the matter with this admirable career; however, the job he was interviewing for was a medical sales representative! I would also interview applicants who had no idea what they wanted to do, which showed little commitment to the company or the field. Employers like it when job candidates are excited about working for them and have a good reason for wanting to join the organization.

What does this all mean? It means you need to look closely at the company or department and see what is vital to the organization and the hiring manager. Find ways to serve your customers. Here are some questions to ask yourself as you dig deeper to find out more about the organization and the position:

- What does the job announcement really say? What does the content tell me about the company culture? What is unique within the announcement?
- What keywords in the job announcement are most prominent when run through a word cloud generator or a chatbot like ChatGPT? Can you identify any themes?
- How does the organization portray the company culture on the website?
- What are the company's values, core competencies, and professional standards?
- What do the company's vision and mission statements say?
- What does the interviewer's LinkedIn profile look like, and what types of connections or credentials do I have in common with the person?
- What do employees or prior employees say about the company or department?
- What do customers say about the company's products or services?
- What is the company sending out on social media, and what does it tell me about the company's services, culture, and overall operations?
- What are the hiring manager's needs and goals?
- What challenges exist in the department and the company?

Find what is important to the employer and present yourself in a way that brings out the skills, experience, training, and qualities that align with the company's needs, goals, and culture. Show employers how you can help them more than any other job candidate.

During the job search process, make sure you can answer "yes" to the following questions each time you pursue a job:

- Do I know the company and the department inside and out, and do I understand the company's and department's needs to the best of my ability?
- Am I doing everything I can to make the hiring manager's job easier and not harder?
- Have I made it easy for the hiring manager to understand why the company should hire me?
- Have I communicated how I can help the department reach its goals and overcome its challenges?
- Have I made it clear why I am different from other applicants and how my unique qualities or skills can help the company?
- Have I demonstrated that I would fit in well with the company culture (values, core competencies, and professional standards)?
- Have I expressed an interest in or passion for the company and the type of work?
- Have I reminded myself that the job search process is all about helping employers get what they want and developing long-term relationships, and have I done everything I can to make this happen?

Steve Krug wrote a book called *Don't Make Me Think* to help people design useful websites.[9] Keep this title in mind when you work on your documents, create your online platforms, or correspond with employers throughout the job search process. Recruiters and hiring managers are far too busy to look for something that should be right in front of them. When you make employers think too much about who you are, what you can do, how to reach you, why you are pursuing the job, or why they should hire you, they will move on to other candidates. Instead, make these things obvious.

Employers are looking for anything that will help them narrow down the applicant pool quickly. To avoid getting eliminated through your résumé, cover letter, and online platforms, lead readers quickly to where you know they want to go. Don't make them burn many brain calories trying to find what they need.

At each stage of the job search process, ask yourself the following question before you submit anything or have any interaction with the employer: "Will I make hiring committee members or recruiters think about anything they shouldn't have to think about?" If you feel you are making employers think too much or forcing them to do extra work to figure you out, go back and rework your documents (cover letter and résumé), refine your online promotional platforms (LinkedIn profile and professional career website), and better prepare for your interactions (phone interview, in-person interview, videoconference, phone conversations, and email correspondence).

You should also avoid making employers wait. Since employers know that just about everyone has a cell phone and most people get their messages instantly, respond quickly to people you reach out to for help, especially if you are unemployed and 100 percent focused on your search. If you want to respond to your friend's text or email message in a couple of days, that's fine. But when you are looking for professional guidance or interacting with employers, act like the person you are corresponding with is your only customer. You need to

- Accommodate employers' schedules and make the process easier on them.
- Respond within one to two hours or sooner.
- Always be aware of the recruiter's or hiring manager's time and exhibit emotional intelligence.
- Send a post-interview thank-you note within two to six hours.

Employers expect you to be at your best during the job search process. They also know that, once you're hired, your best will probably drop down a notch or two. If you aren't meeting or exceeding expectations during the job search process in terms of response time, quality of work, business attire, professional standards, or core competencies, there is a high probability you will not meet expectations when you join the company. You at least want to meet expectations during each stage of the process and then seek to exceed expectations at opportune times.

Providing extraordinary customer service doesn't mean you need to let employers have total control over you. For example, if you answer the phone and an employer wants to interview you on the spot, don't accommodate the request if you aren't ready. You can say that you are thrilled to have the opportunity to talk about your qualifications, but unfortunately, you will need to schedule the interview at a different time.

Many job seekers hurt their candidacy because they do everything the employer wants, and it causes them to perform poorly. Employers respect people who are professional and reasonably accommodating but also have appropriate boundaries. If you say you can't talk for a week, that is a problem. However, if you say you would be happy to speak later in the day or the next morning, that's fine. Sometimes employers will try to catch you off guard, but you don't need to fall for it. They will respect you if you are honest with them and provide reasonable alternatives. Nevertheless, always use your best judgment given your unique situation.

Providing extraordinary customer service should be a priority for you throughout your entire career. One of the quickest ways to be remarkable is to provide excellent service. It isn't difficult to do, but it does take planning, preparation, and action.

Guiding Principle 4: Think Like a Salesperson and Act Like an Artist

As you look to land your ideal job, you must make it easy for hiring managers to understand why they should hire you, and you must know that you have the freedom to do whatever helps you communicate your value. You need to follow the fourth guiding principle: Think Like a Salesperson and Act Like an Artist.

Think Like a Salesperson

While you may not consider yourself a salesperson, you must think like a salesperson if you want to elevate your performance during the job search process. It's about knowing how to package your skills, market yourself, and communicate your value.

Consider Robert, a job seeker who interviewed for a variety of diverse positions as a hobby (really!) over a seven-year period. Robert was invited to interview for 300 jobs, and he received offers from more than 60 percent of them.[10] Interestingly, he was not the most qualified candidate for most of the positions. What was his secret? As long as Robert followed an effective job search process and did all the basics well across the board, he knew he didn't need all the qualifications listed in the job announcement to be competitive. He knew that if he could combine strong job search skills with a likable personality and solid credentials, he would have a good shot at landing a number of jobs. Robert knew how to think like a salesperson and market himself.

Keep sales expert Anthony Iannarino's perspective in mind as you move through each step of the process: "Once I discovered that selling was about helping people get a result that they couldn't get without my assistance, I began to love the game."[11] Think about what you can offer the employer that no one else can offer. What unique value do you bring to the employer and the position? You can think of this as your unique value proposition (UVP): a statement used in advertising to communicate how a product or service is superior to other products or services. Often, in the job search process, your UVP relates to your professional experience, training, or skills, but it can also be a personal experience, quality, or trait. Think about what will give you a competitive advantage over other job candidates as you start to compete for your ideal job, and make sure you communicate it to the employer.

Years ago, I helped a talented PhD graduate from Minnesota with his job search, and I still vividly remember the advising session.[12] The graduate was interested in international consulting. While reviewing his documents—cover letter first and résumé second—I was surprised that he didn't appear to have any language skills highlighted for an international position. As I worked my way to the second page of his résumé and asked him if he had any language skills, he said, "Yes, they're listed at the bottom of the second page of my résumé." I looked at the Skills section at the very end of page two. Here is what he had included: "Language Skills—Fluent in 7 languages, including English, French, Italian, Portuguese, Spanish, Russian, and Mandarin." The graduate was pursuing international consulting positions, yet he had one of his most unique and important skills listed at the very bottom of the second page of his résumé. The hiring manager or recruiter probably wouldn't have made it down that far to see one of his most valuable skills. It was apparent the PhD graduate didn't know his audience, wasn't thinking like a salesperson, and wasn't making it easy for the employer to see one of his most important skills—his unique value proposition.

Make certain your most valuable credentials are front and center. When you begin thinking like a salesperson and finding ways to help the employer see the value you bring, you will seek to understand what is essential to the employer and start to bring your most important skills, training, and experience to the forefront. After our meeting, the PhD graduate had his seven languages highlighted in his cover letter and in a Summary of Qualifications section at the top of page one of his résumé.

How you present yourself is critical. When you watch programs like *The Voice* and *Dancing with the Stars*, you will notice that the most talented people don't always win. Instead, the people who know their audience and present themselves the right way are often the ones who come out ahead in the end. With *The Voice*, for instance, it usually comes down to a combination of how the contestants present themselves, how much the audience warms up to them (likability), and their level of talent—the whole package and not just the "voice." I have seen talented singers lose because they were a 10 on talent but only a 2 or 3 in other areas. I have also seen talented job candidates miss out on offers for the same reason—they were a 10 on technical skills and a 2 or 3 in other areas.

If you want to compete successfully for your ideal job, look for ways to engage and connect with people; don't merely rely on your credentials to land you the job. You want to land the job offer when you are the most talented candidate and when you aren't the most talented.

Most employers value well-rounded candidates over candidates who rank high in only one or two areas. If you think like a salesperson and know what you are really selling, you should be able to close the deal even when you aren't the one with the best skills, training, or experience.

Act Like an Artist

Very few strategies and tactics are black and white during the job search process. In most cases, when it comes to your marketing materials, you have a blank canvas in front of you, and you have the freedom to move content and sections around and do whatever works best for your job search. Your goal is to break away from the norm without incurring much risk. The more you know about the employer (e.g., mission, values, professional standards, needs, challenges, goals, and wants) and the more you are focused on helping them, the safer you will be breaking away from the standard job search rules. Why? Because knowledge is power. The inside information will point you in a direction that more accurately addresses the employer's needs.

Knowledge will allow you to stand out in the right way by implementing tactics that a specific employer values. For example, one consumer products manager from Houston, Texas, spoke to some students at a conference and told them that they should *always* put an objective statement on their résumés. Several of the students came to me quite confused because I had advised them to exclude an objective statement from their résumés. While objective statements are outdated and rarely used on résumés, I was able to use what the manager said to make an important point. The manager was right: If you are pursuing a position with her, you need to include an objective statement on your résumé. If you know what hiring managers want, do whatever you can to show them you are the candidate who is most in tune with their needs and desires.

The more you know about the employer's needs through the job announcement, informational meetings, and your research, the more you can customize your approach and act like an artist with a blank canvas. The less you know, the more you need to follow the rules for your field, and when you do that, you risk appearing like everyone else. If you want to stand out and wow the employer, identify the employer's needs and wants and then act like an artist by uniquely packaging your skills, training, and experience in the best way possible for the employer.

Once you know the employer's needs, you can move essential credentials to the top of your résumé and cover letter. You will be successful if your documents guide the reader where they want to go in the top one-third to one-half of the résumé. Unfortunately, many fancy résumé templates force job seekers to put key credentials in nonstrategic locations. We saw it with the PhD graduate who was seeking the international consulting position. Instead of thinking like a salesperson and then moving the most important credentials to the top of the résumé like an artist, he felt he needed to put his skills at the bottom of page two because that was where the Skills section was located on his résumé template.

One minor change to a résumé—moving one or two credentials or sections around—can often take an applicant from being unmarketable to being extremely marketable. This was the case for Mary, a job seeker from Las Vegas, Nevada, who was interested in going into video and media production right after graduating from college.[13] Unfortunately, Mary had very little in her background related to this field. However, as I was reading through her résumé, I noticed in the Activities section at the very bottom that Mary had developed short documentary films through two summer programs. Given that the first three-quarters of Mary's résumé didn't show any video and media production experience or training, recruiters probably wouldn't have made it down to the Activities section to see her most valuable experience. And if they had, the descriptions were so short that they wouldn't have made much of an impression. As it was, her résumé didn't help her market herself effectively for the desired position.

To make Mary more marketable, I had her create a section below the Education section (in the top one-third of the résumé) titled Video and Media Production Projects. Within this section, she elaborated on the two projects and brought them to life. This minor change moved her from being an unmarketable applicant for a video and media position to a marketable and focused applicant. And it created the halo effect that had employers see Mary's experience in a positive light as they moved down her résumé.

You have permission to change anything during the job search process if it helps you stand out in a positive light and separates you from the competition. Move things around, change things, and adjust. Do whatever showcases your credentials the most. If you use your best judgment, stay flexible, think like a salesperson, and act like an artist with a blank canvas in front of you, you will be more successful throughout the job search process—and throughout your entire career.

Guiding Principle 5: Go Above and Beyond Expectations

Managers don't want to hire mediocre people. They want to hire people like you who are willing to go above and beyond by taking projects off their hands, doing high-quality work, putting in extra time, and completing projects on time. They want people who will deliver and overdeliver. By showing that you have gone above and beyond what is expected of you in previous jobs and convincing employers that you will do the same for them, you will get employers' attention quickly.

You can also show your above-and-beyond approach by how you conduct your job search. If you say you go above and beyond expectations, make sure you reinforce it during the job search process. Here are some ways to go above and beyond as you look to stand out and impress the hiring committee members:

- Adjust your schedule to accommodate the employer's schedule.
- Offer to drive to the headquarters for an in-person interview rather than take part in a phone interview (if given an option or you believe it may be an option).
- Talk to company employees and customers prior to the interview to learn more about the employer's needs and then share ways you can address those needs.
- Respond to messages within one to two hours (or sooner).
- Send a confirmation email the day before your interview to share your enthusiasm for the opportunity and show your professional mindset.

- Develop and share some strategies for how the department can accomplish its goals or overcome its challenges.
- Bring something to share during the interview that demonstrates the quality of your work or the depth of your knowledge.
- Send your post-interview thank-you messages within two to six hours.
- Attach an article that the hiring manager would appreciate when you send a thank-you message.
- Include a report or a paper you wrote with your interview thank-you note or follow-up message.
- Attach a summary of your qualifications (Career Profile—discussed in chapter 5) to your electronic thank-you note after the final interview.

Going above and beyond expectations can still apply even if you make a mistake. In one situation, a 26-year-old job seeker named Kimberly was interested in a position with a company in Chicago, Illinois.[14] Since Kimberly knew she would be competing against many highly qualified applicants, she thought she would impress the hiring manager by sending her application materials directly to the manager through the mail.

A day after Kimberly had mailed her application, she was perusing the company website for some additional information, and she noticed that the hiring manager had the same name as another manager, but they spelled their names differently. As Kimberly took a closer look, she realized she had used the spelling of the other manager's name in her application materials. She was horrified.

Since Kimberly was very interested in the position, she started to think about how she could turn this unfortunate situation around. Given her customer service background, Kimberly knew she needed to get the right product—a quality product—in the hands of the employer as quickly as possible. As a result, she corrected the cover letter and sent another complete application packet via overnight service with a note explaining the situation and apologizing for getting the manager's name mixed up with the other staff member's name.

Kimberly's overnight packet arrived before her original application materials, and she was invited in for an interview. During her interview, the hiring committee members couldn't stop talking about her above-and-beyond approach. Kimberly had wowed the employer even when she had made a mistake.

Kimberly's story illustrates how you can turn a negative situation into an advantage if you use the Slam Dunk Guiding Principles and think creatively. Of course, the story also demonstrates that you should double-check everything before sending out your documents. But, as we all know, sometimes mistakes or errors occur despite our best efforts. In such situations, we have a valuable opportunity to learn from our missteps and try to turn them into something positive.

Going above and beyond expectations will help you stand out and provide better service along the way. You should never come out of an interview without having used stories and examples to show you have a history of exceeding expectations.

Guiding Principle 6: Be Different and Memorable

The final guiding principle is to find ways to be different and memorable during your job search. At the start of each stage of the job search process, ask yourself what you can do to be remarkable. How can you get people to talk about you because you did or said something worth remarking about?[15] You need to be the one who comes to mind at the end of each stage and definitely at the end of the interview stage.

Every part of the job search process has a standard pattern or script that can become boring for many recruiters and hiring managers. Look for ways to make the process more enjoyable and meaningful for them by being different and changing things up every now and then. This will wake up employers and get them to hear, and later talk about, what you have to say. What can you do to impress employers? Can you

- Include a story in your cover letter to grab attention?
- Create a brochure that markets the company's or department's services and exhibits your marketing and graphic design talents?
- Provide recommendations on how the department can reach its goals quicker or address its challenges?
- Bring a portfolio of your work to the interview to impress the hiring committee members?
- Share a training video you created?
- Tell a story during the interview that sticks in the hiring committee members' minds long after the meeting?

- Ask questions during the interview to develop a greater dialogue and uncover important information?
- Answer the weakness interview question in a unique way that wakes up the hiring committee members and showcases your qualifications for the position (see chapter 16)?

By finding effective and appropriate ways to shake up the process, you will reap the rewards of all your hard work and preparation. You will also be remarkable because you took a common occurrence and made it different and memorable.

Tachi, a 26-year-old job seeker from Phoenix, Arizona, is an example of someone who benefited from breaking the script and being different. Tachi knew he needed to elevate his job search performance to land an account executive job with a big brand company that served a unique client base. Despite being invited in for an interview, Tachi learned from an inside contact that the hiring manager was looking for someone with a different background.

To prepare for the interview and shift the manager's thinking, Tachi acted like he was already in the role, and he reached out and interviewed some potential clients to determine their needs and wants. Then, based on his findings, Tachi designed a compact marketing brochure that promoted his services to this target audience and highlighted his expertise in client relations.

During the interview, Tachi presented the brochure, discussed the services he would provide, and outlined his strategy for effectively working with this unique client group. The hiring committee was impressed with Tachi's presentation, marketing talents, proactive approach, and advanced preparation. It was clear to the committee that he was the top candidate for the position.

By elevating his job search to the next level and showcasing his ability to fit in well with the organization and bring significant value to the team, Tachi ensured he didn't leave anything to chance. His approach was different and memorable, giving him an edge over all the other candidates, even those with more desirable "on paper" credentials.

Whatever you decide to implement that is different and memorable, be sure to present yourself in a professional manner for your audience. Some job candidates may take a risk and do something strange to grab attention. You've probably heard stories about job applicants sending résumés to employers in balloons or through singing telegrams. Sometimes these tactics work, but for most companies and positions, they are inappropriate and unsuccessful. In most cases, you don't want to do anything strange that puts you in the "weird applicant" rejection pile. Of course, what is considered strange will often depend on your field and industry. In creative fields, some out-of-the-ordinary tactics could be needed and desired. In most fields and industries, however, you should look to be different and remarkable by focusing your energy on applying the other five guiding principles:

1. Exhibiting quality and consistency.
2. Presenting yourself in a professional manner.
3. Providing extraordinary customer service.
4. Thinking like a salesperson and acting like an artist.
5. Going above and beyond expectations.

These five guiding principles will go a long way in helping you to be different and memorable, and they involve very little risk.

While I was writing this book, I saw a poster that read, "Those who leave a trail of glitter are never forgotten." Leave a trail of (professional and appropriate) glitter at key times throughout the job search process by doing or saying things differently. You don't want to be the job candidate who gets lost in the shuffle. If you find the right time to add some glitter and bring yourself to life, you will be rewarded for your efforts. And, as you will see a little later, the Slam Dunk step will provide you with plenty of specific ways to be different and memorable. But, once again, know your audience, and do what makes the most sense for each employer and field.

Apply the Principles at Every Stage

When you navigate the job search process by following the Slam Dunk Guiding Principles, you will take your job search to the next level and impress employers without implementing risky tactics. As you move through the 6-Step Slam Dunk Job Search Process, think about how you can incorporate the principles so you can stand out at each stage. The more proactive you are in applying the principles, the more you will separate yourself from your competitors—and have fun doing it.

Do you want to know how to get ready to enter the job market and successfully compete for your ideal job?

Step 3

MARKET READY

It's not the will to win that matters—everybody has that. It's the will to prepare to win that matters.[1]

—PAUL BEAR BRYANT

You are about to put an "Open for Business" sign on your job search storefront. But before you do, you need to get the store in order. The basic operations of your job search need to run smoothly and efficiently, and your job search must exhibit quality across the board.

Most job seekers jump right into their job search before they are prepared. They don't have their "store" in order, and you know what happens when products or services aren't market ready: deadlines are missed, quality suffers, inconsistency occurs, products aren't unique and special, customers aren't happy, and potential buyers don't buy.

If you don't have everything in order, you will have a hard time wowing your customers (employers) and getting their business (the job). If you want to be remarkable, you need to get everything ready across the board before you start to compete for your ideal job. You need to be market ready.

During each job search, there is a cost of doing business. As you move through the Market Ready step, keep in mind that the six tasks outlined below are the price of admission to your ideal job. They have been put in place to help you excel once you start to compete.

Market Ready Tasks

1. **Assess Your Marketability:** How do your credentials align with what the market demands within your field? What do you need to add to your credential portfolio to be competitive? What can you do to make yourself even more valuable and appealing to employers?

2. **Determine What Separates You from Your Competitors:** How will you differentiate yourself from the competition within your field? What makes you unique and special? How do you pull everything together in one place so you have what you need to promote yourself?

3. **Follow a Simple Framework for Communicating Your Value:** Do you have a simple diagram you can visualize each time you need to describe the value you bring to your field or a particular job? What will all but guarantee you successfully move through each stage of the job search process and ultimately land the job offer?

4. **Get Your Marketing Documents Ready:** What documents do you need to promote yourself effectively? Are your documents ready to go so all you need to do is customize them for each unique position?

5. **Build Your Brand:** What does your online presence currently say about you? What do you want your brand to communicate? How do you want employers to think about you across the board? What can you do to promote yourself and show your work? What types of promotional platforms are relevant within your field?

6. **Prepare for Contact:** How can you connect with people in nine seconds or less? How will you respond when you meet people and they ask, "What do you do?" or "How are you?" What can you say that will generate interest and curiosity?

If you want to conduct a quality job search from start to finish, you must take the time to establish a solid job search foundation. The stronger the foundation, the more time you will have later to customize your search and find ways to set yourself apart from your competitors.

As you work through the Market Ready step, keep the remarkable Chinese bamboo tree in mind. Even when a Chinese bamboo tree seed is planted, watered, and given fertilizer, you will not see any noticeable growth until the fifth year. But in that fifth year, the tree grows an astonishing 90 feet in six weeks. While there is no upward growth during the first four years, there is significant downward growth as the root system takes hold and expands, setting a solid foundation in place to support the rapid upward trajectory that occurs in year five.[2]

You don't need four years to develop a solid job search foundation, but you do need to understand why you should take the time to go through the Market Ready step. Establishing a solid footing at the start will allow you to do the basics well across the board and spring ahead of your competitors once you start to compete. Always remember that you need to be good before you can be great. And, in your case, you want to go beyond great and be remarkable. The more you can put a solid foundation in place, the more remarkable and successful you will be during your job search and career.

Let's now take a closer look at each of these Market Ready tasks.

Chapter 4

ASSESS YOUR MARKETABILITY

efore you start to compete for your ideal job, you should know where you stand relative to the marketplace. You should know what you want to offer, but you also must know how well you match up with what the market demands.

Identify What the Market Demands

When you are in business, you need to know what your customers desire and then make sure you can offer what they want. Take a close look at your credentials and see how well they align with the market's needs or the core qualifications required in your field. Ask yourself the following questions at the start of—or ideally before— each job search:

- What limitations exist in my background and what can be done to eliminate or circumvent them?
- Can I become more marketable quickly, or will I need to stall my ideal job search or pursue a different job at this time?
- What can I add to my credential portfolio that isn't required by the field or the company but would make me more marketable for my ideal job or more productive on the job once I land it?

Having the right credentials is important. If you don't have critical experience, education, training, skills, and certifications, you may have a hard time opening the door to your ideal job. This will, of course, depend on what qualifications you are lacking and what each company requires.

Lacking a qualification won't necessarily prevent you from being successful. But you need to conduct research to determine whether the lack of a particular qualification is a deal-breaker for the field, company, or position. Also, if you take a long-term view, you will always want to work on getting better for your career so you can have a greater impact now and in the future.

In the Assess Your Marketability task, you will survey the market quickly through your online research. You want to get the lay of the land early and begin to understand your field before you reach out to people for advice in the Relationship Team step. The last thing you want is to contact people and not know much about your field or what you want to gain from your conversations. The more research you can do in advance and the more knowledgeable you are about your field, the more productive you will be conversing with people. During the Assess Your Marketability task, do your best to get answers to the following five types of questions as they relate to your field:

Credentials

- What gaps exist in my background that I need to fill to be competitive?
- What qualities and skills are most important for my field? (Review relevant job postings to determine the most desirable skills and qualities.)
- Is there anything I can add to my credential portfolio (skills, training, certifications, or experience) that isn't required but would make me more marketable? (You will typically uncover this type of inside information later during the Relationship Team step when you contact people and get advice, but sometimes you can locate it online.)
- What are the best self-education avenues to gain technical and nontechnical skills quickly for my field?

Career

- What is the typical career path within my field?
- Given my background, what are the best jobs to pursue now to set me up well for the future?

- What are the best conferences to attend to meet people and learn more about this type of career?
- What are the best professional associations to join?
- What short- and long-term trends are taking place in this field?

Job Search

- What does the job market look like?
- Are there any résumé and cover letter design elements that are unique to my field?
- What are the best job search strategies and tactics to use?
- What are the best social media platforms for promoting my brand?
- How can I add more value to the marketplace than anyone else?
- What will make me stand out?
- What is most important to employers?
- Is there anything I should avoid adding to my résumé and cover letter or saying in an interview that is inappropriate for my field or industry?
- What other online avenues are good for promoting my credentials?

Companies

- What are the big brand companies in my field?
- What small and medium-sized companies exist within my field of interest?
- Are there any emerging organizations I should explore?

Contacts

- Who are the professional leaders in my field?
- Who are the key decision makers within my target organizations?
- Am I connected to anyone on LinkedIn or through my alma mater who is working in my field?
- Who else do I know who could refer me to decision makers in my target organizations?

The answers to these questions will help you understand your field better and enable you to ask the right types of questions when you reach out to professionals during the Relationship Team step. You want all your contacts to be impressed with you and your knowledge, and you want to ask strategic rather than basic questions. If you can't get answers to any of the above questions through your online research or want to confirm what you have already uncovered, have the list of questions available to ask when you contact people as you seek to fill in the gaps.

Ideally, you will have the opportunity to get market ready before you begin to compete for positions. If you are in school or still employed, start getting ready for your job search months before you begin to pursue opportunities. Allocate time to research your field and build up your background to become more marketable. Getting a head start will allow you to adjust your course schedule, take more courses, gain more knowledge, acquire a relevant certification, complete a short training program, or improve essential skills in other ways. Having some lead time is ideal.

If you don't have any lead time and are already in your job search, you will still conduct research on your field, but you will also move quickly to the Relationship Team step as you reach out to people to make connections and get information that will help you become even more marketable. Many job seekers spend too much time online looking for jobs and doing research at the expense of connecting with people. Don't make that mistake. Conduct your online research quickly (two to three days, depending on how much time you allocate to the task each day) and then move on to the Relationship Team step to confirm your findings and gather inside information unavailable online.

Acquire Additional Credentials

As you learn more about your field and how well your credentials align with your ideal job, you may need to find ways to build up your background quickly to become more marketable. The good news is that there are numerous ways to acquire skills in a short amount of time. For example, if you don't have any experience with a particular qualification listed in the job announcement, search the internet to learn the basics about the topic, or find people who work in that area and tap into their knowledge.

You don't need a formal education to become knowledgeable on most subjects. There are plenty of ways to gain both technical and nontechnical skills. For many fields and jobs, you can now acquire a significant amount of knowledge and skills through books, articles, short workshops, webinars, conferences, websites, online courses, certificate programs, and conversations with experts in the field. Self-education is big business. Plenty of inexpensive one-day workshops and short online training programs exist on just about any subject. Professional development avenues will allow you to add skills to your marketing documents and promotional platforms quickly and help you avoid being rejected by an applicant tracking system (an electronic résumé and cover letter review system) or a human resources department that focuses on rigid position requirements. Coursera, DataCamp, LinkedIn Learning, and Udemy are examples of online platforms where you can access professional development courses.

If you lack the critical credentials needed to enter a particular position or field and you can't acquire them quickly, you may need to broaden your job search in order to get into the workforce. If this is the case, expand your search to include jobs that are related to your field but aren't exactly ideal. You should also identify a backup job in case you need to get into the job market quickly before landing a more desirable position.

If you end up in a job that isn't ideal, you will probably need to retool and build up your credentials to land your ideal job further down the line. However, this isn't always the case. It may be that the experience you gain in the less-than-ideal job over the next one to two years is enough to allow you to compete effectively for your ideal job. And, as you may already know, less-than-ideal jobs often serve as stepping stones to your ideal job while also providing you with a wealth of knowledge and skills that can help you excel throughout your entire career.

If you don't end up in your desired position, reach out to decision makers within your field and ask them how you can become more competitive. You can't beat this approach because it also allows you to develop critical contacts in your field. Share your credentials (résumé, LinkedIn profile, and professional career website) with your contacts and ask what is missing and what you should highlight. Whatever job you end up in, assess your situation, adjust, expand your skills, and then work your way back through the 6-Step Slam Dunk Job Search Process to pursue your ideal job when the time is right.

After identifying the credentials you would like to acquire, determine the best ways to obtain them, and then set goals and timelines to achieve them. You don't need to acquire all your credentials immediately and cram in everything during your job search, but you should create three Career Advancement Plans (CAPs). These plans will include a 16-week job search CAP to make you more competitive during your job search, a one-year CAP, and a three-year CAP. Of course, you may find that some of your longer-term plans will change once you enter the workforce and learn more about the field and yourself. Your destination may stay the same, but the path you take to get there could be different than you initially imagined. No matter what happens, your time will be well spent if you continue to develop yourself and find ways to make yourself more valuable to employers.

Chapter 5

DETERMINE WHAT SEPARATES YOU FROM YOUR COMPETITORS

Now that you have your most important and relevant credentials identified and a job search Career Advancement Plan in place, determine how you will set yourself apart in a very crowded job market. You always need to assume that other applicants will come with similar credentials and that at least one applicant will be more qualified than you. When others have similar or better credentials, how are you going to stand out and make your ideal job search a slam dunk regardless of the competition? Ask yourself

- How do I compare to my competitors?
- How will I show that I bring something different to the position that employers value?
- What do I offer that 99 to 100 percent of the other candidates won't offer?
- What makes me unique and special?
- Why should an employer hire me over someone else?

Keep the following definition of competitive positioning in mind as you look to differentiate yourself:

Competitive positioning is about defining how you'll "differentiate" your offering and create value for your market. It's about carving out a spot in the competitive landscape, putting your stake in the ground, and winning mindshare in the marketplace—being known for a certain "something."[1]

Competitive positioning is what it means to have a brand. What are you going to be known for, and why is this important to you and potential employers? Create a story about the unique value you bring to the marketplace. Your unique value may include highlights from your career path to this point, your most important and relevant credentials, your core beliefs or values and how they affect your work, and key aspects of your personality that set you apart.

How many times have you gone into a store to buy a new product only to be confused by all the choices? Don't let employers be confused by all their choices, and don't make them have to spend much time figuring out how your brand is different. Make it very clear why they should hire you over all the other candidates, and don't ever assume your most important credentials will be obvious to them. Remember, you are making their lives easier by clearly conveying your value.

Create a Career Profile

To help determine what value you will bring to each employer and understand how you can differentiate yourself, create a one-page Career Profile at the very start of your job search (focused on your field) and then customize it for each job (focused on the employer and the job).

The one-page Career Profile highlights your most valuable skills, training, experience, certifications, and accomplishments and focuses them on the field and the job you are pursuing. The Career Profile will help you prior to your job search, while preparing your marketing materials and promotional platforms, during the application stage, in your interviews, after your interviews, and as you negotiate for a higher salary. It will provide you with a process to ensure you address each employer's needs and focus your background on the company and the specific position. This is critical since most job seekers fail to ensure the qualifications in their résumés correspond with specific terms and references made in each job listing. How can you win the game when you have the same strategy for each opponent and each employer? You may get lucky every now and then, but in most cases, your plan will align poorly, and you will lose out to someone with a more customized approach. The more you align your background to the field and the employer, the more opportunities you will have to get interviews, wow employers, and land job offers.

Let's take a closer look at the Career Profile to understand how it works and see how it can help you throughout the job search process. As you read through the following sections, please note that you can replace the word "job" with "field" as you prepare your Career Profile and marketing materials before pursuing any position. You will then customize your Career Profile and marketing materials for each job. Below are the eight components that make up the one-page Profile.

1. **Career Value Statement**

    The career value statement is a concise (one- to two-line), powerful tagline placed right below the Career Profile heading (see example at the end of this section) that lets the employer know what is unique about you and what value you will bring to the job and the field. The statement pulls everything together and grabs immediate attention. It isn't an objective; instead, the statement is an advertisement of how you differentiate yourself from others and will provide value to the employer. It reinforces your brand, immediately focuses employers on what you bring to the position or the field, and frames their thinking (and yours) from the very start. Everything that follows should support your career value statement.

    If you have a strong statement already in mind, start with it and then fill in the other sections to support it. On the other hand, if you don't have a refined statement yet, consider writing the statement last. Once you have all the other pieces in place, you can take a close look at the Career Profile content and come up with a statement that pulls everything together and helps you market yourself effectively for the field and each job.

    The career value statement is like the unique value proposition tagline (used at the top of the résumé) and the branding statement (used on the promotional platforms). In the appendix, you will find a simple formula for creating these statements and taglines, and they can be used interchangeably.

2. **Quality of Work Quote (optional)**

    The quality of work quote is an attention-grabbing testimonial that supports your career value statement, highlights the quality of your work, and helps you market yourself within your field. Use a one- to two-line quote and place it under the career value statement (see example at the end of this section). You can often find relevant quotes through past performance evaluations, email feedback, customer comments, or your LinkedIn profile recommendations. Or ask one of your previous supervisors, coworkers, or customers to write one. If you don't have a quote or can't get an appropriate one, then don't include one.

3. **Key Qualifications**

    Within the key qualifications section, add five of the most important qualifications you bring to the position or the field. If you are at the point where you are pursuing specific positions, the key qualifications section will highlight your most relevant qualifications for each specific job.

4. **Key Accomplishments**

    Here you will list three to five of your most relevant and hard-hitting accomplishments. Highlight some numbers here and give employers a picture of what you have achieved. You want them to see what you can do. The more your accomplishments relate to the job, the more the employer can visualize you in the position. Don't just tell employers how good you are; show them concretely how good you are by what you have done or what you are currently doing. Similar to your résumé job description bullets (see the appendix), start each accomplishment statement with an action verb.

5. **Education/Training/Certifications**

    The education/training/certifications section will be the most straightforward section. Don't build up this section as much as you would on your résumé. Keep it simple and straightforward. Also, shorten the heading if you don't have any certifications or relevant professional training.

6. **Skills**

   Here you will add six to nine of the most important skills you have for the job or the field. This section will force you to think about what you bring to the position from a skills perspective. The skills can be both technical and nontechnical, but they need to be relevant to the position, company, and field. The skills and education sections can switch places, depending on which section adds the most value.

7. **Professional Affiliations**

   Next, list one to three relevant professional affiliations. This section shows your commitment to the field and your connection to people within the field. Look to become a member of at least one professional association related to your field; you can search for professional associations during your online research. You can then ask your contacts during the Relationship Team step which professional associations make the most sense for your career path.

8. **Activities**

   Add one or two significant activities you are involved in that are impressive or unique. These will act as a conversation piece and will bring you to life. They also may allow you to bond with the hiring committee members. Don't worry if these initially appear unrelated to the position. Everything is related in some way. Your job is to uncover the link and then show the employer, either in your marketing documents or during the interview, how these activities will allow you to bring a unique skill, perspective, or trait to the position.

Don't wait to put together a Career Profile. As soon as you begin thinking about pursuing a new position, develop a Profile focused on your field. You need to communicate your value, and the Profile will help you highlight your most valuable qualities and credentials throughout the job search process. More than anything, the Career Profile helps you get your credentials focused on the job or the field before you refine your résumé and cover letter. Your Profile is an important part of your job search tool kit, no matter where you are in the process.

Here is an example of a completed Career Profile:

EMILIA SANCHEZ

San Diego, California

esanchez@example.com | (619) 555-1234

professionalcareerwebsite.com | LinkedIn Profile (hyperlinked)

Career Profile

Experienced event planner with a reputation for creating memorable events at half the cost.

"Emilia goes above and beyond expectations to create events that leave people in awe!"

– Vice President of Human Resources, Northbrook Enterprises Inc.

Key Qualifications

- More than 5 years of experience creating, organizing, and coordinating events
- Expertise in event management software and contract negotiations
- Known for producing state-of-the-art events while consistently coming in under budget
- An eye for orchestrating events that appeal to the 5 senses and make people feel special
- Strong interest in the apparel industry combined with advanced textile knowledge

Key Accomplishments

- Orchestrated 30+ board meetings, sales and charity events, and conferences annually for 25 to 2500 people
- Created, organized, coordinated, and promoted an Invitational Games charity event for 1,200 employees that raised more than $100,000 and generated employee goodwill
- Spearheaded a professional conference for 750 attendees at a major hotel. Came in under budget by 28%, with 97% of participants rating the event as "Excellent"
- Designed decorations for numerous limited-budget events and received the following one-word comments: superb, stunning, special, memorable, amazing, incredible, and gorgeous

Education

MS in Hospitality Management (expected May 20XX)

BA in Communication

Skills

- Event Production
- Food Preparation
- Client/VIP Relations
- Social Media Marketing
- Lighting & Sound
- Project Management
- Vendor Negotiations
- Budgeting
- Crisis Management

Professional Affiliations

National Association for Catering and Events

San Diego Arts Initiative Board

Activities

Hiked the entire 2,650-mile Pacific Crest Trail solo at the age of 18

Avid golfer

Using Your Career Profile

Once you identify a specific job you want to pursue, customize your Career Profile so it matches up as closely as possible with the position and the company. Examine the job announcement, company website, and anything you've learned from your contacts to make your Profile as targeted as you can.

In addition to providing you with targeted content for your marketing documents, the customized Profile will give you a one-page snapshot of the key selling points to visualize during the interview process. Consider it your interview cheat sheet.

You will also update your Career Profile after each interview. The questions you ask at the end of your interviews should provide you with plenty of new inside information. (If they don't, consider asking different questions to uncover useful insights.) As you collect additional information about the position and the company culture (values, core competencies, and professional standards), go back and refine your Profile so it aligns as closely as possible to what is essential for the position. By the time you get through the entire interview process, your Career Profile should be very targeted.

Although you will use the Career Profile throughout the job search process, employers will not see it until you attach it to your electronic thank-you note after the final interview. At the end of the interview process, the Profile is a powerful "closing" document that separates you from your competitors and makes it very clear to the employer the value you will bring to the position. If you are up against another strong candidate, the Profile could be just what you need to wow the employer and land the job offer. Submitting the Profile also provides an element of surprise and novelty. It breaks the script and is memorable. Remember, though, nothing is carved in stone. If you feel your Career Profile will be too much and isn't necessary, don't submit it. But it is one more tool you can use at the end of the process to help seal the deal.

Finally, once you receive the job offer, you can use the Career Profile information to support your case for a higher starting salary.

Marketing Yourself

Before you start using your Career Profile to develop your marketing documents and promotional platforms, let's put a simple sales framework in place—the Slam Dunk

Triangle Offense—that you can quickly visualize in your mind whenever you need to communicate your value on paper or in person. While the Career Profile will give you the content for promoting yourself, the Slam Dunk Triangle Offense will give you the framework for effectively sharing your most relevant and prized qualifications with others.

Chapter 6

FOLLOW A SIMPLE FRAMEWORK FOR COMMUNICATING YOUR VALUE

How do you feel when a hiring manager asks you, "Why should we hire you?" or "Why do you think you are the best candidate for the job?" Most job seekers have a difficult time answering these types of questions because they have no idea where to begin, what to say, or how to promote themselves. If you want to land your ideal job in any market, you must inspire employers with your answers to these types of questions. You can't leave anything to chance.

Your next Market Ready task is to plant a simple sales framework in your mind that will help you answer any qualification-related question. Something you will see in most job search books is a long list of strategies and tactics to use, and this book is no exception. It can be quite overwhelming, and it's even harder to remember everything when you are under pressure. The Slam Dunk (SD) Triangle Offense will simplify the process.

The Slam Dunk Triangle Offense

The SD Triangle Offense (Figure B) gives you a visual image you can quickly bring to mind to help communicate your value at every step. You can use it as a guide when you are creating your marketing materials, building a relationship team, preparing for your interviews, talking with employees in your target organizations, chatting with people at a conference, interviewing, and interacting with anyone else during the job search process. When you combine the SD Triangle Offense with strong credentials, the right mindset, and the Career Profile, you should be unstoppable.

The SD Triangle Offense is included in the Market Ready step so you can get used to referring to the framework as you prepare to enter the job market and compete for your ideal job. The Offense has four parts:

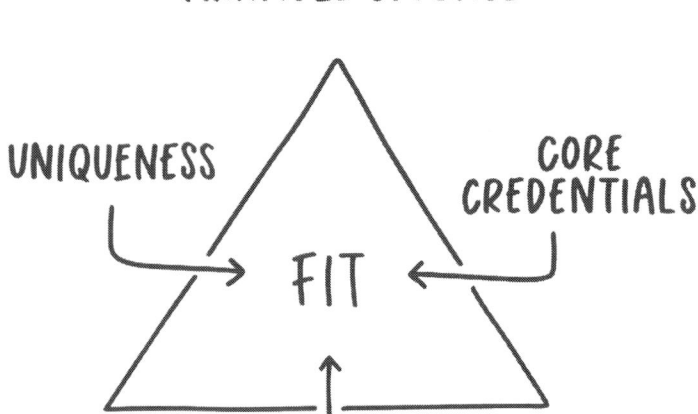

Figure B: Slam Dunk Triangle Offense

Bottom: Interest
Why do you want to work for the organization and within the field?

Right Side: Core Credentials
How well do you match up with the core job requirements?

Left Side: Uniqueness
Why should the company hire you over someone else?

Middle: Fit
Will you fit in well with the company culture, employees, clients, and hiring manager?

The three sides of the SD Triangle Offense (interest, core credentials, and uniqueness) feed into the middle of the triangle and help show your fit with the company. If you can show the employer you will bring all these components to the organization, you will elevate your job search performance and often move along in the process.

As you read through the four parts in more detail below, contemplate how you could use this framework to describe yourself, design your résumé, write cover letters, and answer interview questions. Then, take a moment to brainstorm and outline your SD Triangle Offense as it relates to your field, using your Career Profile to help you think through all four parts of the Offense.

Interest

First, show employers you are interested in or passionate about the work and the company. Convince them that you want to work for the organization and that you have a good reason why. Expressing your interest through a story will help make you memorable: "I became interested in working at the Monterey Bay Aquarium when I was six years old and living on a farm in Iowa." Your goal is to create curiosity while also expressing interest.

One large study showed that candidates interested in and committed to a particular organization are the candidates who often get hired and succeed within the company, which is a trend I have seen clearly in my decades of experience.[1] Employers like job candidates who express interest in the company and have a good reason for wanting to work at the organization. Spend some time researching the organization and coming up with reasons why you are interested in joining the company. The more you can show your commitment to the company and the job, the more confidence the employer will have that you will excel and stay with the organization long-term.

How can you express passion or interest? Can you

- Highlight experience you have that is related to the position?
- Demonstrate that you can do the job and do it better than anyone else?
- Show your connection to the organization?
- Express your knowledge of the company and the operations?
- Indicate that you went out of your way to talk to company employees and customers?

- Explain why you are interested in or passionate about the company?
- Describe some personal projects you have worked on that relate to the job?
- Exhibit a high level of preparation at each stage of the job search process?
- Share a respected referral?
- Show you know the field and the ins and outs of the company?
- Mention how you have used the company's products and services?

Use your best judgment when it comes to expressing interest. Too much talk about passion or interest in the company can be a turnoff if you don't appear authentic. Rather than repeating your interest in the organization, find ways to back up your passion or interest with something tangible:

- I worked in this sector.
- I collaborated with the company employees at my last job.
- I worked on projects that brought me in contact with the company.
- I have several friends who work in this sector, and I have talked to them about the field.
- My mother worked in this field for 30 years, so I am quite familiar with this type of work.
- I have wanted to work in this field ever since I completed a transportation-related cost-benefit analysis class project.
- I love the company products and have used them ever since I played tennis at the University of Northbrook.
- I once interviewed Frank Smith in your compliance department for a class project.
- I recently talked with Kira Humphrey in your sales division.
- Ever since I was 12 years old, I have wanted to work for the US Department of Homeland Security.

Find something that's part of your background that shows the employer you know what you are getting into and are genuinely passionate about coming on board.

Core Credentials

Next, show the employer you have the core knowledge, skills, education, experience, and certifications needed to do the job and do it well. The more qualifications you have that align with the position, the better. Know what is important and bring out your core credentials at each stage of the process.

How can you guarantee you highlight your core credentials? Create a Career Profile for each position. As you read in chapter 5, the Career Profile will force you to take a close look at each job announcement and then highlight your most important credentials for the position. And don't forget to paste the job announcement content into a word cloud generator to let you know what core credentials and skills are most relevant and valued. This information will help you focus on what is most important. But don't rely solely on what is listed in the job announcement. Reach out to employees, prior employees, and your relationship team to get inside information that isn't listed in the job announcement. Inside information can set you apart because employers often leave out relevant requirements from official job postings.

With a list of the core credentials you bring to the job, you will be able to weave them in as you promote yourself. In most cases, you will not get hired unless the hiring manager is convinced that you can do the job and do it well. And never assume employers have this all figured out. Instead, make their jobs as easy as possible by showing them that you have what it takes to excel in the position.

Uniqueness

Third, show employers you will bring something unique and special to the position and the organization that sets you apart from your competitors. Select something that employers value and will not get unless they hire you.

Unique and special doesn't mean you need to do or share something peculiar. It may simply be something like one of the following:

- You have acquired an important skill or learned an essential process.
- You have received advanced training related to your field and the position.
- You bring a diverse perspective or a diverse set of skills.
- You have a natural talent related to the work.
- You have experience with the company's products or services.
- You completed a class project related to the company or the field.
- You will bring clients to the company.
- You always go above and beyond expectations.

- You have a combination of experience, training, and skills that creates a unique and relevant overall package.
- You have a personality trait that is highly valued.
- You have many connections.
- You have a strong customer service background.
- You are very creative.
- You have a valued certification.
- You accomplished a significant personal feat that highlights transferable skills.
- You traveled around the world and have a broader perspective.
- You are an accomplished performer (artist, musician, athlete, singer, etc.).

With every job search, assume you will be competing with many applicants who have both a passion for the position and the core credentials to do the job and do it well. Given this assumption, you should always identify what you will bring to the position and the company that is unique and valued. What will separate you from other job candidates and give employers something they will not get from anyone else? Make a list of everything that is unique about you and add to the list by getting input from friends, family members, and colleagues. Select two or three that present something that the employer will value, and then develop a story that ties the value of these experiences or qualities back to the position or the field.

Make sure the link is obvious or that you connect the dots for the employer so the value is clear. For example, being an accomplished painter might give you an eye for design that would help you create visually appealing event spaces in your event planning position. You can usually find a way to connect most experiences or qualities to your ideal job, but if you can't, don't include it. Keep looking and think creatively.

Fit

Once employers know you are interested in the position and the company and can do the job, they make sure you align well with all areas of the organization (e.g., values, core competencies, professional standards, and people). The best organizations will go to great lengths to ensure candidates match up well with the company, department, and position. Fit is one of the most important reasons an employer feels comfortable extending a job offer.

If an employer hires someone who doesn't match up well with the company culture, the new employee can destroy the morale of the department. As a result, effective managers rarely extend a job offer unless they

- Know they like the top candidate and feel there is good chemistry.
- Believe the candidate will fit in well with the company culture.
- Know the candidate will work well with both employees and clients.
- Know the candidate matches up well with the position requirements.

Fit is also essential for your satisfaction in the position. Take a close look at each organization and ensure your values align with the company culture and you feel comfortable working for the organization. When you research the organization, collect information that can help you market yourself better and determine if you match up well with the company. Always spend time researching the organization. It will pay off for you in numerous ways.

Since hiring someone who is a perfect fit is easier said than done, your goal as a job seeker is to help the employer clearly see that you are a strong match with the organization. And you need to do it quickly. Here are some ways to demonstrate your fit with the company and position:

- Tell a compelling story about what attracted you to the company.
- Get a referral and have the person who referred you to the position talk about how well you match up with the organization and the job.
- Indicate that you have done research on the company and know the company's vision, mission, and values (whatever is important to the company: principles, pillars, commitments, beliefs, or ethics).
- Share your experiences working with people in the company or the industry.
- Get inside information on the company culture (values, core competencies, and professional standards) and share stories that show you fit into the culture and would flourish in such an environment.
- Collect inside information on what is most important for the company, the position, and the hiring manager, and then address these important elements during the process.
- Make sure your social media sites and all your promotional platforms match up well with the company culture.

- Wear attire that is appropriate for the company culture and the position.
- Develop good rapport by smiling, shaking hands firmly, making eye contact, and exhibiting good posture.
- Mimic the company work ethic by how you perform during the job search process and by sharing how you have performed in prior jobs.
- Exhibit emotional intelligence.
- Speak highly of everyone.
- Apply the six Slam Dunk Guiding Principles throughout the job search process.
- Mirror the hiring manager's body language and tone.
- Be likable (pleasant, prepared, positive, engaged, professional, cheerful, etc.).
- Use good manners, say thank you, and always be polite.

Based on your research, you will know the job, field, company, and industry quite well, so use your best judgment on the most effective ways to communicate fit. Within some fields, being different in an unusual way may help you fit into the company. Know your audience and do what works well for your audience and industry.

Pulling it All Together

Once you have outlined all four parts of the SD Triangle Offense, come up with one or two stories related to each part, and make sure your stories include accomplishments—the impact you have had in a particular role or with a relevant project. If an employer asks you any of the following interview questions, you can go right to your SD Triangle Offense to answer them, and you will have a story or two to share as well:

- Why should we hire you?
- Why do you think you are the most qualified candidate for the position?
- Can you tell us about yourself? (You can also use the Ice Cream Cone Approach, described in chapter 9.)
- Why are you interested in working for our company?
- How can you help us?
- What makes you a strong fit for the position?
- If hired into the position, what would you bring to the job that no one else would bring?

- What are your strengths?
- What attracted you to this position?

You won't use the same response for each of these questions, but you can take parts of the SD Triangle Offense to help you answer different ones. Practice answering the questions using the SD Triangle Offense, and you will be well prepared for most interview questions.

As you begin to pull everything together, notice that "core" has been added to "credentials" to emphasize that you often don't need to meet all the position requirements to get the job offer. In most cases, you only need to have the critical (core) credentials demanded by employers and then demonstrate why they should hire you over all the other candidates. Remember, your goal is to land the job offer when you are the most qualified candidate and even when you're not the most qualified. The 6-Step Slam Dunk Job Search Process, along with the SD Triangle Offense, will help you achieve this goal.

Answering with the Slam Dunk Triangle Offense

Below is an example of how you could answer the "Why should we hire you?" question using the SD Triangle Offense. You can pick and choose what you incorporate into your answer, but this will give you a framework to use.

Question: "Why should we hire you?"

Interest (Opening)

"Well, first, I want to work for Northpoint Healthcare. My interest in the company began when I read an inspiring article by your CEO, Avery Everson, about the company's passion for driving change within the healthcare industry. The article was meaningful because I grew up in a family dedicated to the medical field. My mother, father, and uncle all worked at Eagleton Hospital, and I feel like healthcare is in my genes. I want to be part of an organization that drives change within this industry. And given my education, experience, and interest, I have continued to monitor the jobs within Northpoint's Information Technology (IT) Department."

Core Credentials

"In addition to my interest in the company, I also match up well with all the core requirements of the Systems Analyst position, especially with my skills in _____, training in _____, and my experience in _____. And I have a proven record of _____. When I worked at _____, I took a lead on _____ that resulted in _____ [add numbers here if you can]."

Uniqueness

"Besides these credentials, I believe I would bring something unique to the position. I have _____."

Fit (Close)

"As you can see from my education, experience, and accomplishments, I am committed to this line of work, and I believe my work ethic aligns well with the company values. For example, I _____. Additionally, I know I would enjoy working at the company and within your department given that two of my close friends are employed at the organization and love their jobs. I am thrilled to have the opportunity to talk to you today about how I can make a strong contribution to the Systems Analyst position within your IT Department."

Always address all parts of the SD Triangle Offense by the time the interview is over. The first two parts—interest and core credentials—help make you competitive, while the other two—uniqueness and fit—help you seal the deal. If you match up well with the position and communicate all four parts of the SD Triangle Offense effectively, you will be well on your way to wowing employers and making your job search a slam dunk.

Chapter 7

GET YOUR MARKETING DOCUMENTS READY

When you start to compete for your ideal job, you should have all your marketing documents ready to go at a competitive level. Then, all you need to do is tailor them as you seek to stand out and wow each employer. You may occasionally find that there are some companies and positions that demand something entirely different from what you have already put together during the Market Ready step. That is fine. You should expect to make changes to your documents. Remember, you are in the business of landing your ideal job, and you will need to adjust and do whatever makes the most sense for each organization and position. But, in most cases, you will only need to refine your documents a little for each unique opportunity. Have the following marketing documents ready to go early in the process:

- Résumé and cover letter
- Email correspondence
- Work samples (portfolio)
- Thank-you note
- Reference sheet

Preparing these documents early in the process will allow you to concentrate on customizing them once you start to pursue specific jobs. And the more you tailor your documents, the more you will separate yourself from your competitors—right from the start.

Résumé and Cover Letter

Résumés and cover letters rarely close the deal and get you the job offer, but they are critical components of the job search process, especially when they may be the first contact you have with employers. They are also the first tangible materials you share with employers that let them know how well you can create and market something. Don't let anyone tell you that these documents can't help you differentiate yourself from other candidates. If you want to land your ideal job, never assume employers will overlook any marketing document or online platform. Everything you do during the job search process needs to be done in a high-quality and effective manner.

Having a Career Profile in place at the very start of your job search will provide you with enough content to get you started on creating all your documents. You will begin by focusing your résumé and cover letter on your field, and then you will customize them for each opportunity as you start to compete for specific positions. But the question is, how do you put the content down on paper in a way that grabs attention and demands action?

With each document, act like you have a blank art canvas in front of you, think about what adds the most value for each position, and then act like an artist and place your credentials on the canvas in a way that best markets your qualifications for the position. Your goal is to design your documents so the hiring manager or recruiter visualizes you in the position and invites you in for an interview. To do this, your résumé and cover letter should accomplish the following:

- Show your personality and bring you to life.
- Present you in a professional manner.
- Showcase your writing ability.
- Exhibit quality across the board.
- Express your interest in or passion for the field, type of work, and company.
- Highlight your qualifications for the job.
- Differentiate you from other candidates.
- Show you are a good fit for the organization and the position.

To ensure your résumé and cover letter address these areas and are compelling and appealing, design them to be change-friendly, reader-friendly, and employer-focused (field-focused at first, then customized for each position).

An effective résumé and cover letter will help you create a strong first impression and land you a job interview. As you will see in chapter 14, in some cases they may even help you seal the deal and get an offer. If you want to create effective documents, prepare them early (in the Market Ready step) using the general guidelines laid out in this section and then finesse the documents later once you know about the position requirements, department challenges and goals, and company culture.

While the sections below will explain the general approach for designing your documents, you will find a more comprehensive list of résumé and cover letter design guidelines in the appendix.

Change-Friendly

> **Can you modify your documents easily and quickly without the help of others?**

Your résumé and cover letter are living documents that must be modified for each position. When documents are too difficult to change, applicants will often use the same résumé and cover letter for all positions. When they do, they will have difficulty competing for their ideal jobs as their competitors pass them by with more targeted and customized marketing materials.

Make sure you can modify your documents quickly and easily. Unless you are pursuing opportunities in a creative field (e.g., graphic designers and multimedia artists), avoid columns, boxes, highlighting, and other elaborate features. Promote yourself with the content and not a fancy design. If you are in a creative field or just want to add a little more creativity to your materials, consider sending two versions of your résumé—a standard version and a more creative version—to cover all your bases and make the evaluation process easy for recruiters and managers.

While some fancy résumés and cover letters might look nice, they become problematic when they are difficult to modify or when creativity dictates the design. Recently, a 23-year-old job seeker named Cole came to me for some help with his marketing documents.[1] I reviewed his résumé and liked it. I could sense he had some graphic design or art background because it was graphically pleasing. There were a few aspects

I didn't care for (dates highlighted on their own on the right side, awards disconnected from where he received them and too far down the page, and a bulkier job description section), but I thought it was tastefully done. The problem was that the fancy design had forced Cole to put content into nonstrategic and ineffective locations.

Here is an important tip: Never let a design determine where you place your credentials on the canvas (page). During the application stage, your primary goal is to land the interview. To achieve this goal, get to know your audience and then place your credentials on your résumé and cover letter in a way that best promotes you for the position and the company. In Cole's case, this required moving a few elements around. However, when I asked him if the résumé was easy to modify, he said, "No!" I then asked if he had a graphic design or art background, and he said, "No, but my mother does, and she was the one who designed the résumé in Photoshop." Cole's résumé failed the change-friendly test. Why? Because he would constantly need to go back to his mother to make modifications.

Since your résumé and cover letter are living documents that need to be customized for each position, you must be able to change them easily on your own. If a task is difficult to do during the job search process, you will either put it off or not do it. By making your résumé and cover letter change-friendly, you will be able to make modifications to your documents quickly and easily throughout the entire process. See the appendix for a more comprehensive list of change-friendly guidelines.

Reader-Friendly

> **Are your documents engaging and easy to read, and do they quickly get the readers where they want to go?**

Design your résumé and cover letter in a way that gets readers to go quickly where you want them to go and where you know they want to go. Recruiters and hiring managers have limited time and will initially glance at a résumé and cover letter for a matter of seconds to make a "first impression" decision.[2] When you make your documents too complicated, you may not move on in the process if employers have a difficult time finding what they need or use some type of evaluation recruitment software that can scramble or reject complex documents.

According to Jobscan, 98 percent of Fortune 500 companies use applicant tracking system (ATS) software during the recruiting and hiring process, and 66 percent of large organizations and 35 percent of small companies use some type of recruitment software.[3] Electronic recruitment software could misread or garble complicated and fancy documents that contain the following:

- Columns, tables, logos, images, shading, abbreviations, and acronyms (To avoid problems with acronyms, spell out the words the first time and then put the acronym in parentheses at the end. On repeated references, you can use just the acronym.)
- Nonstandard bullets (Avoid stars, check marks, check boxes, and diamonds.)
- Headers and footers (Use Microsoft Word without any headers and footers.)
- Nonstandard date formats that only list the year (List both month and year.)
- Unique fonts (Use Calibri, Arial, Helvetica, Times New Roman, Cambria, or Garamond.)[4]

To be safe, keep your documents simple (uncluttered, organized, and strategic) and then use an ATS online résumé scan program to provide feedback on whether your résumé and cover letter will pass the ATS.

Even if the company doesn't use an ATS, there are additional reasons why you shouldn't get too creative with your documents. Hiring managers and recruiters like a standard format where they can find what they are looking for quickly. They don't have the time to sort through creative and unique documents to find what they need. Additionally, hiring managers may view fancy documents as a warning sign. Similar to how publicly held companies sometimes develop fancy annual reports to hide weak financial numbers, creative and complicated résumés could be a sign that job candidates are hiding something. If the numbers are good (training, experience, and skills), you don't need to hide them behind an elaborate design.

Developing reader-friendly documents also means your résumé and cover letter are engaging. They should start and end with something different and memorable. Pull the reader into your documents with impressive credentials, a referral, an engaging story, a focused tagline, a testimonial, or anything else that wakes up employers and gets them to read your documents and bring you in for an interview. You will see many of these "grab-attention" tactics throughout the book, and you can access additional tactics in the appendix.

Be proactive and look carefully at each section of your résumé and cover letter to ensure everything will be clear, straightforward, and interesting to the reader. Run confusing passages by others if you are unsure and need additional feedback. Having to read something more than once to grasp it is one sign that it is not clear. If something is too complicated, unclear, or dull, change it.

Always know your audience and use your best judgment when it comes to résumé and cover letter design. If you are in a creative field, you will probably want to develop more eye-catching and creative documents, such as an infographic résumé or one with more design elements. But in most other cases, you need to focus on incorporating the right content, selecting the right headings, and placing the information and sections in the right places. If you care about employers, you will find ways to make their jobs easier through things like reader-friendly documents, and, in the process, you will promote yourself more effectively. See the appendix for a comprehensive list of reader-friendly guidelines.

Employer-Focused

> **Do your documents focus on employers' needs and help you market yourself in the best way possible for each position?**

If your résumé and cover letter are employer-focused, they will bring out the education, training, experience, and skills that most closely align with the position requirements and the company culture. They will also convince the employer throughout the entire document—and especially in the top one-third to one-half of the résumé and cover letter—that you have the potential to add considerable value to the position and the organization.

As you start to make your résumé and cover letter employer-focused, do your research and use the tools you have in place to make your documents more targeted:

- Find out as much as you can about the field, employer, and position, and then update your Career Profile with the credentials and accomplishments that most closely align with the employer's needs and desires.
- Paste the job announcement content into a word cloud generator or a chatbot like ChatGPT to determine what is most important within each position, and then incorporate the most prevalent terms into your Career Profile.
- Look closely at your Career Profile and move your most relevant credentials and accomplishments into your résumé and cover letter for each position you pursue.

The more you know about the position, company, and hiring manager, the more you can make your documents employer-focused and the more you will stand out. As mentioned earlier, you will initially focus your résumé and cover letter on your field and then later customize these documents for each company and position you pursue. To help focus on your field, you can find a job announcement that reflects the types of jobs you plan to eventually pursue and use it to create your initial résumé and cover letter.

With both your résumé and your cover letter, don't be afraid to move content around and change headings to market yourself more effectively for each job and organization. You have permission to make changes if a different structure helps you get better results and makes your documents more employer-focused.

An employer-focused strategy can be a game changer. I worked with one job seeker named Steven from Ventura, California, who was pursuing a PhD in political science but wanted to pivot out of academia and find a job in the information technology (IT) field.[5] When Steven contacted me, he had been pursuing jobs for months without success. After reviewing Steven's résumé and understanding his goals, I had him move his education down to the bottom of his résumé. I then had him create a short, four-bullet Summary of Qualifications section at the top that packaged his most relevant credentials and got employers thinking the right way from the start. He then added an Information Technology Skills section right below the Summary of Qualifications section to bring out more IT technical skills. I had him keep the Experience section in the middle. And I made sure Steven minimized his PhD education and displayed it differently. I didn't want the reader to be confused about why Steven had been pursuing a PhD in an unrelated field.

By moving the vital information to the top of the page and reframing his narrative, the résumé became more focused and appealing to the target audience. The changes led the readers where they wanted to go and focused attention on what marketed Steven the most for the field he wanted to enter. As a result of targeting the résumé more, elevating his most important credentials, and minimizing any concerns about his background, Steven went from being unmarketable to being very marketable. After implementing these changes and using the redesigned résumé to pursue several IT-related positions, Steven had an offer on the table in three and a half weeks.

No matter what résumé or cover letter format you use, give yourself permission to modify your documents. And when you reach out to your contacts during the

Relationship Team step, ask them for their feedback on your résumé and cover letter. Always seek inside information. Then, think like a salesperson, act like an artist, and move content and sections around to help the employer clearly understand your value. See the appendix for a comprehensive list of employer-focused guidelines.

Email Correspondence

As with your résumé and cover letter, start developing email messages early so you only need to customize them right before you hit the send button.

If you prepare your email correspondence in advance, you will avoid many of the errors and inconsistencies caused by crafting messages at the last minute. Think about how many times you have caught a mistake or found a better way to write something after you have set a document aside and come back to it. Getting documents or messages ready in advance builds in your own quality control system.

While you will see plenty of email correspondence examples as you move through this book, the example below will get you thinking about how you could craft your own introduction messages.

Hi Agatha,

Nice to meet you online!

I am a training and development manager at Emerald Hotel Group, and I am interested in transitioning into the apparel industry. I noticed on your LinkedIn profile that you made a similar career move, and I thought you would be an excellent person to reach out to for some advice on making such a transition. Would you happen to have a few minutes to answer some questions I have about working my way into the apparel industry?

If you are available for a quick phone call, I have a flexible schedule on Tuesday and Thursday mornings, and I would be happy to rearrange my schedule on other days to accommodate your availability.

By the way, it appears we both know Bob Smith. Bob was the one who got me involved in training and development when we attended the University of Colorado Boulder, and we are still close friends.

Thank you in advance for your help!

Have a great week,
Bret Sammons

Bret could also try to leverage his relationship with Bob Smith and open with this connection, or he could contact Bob and ask to be introduced to Agatha. As you know, however, going back and forth with people can take time, so you will need to use your best judgment on which approach to take given your situation and time frame. Ideally, you will send your messages through email and not just LinkedIn. Some people don't monitor their LinkedIn messages, so you should try to find the person's email address and use this communication avenue whenever possible. If you are connected to the person on LinkedIn and you have a premium service, you should have access to the person's email address. If you aren't connected, visit slamdunkjobsearch.com for complimentary tips on how to locate a person's email address.

As you will learn in the Relationship Team step, most introduction messages have a similar framework that can be used for a variety of audiences. By creating email correspondence messages in advance that can be adjusted for specific people, you'll increase the quality of your communication and make the process easy for yourself.

Work Samples

People tend to remember 80 percent of what they see and only 10 percent of what they hear.[6] As a result, if you want to stand out during your job search, be prepared to give the hiring manager something tangible. In most industries, this will be handouts showcasing your previous work.

Depending on your field, work samples could include writing samples, artwork, designs, reports, articles, marketing campaigns, training materials, code samples, grant proposals, photographs of culinary creations or clothing designs, press releases, graphic presentations, lesson plans, or blog posts. Compile the most relevant samples into a polished packet, such as a professional folder or cover sheet.

To create a memorable impression, design visually appealing work sample handouts. The visual impact of your work samples is essential. Why? Because visuals are processed by long-term memory, while words are processed by short-term memory with limited retention.[7] Also, the brain processes visuals 60,000 times faster than text, which is crucial when the average attention span is only six seconds.[8] If you need help creating a visually appealing work sample packet or cover sheet, consider using freelance services like 99designs, Fiverr, or Upwork for assistance.

When you pull your work samples together early in the process and put them in a professional format (a well-designed packet with a professional cover sheet), they will be ready to use at any point in the process—application, interview, or thank-you note stage. Moreover, some employers may ask for work samples. Having samples available will allow you to quickly provide an employer with one or more at an opportune time.

Thank-You Notes

Like activating your car turn signal or brushing your teeth, sending a thank-you note should be a habit and considered a necessity. Timely and well-written thank-you notes are memorable, professional, and often expected. These days, email is a perfectly acceptable way to send a thank-you note. (Reminder: Unless otherwise stated, thank-you notes and messages refer to thank-you "email" messages in this book.)

What happens if you don't send a thank-you note but your competitors do? You may stand out in a negative way. When employers don't get a thank-you note from job candidates, questions surface:

- Are the candidates all that interested in the position?
- Do they have strong follow-up skills?
- Will they exhibit proper business etiquette on the job?
- Are they lacking time-management and organizational skills?
- Will they approach the job in a professional manner?

If you don't send a thank-you note, you will also miss out on another opportunity to develop a stronger relationship with the hiring committee members. Never give up an opportunity to develop a closer relationship with people in your field, particularly hiring managers in your target organizations.

According to CareerBuilder, 57 percent of job seekers don't send thank-you notes following an interview.[9] Another survey conducted by Accountemps found that only 24 percent of human resources managers received thank-you notes from candidates they interviewed. This same survey showed that 80 percent of the managers said thank-you notes were useful during the evaluation process.[10] Somewhere along the way, strong follow-up etiquette got lost. But when something is lost or rarely used, it means you will stand out if you do it and do it well.

If you want to conduct a competitive search, learn how to write effective follow-up letters for a variety of audiences and situations. If someone helps you or interviews you for a position, send a thank-you note. If someone turns you down for a job, still send a note expressing your appreciation for the opportunity to interview for the position. Why? Because no one else will, and you need to go above and beyond everyone else. A thank-you note makes people who receive the note feel good and appreciated. And when people feel this way, they will be motivated to help you even more. You need to take a long-term perspective and remember the importance of developing and maintaining relationships.

If you take the high road and effectively follow up no matter what happens, people will be impressed with you and want to find ways to help you. If you get turned down for a position but then the company's top candidate decides to pull out of the job for some reason, whom do you think they will call? If you sent a nice follow-up message and you are the second- or third-choice candidate, you will often be on the short list for a call. Or if another position comes up in the same department down the line, whom do you think they will remember? You! When you are focused on developing your reputation, expanding your relationship team, and maintaining long-term relationships, you will see the importance of expressing gratitude in both positive and not-so-positive situations.

Spend time in advance putting together a few competitive post-interview thank-you notes so you can then customize them as you move through the process with each job search. Here is an example of a post-interview thank-you note:

Dear Jackson,

I want to take a moment to thank you, Ada, and Mateo for meeting with me earlier today. I know how busy you are, yet you made me feel like I was your only candidate. Thank you!

I appreciated hearing more about the Speech-Language Pathologist position. Our conversation reinforced my interest in the opportunity and convinced me that my four years of experience, along with my Certificate of Clinical

Competence in Speech-Language Pathology, would allow me to help Horizon West Rehabilitation Center reach its goals.

I was particularly intrigued by the challenges you face with your high patient caseload and the level of stress generated by the overall process. With my experience working with a caseload of more than 65 patients and helping develop a highly efficient report writing system, I believe I can add considerable value across the organization.

Given my keen interest in helping people of all ages with speech and language disorders, I know I would enjoy working for the Horizon West Rehabilitation Center. Additionally, with family and friends residing in Massachusetts, I would be thrilled to have the opportunity to live in the Boston area.

Thank you again for the opportunity to share my background and qualifications. I look forward to hearing from you, and I hope I am your top candidate. In the meantime, please let me know if you have any other questions or would like additional information.

Sincerely,
Gloria

P.S. I had a chance to read the reviews of Jill Bolte Taylor's book *My Stroke of Insight*, and I can see why it has had such an impact on your career. Thank you for recommending it!

The more you customize your thank-you notes, the more you will stand out, especially when most job seekers send generic thank-you messages. If you want to make your ideal job search a slam dunk, seek to add at least one sentence that references something you and the hiring manager discussed in the interview. Your goal is to bring your thank-you notes to life and separate yourself from your competitors. Every moment of contact is an opportunity to stand out, so make sure you don't let this post-interview moment go without taking advantage of it.

If you know that a shorter thank-you message will be more appropriate given the type of job and company, then go with a shorter version. Here is an example of a shorter message:

Hi Sandra,

It was a pleasure speaking with you and Sam earlier today about the Assistant City Planner position within your department at the City of Westnorth. Thank you for treating me so well during my visit.

I am excited about the possibility of being a part of such important work related to the city's redevelopment initiatives. Our conversation convinced me that my planning experience with the City of Augustine, along with my degree in city and regional planning, would allow me to help you and your team meet or exceed the department goals.

I look forward to hearing back from you next week. In the meantime, please let me know if there is anything more I can do to help with the hiring decision. Thank you!

Sincerely,
Ray

P.S. I have attached an article I found that addresses the need for more green space in redevelopment projects. Based on our conversation, I think you will find the information very interesting.

Use the basic framework of these thank-you note examples to help you develop post-interview messages that will work well for your background and unique job search. You will then modify your message after an interview once you know more about the company and the position. To help you customize each note, listen for something that intrigues or impresses you in the interview and record it on your phone, notepad, or the reverse side of the interviewer's business card soon after the meeting. You can then incorporate this information into each thank-you note: "I was particularly intrigued by . . ." or "I was particularly impressed by . . ." Customizing your messages will separate you from your competitors, and it is easy to do if you plan and look for content.

If you are sending a thank-you note after an interview, try to send it within two to six hours. If you have your interview late in the day, the following morning is fine, but always send a thank-you note within 24 hours following an interview.

At every turn, you need to do the basics well. You don't know if an employer will value a thank-you note, but you do know that there is rarely a time when sending a professional thank-you note would be a bad thing. When you have come this far in the job search process, never give the employer any reason to offer the job to someone else. Don't leave anything to chance by assuming the hiring manager will not value a thank-you note. Always send one!

Professional Reference Sheet

Have a professional reference sheet prepared before you start pursuing opportunities. You never know when an employer may ask for it, and you don't want to throw anything together at the last minute during the job search process, particularly your list of references.

Your professional reference sheet should have the same heading, font, and margins as your résumé and cover letter. Here are the typical reference sheet sections and headings:

NAME

City and State

Email Address and Phone Number

Professional Career Website URL and LinkedIn Profile URL

Professional References

Name

Title

Organization

Address

Phone Number

Email Address

If an employer could be confused by how you are connected to the people listed on your reference sheet, add a one- or two-line statement explaining the relationship you have with each person: "I worked with Natalie Akina on a two-year consulting project, and she later became one of my clients when I started working for Greenfield Enterprises."

List at least three references. But, ideally, have five in case an employer asks for this many or you would like to swap references in and out depending on the type of position. Include people who will rave about you, and make sure you ask for permission to use the people as references before you add them to your list. You don't want to have to contact your references at the last minute when they may not be available or aren't comfortable being on your list. Complete your reference sheet early so that everything is ready to go. Then, all you need to do is notify your references each time you anticipate that an employer may contact them.

Add at least one reference who will seal the deal for you. While everyone should rave about you, you need a closer who will take it to the next level—someone you can feed important information to and who will say all the right things and make it seem like the company would be crazy not to hire you. And this person doesn't need to be in a position related to what you are currently pursuing. Regardless of whom you select for this role, the person should rave about your professional work ethic, extraordinary customer service, teamwork, above-and-beyond approach, and ability to consistently produce high-quality work.

Use the Antique Store Editing Approach

Never send your marketing documents without first putting them through a quality control process. Quality control is vital for your reputation and brand. You may remember that "Exhibiting Quality and Consistency" is the foundational guiding principle outlined in the Success Mindset step. Most job seekers fail to exhibit quality and consistency across the board, so you can separate yourself quickly from the competition by living up to this principle.

You may be surprised to hear that I have found wrong phone numbers and email addresses on résumés and cover letters. I have also seen obvious spelling errors within section headings. Errors exist because job seekers fail to double-check all the content within each section. They assume the information within certain sections is accurate, and they tend to review documents globally rather than systematically.

People will tell you to read a document two or three times before you send it. Beware! This editing strategy isn't the way to avoid all mistakes and inconsistencies. It may help if you look at a document one day and then wait a day or two to look at it again. It also may help if you look at it one time online, then print it and look at it in a different form. Another trick editors use is to read things aloud. Even with these tactics, however, you will often miss inconsistencies and errors. So, outside of hiring an editor or proofreader, the question is, how can you avoid errors and inconsistencies on your documents? You should use the Antique Store Editing Approach.

The Antique Store Editing Approach has helped thousands of job seekers eliminate 99 to 100 percent of inconsistencies and errors on their job search documents. The approach works because it forces job seekers to look closely at everything in a systematic manner.

One day when I was on vacation and walking through an antique store in Encinitas, California, I figured out an effective way to edit job search documents. I know—it does seem strange that I would be thinking about editing résumés while strolling through an antique store on vacation. I had my editing filter on because I was baffled as to why as many as six résumé reviewers missed errors and inconsistencies on résumés before they were published in a résumé book. I was concerned about the ineffectiveness of this type of editing process, so I was motivated to find a means for job applicants to examine their own documents and get better results than external reviewers.

As I walked around the antique store, I quickly realized how difficult it was to see everything in one walk-through. Being that the store had many interesting items, I decided to walk it multiple times, focusing on a different set of objects each time. One time, I focused on the paintings, then on the sculptures, then on the furniture, and finally, on the trinkets. When I observed the store globally, I missed many items. However, when I broke the busy store down into compartmentalized areas and categories, I noticed many items I didn't see during my initial, global walk-through.

The document editing process works the same way. When you look at a résumé or cover letter globally, you tend to miss errors and inconsistencies because your eyes view the documents broadly and don't focus on the details. To train your eyes to see specifics, break your documents up into compartmentalized sections and categories, and focus on one thing at a time for each pass. This means you will read through each document multiple times. Here is an example of how you would review compartmentalized sections of your résumé:

1. Check your phone number and email address. Are these correct? Don't assume they are accurate.

2. Scrutinize the headings for spelling errors. Often, spellcheckers aren't set to review headings or will treat words in all caps as acronyms and assume they are accurate. Also, your eyes often skip headings during a general review. Always check the headings separately.

3. Look over all the commas and colons to confirm consistent usage and formatting (including bolding and italics) throughout the document.

4. Check all the dashes and hyphens to ensure consistent length and spacing.

5. Review the dates to make sure they are presented in a consistent manner, and check for accuracy.

6. Ensure information is presented in a consistent format within sections. In other words, keep the order and formatting of information the same.

7. Make sure the spaces after periods and colons are consistent. One space is considered standard.

8. Take a close look at all your bulleted sentences in the Experience section to ensure they either all end with a period or all end without a period. Since there are no strict résumé rules for using periods after bullets, feel free to use periods, but always use them the same way throughout your documents. Consistency is vital.

9. Confirm all acronyms are spelled out the first time to avoid ATS confusion. For example, instead of LCA, write Life Cycle Assessment (LCA).

10. Check technical terms to ensure they are spelled correctly, including software programs. Remember that "PowerPoint" is spelled with two capital letters, and "Photoshop" is spelled with one.

11. Look for obvious errors that are seen on many job search documents and not picked up by spellcheckers: led vs. lead, met vs. meet, complement vs. compliment, manger vs. manager, principle vs. principal, to vs. too, and role vs. roll.

12. Make certain all company and school names are spelled correctly.

13. Ensure font size and style are consistent.

14. Double-check the margins to ensure nothing looks too cramped (0.5 top and bottom margins and 0.9 left and right margins are just about right).

15. Confirm that each bullet begins with a different action verb within each job description area.

16. Check the hooks (numbers and percentages) to ensure they are all presented as numerical digits to grab attention.

17. Make sure all links (LinkedIn, professional career website, GitHub, etc.) work.

18. Run the spellchecker over the document one more time.

Most tasks on this checklist can be used for all your documents, including your cover letter, to help you spot errors and inconsistencies that you could otherwise miss during a more general review. Add to the list if you feel something would be useful for your documents. And, as mentioned earlier, it is a good idea to set your documents aside and review them later. To cover all your bases, go one step further and print your documents to view them in a different form and then read them aloud. Although you will pick up 99 to 100 percent of all errors and inconsistencies using the Antique Store Editing Approach, always have another set of eyes review your documents.

In addition to checklists, there are many other tools available to maintain quality control during your job search and within your career. If writing isn't one of your strengths, sign up for programs like Grammarly and QuillBot to double-check your email messages and help you polish your marketing documents and online promotional platform content. Also, consider using ChatGPT to proofread your work and identify any unclear or confusing passages. Don't feel you need to go it alone. Do whatever will help you maintain quality throughout the entire job search process.

A Strong First Impression

Your documents may not close the deal and get you a job offer, but they can go a long way in creating a strong first impression and landing you an interview. If you want to create effective documents, prepare them early using the guidelines described and then customize them later once you know the job requirements, department challenges, and company culture. And always use the Antique Store Editing Approach and other relevant tools for quality control.

Chapter 8

BUILD YOUR BRAND

Now is the time to develop and communicate a consistent brand that tells employers, contacts, and other professionals who you are and what you will bring to the marketplace. Your brand should represent the career and job you want, not the career and job you currently have. The more an employer can visualize you in the position at every turn and the more targeted and professional the message, the more the employer will want to interact with you and advance you along in the process.

A professional brand is a general perception people have of you based on your experience, expertise, behaviors, and actions. When summarized into a branding statement, it lets employers and others know who you are, what unique value you bring to the marketplace, and why someone should hire you. It lays the foundation for your reputation.

Your brand, communicated by your marketing materials and promotional platforms, should be professional across the board, relevant to the field, true to who you are, and visible to employers. It also needs to separate you from your competitors. If you have branded yourself effectively, you will stand out above your competition in your own unique and special way. Start to develop a professional brand by first cleaning up your existing online presence.

Clean Up Your Online Presence

Believe it or not, you already have a brand: your online presence that is visible on Facebook, LinkedIn, X (formerly known as Twitter), Instagram, Pinterest, YouTube, personal blogs, and elsewhere on the internet. What do you think employers do the minute they want to know more about you and the value you could add to the position and the company? They check your online presence.

According to CareerBuilder, 70 percent of employers explore a job candidate's social media sites before making a hiring decision, and more than half of the employers find something online that causes them to reject job candidates.[1] What does your Facebook page say about your personality, habits, values, and interests? Go back through the past six months with all your social media sites and evaluate yourself from an employer's perspective. If you feel you will have a hard time critiquing yourself, have someone else review your online presence and provide honest and constructive feedback. Ideally, you will find a hiring manager who can provide this type of feedback.

Know your field and industry, and then put on your public relations hat and ask yourself if your social media sites present you in a positive and professional manner for what you want to do. Do they show you as a hardworking, likable, stable, and focused individual? Delete or hide anything that could tarnish your image and cause the employer to run the other way. If someone tags you in an unflattering or inappropriate post, ask your friend to remove or hide the post. You should also deactivate old social media accounts and work with Google and other search engines to remove anything on the internet that is inappropriate or doesn't support your brand.

Don't think you need to stop having fun or stop posting personal images. If the posts are fine from an employer's perspective, you are good to go. However, if they show you engaging in inappropriate or unprofessional activities, make sure your privacy settings are enabled or the images or tags are removed. Don't take any chances when it comes to your reputation.

One of the best ways to establish and maintain your brand is to control the narrative. You can start to do this by using a unique and consistent name throughout your career. Google search your name and see what surfaces. You want the name you use to be unique so a Google search will not generate a long list of names or uncover some questionable people with the same name. If this does happen, add a middle name or middle initial: Bob William Smith or Bob W. Smith. Once you have chosen your branding name, secure a Gmail address and a website domain with the same name so you can use it for your professional career website. Do the same with other social media sites.

Cleaning up your online presence doesn't mean eliminating your online presence. Not having a presence online can be as bad as having an unflattering online presence. A CareerBuilder survey showed that 47 percent of employers were less likely to interview applicants if they couldn't locate them online.[2] The absence of an online presence could be an indication that the person lacks marketing skills, is out of touch with the real world, doesn't value connections, or doesn't have any connections. Unless there is a good reason not to have an online presence, make sure you have one.

Develop Your Brand

Once you have cleaned up your online presence and any other areas in your background that could create a problem, turn toward creating a premium brand that focuses on how you will be viewed by the professional world throughout your career. Your brand is the promise to your customers that you will present yourself, behave, and perform a certain way all the time. How do you want to be known in your field and throughout your career? What will you bring to your field that is unique and special? What will employers get from your brand (you) that they won't get from any other brand? Develop a focused, unique, and consistent brand that employers will relate to and want to engage with on a daily basis.

> How do you want to be known in your field and throughout your career?

An effective brand should help you develop a positive relationship with employers even before you have any contact with them. And, once you do have contact, your brand must be reinforced across the board by how they see you in person. Here is an example of what an unprepared job seeker could discover following a job interview:

> "I had a phone interview this morning, and the interview went quite well. However, when I looked at my LinkedIn profile 30 minutes after the interview, I noticed that the hiring manager had already looked at my profile. I was excited that she was interested, but I was concerned because my profile was focused on pursuing a writing/journalist position, and I was interviewing for a sales position."

This example illustrates the disconnect that exists for many job seekers. What do you think happens when employers uncover these types of inconsistencies? The employer moves you to the sidelines because of concerns about your long-term commitment to the field and the position. If one part of you is inconsistent with another part, you don't have a trustworthy brand. And, without a trustworthy brand, you will have a hard time developing a strong and lasting relationship with employers.

Based on my experience, managers tend to hire the safest candidates (candidates with minimal risk of leaving the company early) and not necessarily the most qualified candidates. What does this mean? It means you need to minimize any concern an employer may have about hiring you and then losing you in the near future. If there are concerns about your commitment and stability, the employer will often eliminate you. By having a consistent and relevant brand in place to reinforce your commitment to the field, you will minimize these types of concerns.

The sooner you can develop a consistent brand that communicates how you want to be seen by employers, the sooner you will attract the people and jobs you want into your life. But don't think your brand will magically appear. Take time to think about what you want to be known for in your field and life, and then take steps to communicate your brand and reinforce it throughout your career.

Start with a branding statement that sets the stage for how you want employers to see you. Here is an example of a branding or career value statement pulled from the top of the Career Profile example: "Experienced event planner with a reputation for creating memorable events at half the cost." This statement communicates what the event planner is known for and what the planner will bring to the job that no one else will bring. It differentiates the planner from the other candidates and lets employers know how the person will add value to the company. See the appendix for information on how to develop branding and career value statements.

After establishing your branding statement, identify qualities and values that closely align with your desired brand. These will guide your behavior, ensuring you maintain your brand over the long run. For example, the event planner might list fun, unique, personalized, efficient, and prompt. With your qualities and values in place, write down all the strengths, skills, and accomplishments that add credibility to your brand. You can use these to support and sell your brand. Work them into all your promotional platforms and marketing documents.

With a well-defined brand in place, you now need to reinforce it in all areas of your life. To help you maintain your brand, establish standards for how you will function. If being trustworthy is one of your most important qualities, put standards in place to make sure you are seen as a trustworthy person all the time (e.g., I will maintain consistency in everything I do). You can then break these down into more detailed standards that will guide your daily actions (e.g., I will respond within 24 hours to every email).

Since your brand will shape your reputation and guide your behavior, take this process seriously; spend plenty of time thinking about what you want to be known for and how you want others to think of you. Early on, use your Career Profile to help you define your brand. Once you have a premium brand in place, you can then use your brand to help you develop or refine your Career Profile each time you begin a job search.

Remember that everything the employer encounters related to you and your background defines and reinforces your brand. This includes how you communicate, what you wear, how you write, what you bring with you to a meeting or interview, what your business cards look like and say, the design of your résumé and cover letter, your follow-up skills, and on and on. You are your brand. What you do in all areas of your life and during your job search and career defines your brand.

Put yourself in the employer's shoes and view yourself through the employer's eyes. Don't leave anything to chance when it comes to your reputation and brand.

Promote Your Brand

You may have all the qualifications needed for a job and be the best at just about anything, but you will never get what you want if you're unable to promote yourself and show your work. Employers rely on what they can see, and the more they can see you in the right light, the better.

If you want to become more likable in the eyes of the employer, take advantage of any opportunity to increase an employer's sense of familiarity with you.[3] An effective way to do this is to display your picture on your promotional platforms when appropriate. Do you have a friendly photo on your LinkedIn profile? Do you have a professional career website with photos that help employers visualize you working for them? Are your other social media sites professional and visible to employers? Can employers easily locate these sites and access them? What about having your photograph on your professional business card and next to your email signature line? Of course, use your best judgment, but appearing personable and approachable will often pay off for you.

You may be wondering if all of this is worth it for a job search that may only take one to three months. If you're thinking this way, think differently. Times have changed, and the job search process has changed. No longer do you want to rely on résumés and cover letters to land you job interviews. You want to get employers to gravitate toward you because of what they have observed online about you and your work.

Primary Avenues to Promote Your Brand

Rather than think you need to continue to search and apply for jobs throughout your career, put a foundation in place to drive people to you by sharing your work. Remember, you're pursuing connections and opportunities, not applying for jobs. Attract people through your blog, a project you posted online, your LinkedIn profile, a professional career website, a talk you gave at a conference, or social media posts.

Use the following avenues to show your work and promote yourself and your brand:

1. Create a well-designed LinkedIn profile.
2. Develop a professional career website.
3. Establish a presence on other relevant online platforms (e.g., X, Facebook, YouTube, Instagram, Medium, Pinterest, GitHub, or alumni social networking platforms).
4. Use face-to-face avenues (e.g., conferences, information meetings, internships, volunteer work, or professional association events).

If other promotional avenues are relevant within your field or industry, add them to the list. Some people may conduct a webinar, submit personal press releases (you can search the internet for free online press release distribution services), start a podcast, or write articles.

How many promotional avenues you use will depend on your field, level of expertise, social media talent, and overall capacity to pull off something of quality. Regardless of what you do, follow the Slam Dunk Guiding Principles whenever you design any marketing document or promotional platform. Quality and consistency should be at the top of your list. If something doesn't pass the Slam Dunk Guiding

Principles test, don't put it in front of people. Your goal is to create simple, clear, and consistent messaging. Show your work but show it right.

Let's now look at each of the promotional avenues recommended for your job search and career.

1. **LinkedIn profile**

    To be competitive, create a LinkedIn profile. When employers go online and search for an applicant's profile and can't locate one, their impression of the candidate drops. If you make a commitment to be competitive, you need a LinkedIn profile to show you're living in a contemporary professional world and you value connections and people. Allocate time to set up a robust profile. Consider your LinkedIn profile as a critical job search tool that should be complete, visually appealing, focused, and error-free.

    Here are some tips that should survive the test of time and help highlight your most valuable credentials and bring your profile to life:

    -   Complete as much of the profile as you can without overdoing it. Eye-tracking studies have shown that a busy LinkedIn profile will distract the reader's eye away from important skills and other content that add the most value to the position.[4] A few strategic documents and photos are great if they reinforce your brand, but too many can be distracting and make your profile look busy. You can include more information than you have on your résumé, but don't overdo it. Employers will not spend much time on your LinkedIn profile if it is overwhelming and complicated. More than anything, use your LinkedIn profile to create curiosity so employers are excited to contact you to learn more. You will read more about developing curiosity in chapter 9.
    -   Make your LinkedIn profile change-friendly, reader-friendly, and employer-focused. It should have short readable nuggets of information (descriptions of three to seven lines in length) rather than long, dense paragraphs. It should also quickly lead readers to where you know they want to go. There should be no question about how you can help the employer and what value you will bring to the marketplace.

- Incorporate keywords. Identify 10 to 15 keywords related to the positions you plan to pursue. Add them to your headline and summary (the About section) and sprinkle them throughout your profile. Also, pull up your branding qualities, values, strengths, skills, and accomplishments and weave them into your profile to reinforce your brand and communicate your value.

- Use your headline, summary, and banner to engage employers, communicate your value, and frame your narrative. Here is an example of a career value statement (taken from the Career Profile in chapter 5) that could be used in the headline or summary as a LinkedIn framing statement: "I create memorable events at half the cost." Or in my case, "I help job seekers become 'the candidate' employers can't wait to hire." Alternatively, in the headline, you could include your current job title and your top two or three skills or areas of expertise. If you use this approach, make sure you incorporate a framing statement in your summary along with a complete list of relevant skills or areas of expertise. To pull everything together, add a banner image that reinforces your brand.

- Add a well-thought-out and professional photo. Studies have shown that a LinkedIn profile with a picture will get 21 times more views and 9 times more connection requests.[5] Consider your LinkedIn photo as your virtual handshake.[6] Since this could be the first time most employers will see you, you want to use a photo that will show employers you're someone they would enjoy working with—someone who looks happy, friendly, and approachable. Your LinkedIn photo should also be relevant to your field. Use a headshot in which people can see your face clearly without any distractions. Wear something nice but not too formal. Of course, what you wear will depend on your field. Unless your field is extremely formal, wear business casual attire.

- Be active on your profile. Connect with people on LinkedIn after you meet them, endorse others so they will endorse you, seek recommendations, add relevant documents to show examples of your work, post field-specific content that reinforces your brand, and continually update your profile with new information that is focused on the job you want.

- Identify LinkedIn buddies who are willing to modify their LinkedIn recommendations on short notice to help you market yourself better for each position. This could be a supervisor you developed a good relationship with or a close colleague. Find at least one person who would be happy to put in extra time to help you customize your job search. This could also be the person listed on your reference sheet who acts as the closer.
- Bring yourself and your background to life by completing all or most of the sections on your LinkedIn profile. Also, consider following people, companies, schools, and groups in the Interest section to help develop an instant connection with people you don't know.
- Use the Antique Store Editing Approach to ensure your profile is error-free and consistent throughout.

A well-done LinkedIn profile is a critical component of an effective job search. Take time to create an impressive profile that will attract employers and give you a competitive advantage during the job search process.

2. **Professional career website**

If you want to grab attention and impress employers, develop a professional career website in which you will include documents and images in a more visual and targeted manner. Since your job search is really about your career, the time you put into a professional career website is well worth it. You can continue to refine and update the website as you move through your career so it will be ready each time you decide to make a transition.

Many excellent website design platforms are available for you to develop a professional-looking website where you can drag and drop text and images into the site without much effort. You have much more space and flexibility with websites than you do with your LinkedIn profile and résumé. You can add larger photos that grab attention and create your visual brand without distracting from your credentials. A website also allows you to create a simple and visually impressive front landing page and then set up a menu that leads readers to additional information.

Here are some content areas you could add to your website menu:

- Vision/Mission
- Areas of Expertise
- Credentials
- Bio
- Résumé
- Courses
- Professional Workshops
- Awards
- Conferences
- Publications
- Reports
- Projects
- Articles
- Testimonials
- Clients
- Videos
- Blog
- Podcast

When you design your website, think of yourself as a consultant. Why should clients hire you to do work for them? An elegant, simple, and attention-grabbing home page is important. If the website extends vertically (deeper on the landing page), consider the top part of the website as your key promotional real estate. Include a larger photo and branding tagline along with a quality of work quote that will have employers see you in the right light from the start. You could also consider adding some relevant areas of expertise. The key is to know your audience and then design your website to appeal to them. Form follows function.

3. Other relevant online platforms

Besides a LinkedIn profile and a professional career website, get to know your field and industry and then add other online platforms that are relevant for your unique job search and career. If you are in a highly creative and social media savvy industry, you should have a professional presence on other relevant social media sites. For example, if you work in a knowledge industry, you will want to build a brand by sharing your expertise and knowledge through X (formerly known as Twitter) or blogging platforms like Medium, LinkedIn, and Facebook. And if you are a data scientist, software engineer, or computer programmer, you will add GitHub to your promotional platform repertoire.

Posting relevant content on your social media sites is a great way to promote your brand and get people to gravitate toward you. You can post the results of one of your side projects, share a relevant and intriguing article, post your own articles, share your opinion or knowledge on a subject, or publicize an award or milestone. Start with something you feel comfortable sharing, then gradually increase the number of posts.

4. Face-to-face avenues

Online avenues are one way to show your work and tell people about your brand; however, you also need to show your work by coming face-to-face with people. If you really want to wow potential employers and close the deal, find ways to interact with them. You can do this through informational meetings (BQAA Sessions, discussed in the Relationship Team step), conferences, mixers, alumni events, internships, volunteer work, and many other avenues. Since you have limited time during your job search, use the face-to-face avenues (virtual or in-person) that make the most sense for you, your job search, and your field. But always look for ways to diversify your job search and promote yourself and your brand.

> "If you don't give the market the story to talk about, they'll define your brand's story for you."
>
> —David Brier

Brand Maintenance

A well-developed and pertinent brand will not appear by itself. You must work hard to build and maintain it over the long run. As David Brier, an award-winning expert in identity branding, said, "If you don't give the market the story to talk about, they'll define your brand's story for you."[7] Keep this quote in mind throughout your career and always perfect, protect, and promote your brand.

Chapter 9

PREPARE FOR CONTACT

Be prepared to talk about your career and reinforce your brand to anyone you meet during your job search. You never know when you might have an opportunity to establish a meaningful connection with someone—not just when you reach out for an informational meeting, but also when you strike up a conversation in a store or at your child's soccer game, mingle at a mixer or conference, get introduced at a barbecue, meet someone in an art class, or even run into a friend on the subway. Every interaction is an opportunity, so you must be prepared for any type of contact.

In one situation, Nash, a talented engineering student, connected with three different decision makers within less than two hours, and he benefited from being prepared for both strategic and spontaneous interactions.[1] On the last day of his engineering internship, Nash went to his manager's office to thank her for the opportunity. Unfortunately, the manager had been called out of the office on an urgent matter and was unavailable. Rather than leave, Nash went out of his way to stop by the office of another executive—the operations manager—and thanked him for the opportunity. As Nash was leaving the office, the manager told him to stay in touch and then asked Nash to reach out when he got closer to graduation.

As soon as Nash left the building, he headed over to another engineering company he was interested in where he had scheduled an informational meeting and a company tour. After the tour, he had a nice conversation with the chief engineer about the engineering field and potential opportunities at the company.

On his drive home, while at a stoplight, Nash recognized the woman in the car next to him. It was the mother of a student he knew from high school. He lowered the passenger window and said hello. The mother asked him what he was doing, and Nash said he was studying mechanical engineering and had just finished an internship at Franklin Engineering. The mother worked at another engineering firm in the local area, and she told Nash to reach out to her when he was getting closer to graduation.

These three interactions all happened within an hour-and-a-half span: one because Nash got in front of a decision maker to say thank you, one because he set up a meeting in advance through a family connection, and one because he lowered his car window to say hello to someone he knew.

One month into his senior year of college (just a couple of months after his internship), the operations manager at Franklin Engineering contacted Nash and offered him a job. Good things will happen when you get in front of people. Nash also added all three people to his LinkedIn profile and continues to stay in contact with them.

When you meet people during your job search, you don't want to get caught off guard. You want to be strategic, and you want to be excited to connect with people. Since most hiring takes place through referrals and connections, you must capitalize on all the interactions you have with people inside and outside the workplace. You want them to be curious about you and your work.

Curiosity Statements

During your interactions, try to create intrigue that will prompt people to want to know more and continue talking with you. You need to know what to say to someone at a conference, mixer, or lunch meeting when you're asked one of the following questions and might have limited time to generate interest and start a conversation:

- How are you doing?
- What business are you in?
- How is your day going?
- What brings you here?
- What is your story?

If you haven't thought about how to answer these types of questions, you may be caught off guard and not know what to say. If this happens, you will miss an opportunity to connect with a person who may be able to help you. Sally Hogshead, in her book *How the World Sees You*, says the following:

Every time you introduce yourself, you have about nine seconds to engage your listener. This is your window of opportunity for a connection. If you earn their interest during those nine seconds, people will be more likely to engage further. If you fail to add some value in that golden window, they're less likely to listen to what you say, let alone remember it or act on it.[2]

People will often ask open-ended questions like "How are things going?" or "What do you do?" This is a great opportunity to grab their attention, but it can be easy to push people away by indicating that you are busy or by using vague, dead-end statements, such as

- Things are quite busy with my work.
- I'm swamped.
- I'm a stockbroker.
- I'm a graduate student.

Will these statements generate a conversation and engage people? Probably not. Instead, you need to create curiosity that will help people connect with you and want to learn more about you and your work.

On the other extreme, some people have learned to use an "elevator pitch" to quickly share their brand. However, the elevator pitch—a 20- to 30-second statement about your career, job, service, product, or project—immediately conjures up the notion that you are selling or pitching something. How can you effectively sell something to someone when you haven't developed a relationship with the person and don't know the person's needs? An elevator pitch is difficult and uncomfortable. Brief Curiosity Statements should replace the elevator pitch as your go-to approach for connecting with people. They are the gateway to more fruitful conversations.

Instead of pitching or selling yourself, share a brief statement that generates interest and intrigue in nine seconds or less. Your goal is to get people to want to hear more about you and what you have to say. Ideally, your statement will generate a dialogue where people learn more about you and you learn more about them.

Here are four examples of brief Curiosity Statements that generate intrigue quickly:

"As a graduate student at the University of Northbrook, I am developing a state-of-the-art water action plan aimed at saving the university $250,000."

"I'm preparing a talk for a unique workshop I am co-facilitating at a career development conference in Reno, Nevada. The title of our presentation is 'How Does Your Office Space Influence Your Interaction with Clients?'"

"I'm rolling out an innovative sales campaign that should increase sales by as much as 25 percent in one year."

"I run all the events for a Fortune 500 company, and I focus on making events special and memorable at half the cost."

The conversation continues because these statements generate intrigue. You want to have the person you are talking to say, "How do you do that?" or "Tell me more about that." If you are more entrepreneurial-focused, you can use a story approach:

"I went through _____ experience. I developed a _____ solution to overcome my challenge. And I'm now helping people confront similar problems by _____."

Preparing Curiosity Statements allows you to connect and engage in a more natural way while still sharing essential information about your work and your brand.

Your Needs

Once you have established a connection with the person you are speaking with, you can share information about your needs. If you don't put your needs out there at some point or ask questions to uncover additional information or resources, you will never know if the person can help you. However, you don't always need to ask for immediate help, especially if you have limited time to talk. Your "ask" could come after you have developed a deeper relationship. You could get a business card and then follow up later.

If you have created intrigue and engaged the listener, you can provide more information on your situation. Here is an example if you are looking for a job out of college:

"I'm about to graduate from the University of Williamson with a degree in renewable energy. My goal is to help companies reduce their energy consumption by at least 20 percent without impacting their operations, and I'm looking to land a position within an energy-related consulting firm in the San Francisco Bay Area."

You can use a formula and fill in the blanks:

Example 1

"My goal is to find a job in _____ and help a company _____ by _____."

Example 2

"With my skills and experience in _____,
I am pursuing jobs in _____ where I can
help companies solve _____. I'm specifically
looking for _____."

Example 3

"I help people with _____ by _____
so they can _____. And I'm pursuing _____."

If you don't share enough specifics, you will rarely develop a connection or generate interest and curiosity. Stories, specifics, and Curiosity Statements stick with people. And, if you want to be memorable, you need to have things stick.

No matter how you do it, the key is to grab attention early and draw people in to hear more. Take time at the start of each week or before a conference or mixer to plan your response to questions you might get about you and your work.[3] By turning moments of contact into opportunities for some useful exchange of information, you will often get something valuable out of the conversation. Curiosity Statements can open the door to more meaningful interactions and help you in any setting, including at work, receptions, conferences, talks, and during everyday interactions. If you take the time to prepare, you will never let a moment of contact go to waste.

Give and Then Take

While Curiosity Statements will create intrigue and allow you to share your needs, there are times when you might want to approach a moment of contact from the opposite direction. For instance, before sharing your needs, try to learn more about the people you meet and find ways to help them. This is such an obvious and simple tactic that most of us, including most job seekers, fail to use it. Many people think it's too simple to work. Well, it does work, and you should find ways to use this tactic.

Instead of waiting for people to ask you how you are doing while you are standing in the elevator, ask them how they are doing or find out what brings them to a conference or mixer. Spend time trying to find out what people's needs are and how you can help them. When you help others, you will be rewarded in so many ways. As author and motivational speaker Zig Ziglar said, "You can get everything in life you want if you will just help enough other people get what they want."[4]

> "You can get everything in life you want if you will just help enough other people get what they want."
>
> —Zig Ziglar

Seek to give first and take second. The job search process is all about connecting with people, developing relationships, helping people get what they want, and finding ways to get what you want. The more you remind yourself that your job search is about the people you interact with and then act in this manner, the more success you will have.

The Ice Cream Cone Approach

At some point during the job search process, someone will ask you the (implicit) question, "Tell me about yourself," perhaps during an informational meeting, conference, event, or job interview. Unfortunately, the question is difficult for many job seekers because it is so broad. Where should you start? How much of your background do you incorporate? What do you need to accomplish with your response? How can you promote yourself while also being personable and memorable? If you want an easy-to-follow structure to pull up in your mind each time you get the question, use the Ice Cream Cone Approach shown in Figure C.

The Ice Cream Cone Approach helps you remember that everything you say should be strategic and tell the story of why you are where you are right now—either interviewing for the position at this company or pursuing jobs within this field. To help you remember this strategic approach, visualize the ice cream cone as a funnel that starts out broader and then narrows down to the position or the field.

Figure C: Ice Cream Cone Approach

To use the Ice Cream Cone Approach to answer the "Tell me about yourself" question, start at the top of the cone and work down, covering each part as detailed below.

Frame Your Narrative

Frame your response by saying what you are passionate about or interested in that ties back to the position, company, and field. This framing statement allows you to set the stage for how you want employers or your contacts to think about you and your focus from the very beginning. Then, everything that follows will support this statement. If you are interested in event planning and are asked the "Tell me about yourself" question, here is an example of how you might respond:

> "I am passionate about organizing special events that wow participants and come in under budget."

Here are some other ways to frame your narrative with an opening statement:

> "I want to help people _____."

> "I have strong interest in _____."

> "I see a need for _____, and I want to _____."

Tell Your Story

You will then tell a story that supports why you became interested in this field. What was the turning point that got you to gravitate toward this career? Stories are memorable, and employers are interested in hearing what motivated you to enter the field. Employers and contacts may not remember your credentials (unless they are unique or impressive), but they will recall your stories. As a result, add a story somewhere in your answer. In most cases, the story will immediately follow your framing statement. The story can start when you were young or begin when you were in school or working in a job. The more interesting and unique the story, the better. Here are two event planning examples:

> "My passion for the event planning field began when I was completing my undergraduate degree at the University of Northbrook. During that time, while I was pursuing a communication degree and searching for part-time work, I applied for and landed a student assistant position with an events

manager in the College of Innovative Design. The minute I started working in the position, I fell in love with event planning, and I found that I had a knack for the work."

"My passion for event coordination began when my supervisor at Western Enterprises Inc. approached me about managing an event for more than 900 employees shortly after the events manager unexpectedly left the company two weeks before the event."

Here are some examples within other fields:

"My interest in film started when I grew up in Alaska and worked part-time with a documentary filmmaker who was filming endangered species in the Yukon-Kuskokwim Delta."

"My interest in air quality started when I grew up in Covina, California. I vividly remember when my classmates and I had to come in from recess because our lungs hurt so much from the thick smog. This experience led me to . . ."

"I became interested in engineering when I was chosen to participate in an innovative high school engineering program that combined art and technology."

"I first became interested in working in the outdoor apparel industry when I hiked the entire Pacific Crest Trail with my parents when I was 15."

Your story should engage the employer. It can begin at any time in your life, but you need to show how it laid the foundation for all the steps you have taken since to prepare for your field and the desired position.

Highlight Your Preparation

Once you have framed your narrative and engaged the interviewers with your story, you will describe what you have done strategically to prepare for this field and the specific position. This part of the ice cream cone is typically told in chronological order and showcases the most important steps you took (experience, education, training, and certifications) that have brought you to where you are today (either pursuing an available position or talking to one of your contacts).

You'll notice that "experience" is listed twice in this part of the Ice Cream Cone Approach figure. This is because people typically gain experience in one job or volunteer opportunity, then pick up a certification or training, and then go on to get some other type of experience, like a new job. In other words, you probably have more than one kind of experience to include as you walk your listener through the important steps of your career journey.

Make sure you incorporate specific, relevant examples of your work and accomplishments, including significant numbers and awards. You want to bring your story to life and avoid repeating your résumé within this section. You don't need to discuss every job you have held or every credential you have acquired. Instead, talk about the credentials that most closely align with the position. The ice cream cone funnels downward because everything you have done in your past (all the credentials you mention) has prepared you for the field and the available position in some important way.

Here is an example of how the event planner might highlight the steps taken to prepare for the field and the current opportunity:

"I worked alongside the events manager all four of my undergraduate years, and then, shortly after graduation, I accepted an event planning job with Square West Services, where I helped increase event attendance by more than 30 percent and worked my way up to events manager within two years.

"During my second year at Square West, I realized I wanted to get more training in all areas of event planning and coordination. As a result, I completed a one-year intensive master's degree in event management through the BCT School of Professional Studies, and I graduated in the top 1 percent of my class.

"Immediately after graduating from the program, the Smithton Hotel Group hired me to oversee the company's large events and manage five staff members. I have continued to work for Smithton for the past four years. During this time and with a great team, I organized numerous innovative employee activities, including several 'Fun at Work' employee satisfaction events that resulted in a Peak Performer Award, which is only presented to two employees each year."

Note that each paragraph ends with a selling point: promoted in less than two years, graduated in the top 1 percent of the class, and received the Peak Performer Award. It also incorporates a Curiosity Statement: "organized several innovative 'Fun at Work' employee satisfaction events."

If you feel you need to bring your narrative to life, weave in more accomplishments, speak about projects that would be of interest to the potential employer, and incorporate metrics whenever possible. And always find ways to use brief Curiosity Statements to generate additional interest.

Funnel Everything Down to the Position

Once you have highlighted the most important steps you have taken to get to where you are, tie them back to the job and the organization. Here is a simple example of how you might connect your preparation to the job:

> "All my experience and education have prepared me for this type of role, and that is why I was excited when I heard about this opportunity."

Close with a Personal Quality, Talent, or Unique Experience

Bring yourself to life and get people to relate to you by adding some unique quality, talent, or experience at the end of your answer. It can be an achievement in arts, music, sports, outdoor activities, volunteer or charity work, or some other activity. It can also relate to a personal quality or unique skill. Whatever you select should be interesting and should show off your talents in a different way. Ultimately, you will relate your uniqueness to the job. Here is an example:

> "And, on a more personal note, I enjoy oil painting, and I have won a couple of art contests for my work. In all my jobs, I try to use my artistic and creative experience and training to enhance my problem-solving and marketing skills. For example, when I worked at Square West Services, I was recognized for a marketing event I organized. By incorporating some creative elements into the event and the promotional materials, I helped increase overall participation by 34 percent over the previous year. I know I would bring this same type of creativity to the Events Director position."

If you don't have anything relevant to say about a unique quality, talent, or experience, come up with a one- or two-line closing statement that expresses your interest in working in the position and for the company:

> "Not only am I interested in the Events Director position, but with my experience in the hospitality industry, I am also very excited about the possibility of working for Emerald Hotels. And I am thrilled to have the opportunity to talk to you today about how I can help the company achieve its goals."

If you do talk about a unique quality, talent, or experience but feel you need to end with a closing statement, here is a shorter close:

> "I believe my background aligns well with all parts of the job, and I am thrilled to be able to talk with you today about my qualifications."

Practice Your Response

The Ice Cream Cone Approach is straightforward and simple, but you will need to spend some time running through the approach so it comes naturally to you. Feel free to change the order of the five levels if an adjustment will help you tell a better story. No matter what you do, always remember that the Ice Cream Cone Approach presents a story that funnels your most important credentials down to the position and the company (or the field you are entering if you are talking to one of your contacts).

As you prepare your Ice Cream Cone Approach response, try to keep your answer between a minute and a half to two-and-a-half minutes long and grab attention in the first nine seconds through your opening line and story. Most of your interview responses should be between thirty seconds and two minutes, but your answer to the "Tell me about yourself" question and other complex questions can go a little longer (between two and four minutes) if you make them interesting for the hiring committee members. You can make longer responses more engaging by incorporating stories, examples, or accomplishments into your answers, or by breaking your answers up into sections (e.g., First, Second, and Third).

Refine, Customize, and Strategize

The Market Ready step was created to help you become proactive and strategic. The more you can prepare for the job search process in advance, the more time you will have to refine, customize, and strategize once you start to compete for your ideal jobs. The candidates who do well are the ones who take the time to determine what is essential to employers. They then modify their marketing documents and promotional platforms to present a consistent brand and show employers that they will add more value to the position and the organization than anyone else.

After your initial market-ready preparation, you will begin reaching out to people to get inside information, which will enable you to target your marketing documents and "Tell me about yourself" response even more. The Relationship Team step (presented in chapters 10 through 12) will help you feel more comfortable reaching out to people and getting the help you need to increase your market readiness.

Do you want to connect with key people in your field, build a relationship team, learn more about your industry, become more marketable, and get in the door at your target organizations?

Step 4

RELATIONSHIP TEAM

If you believe business is built on relationships,
make building them your business.[1]

—SCOTT STRATTEN

An empty Halo Top ice cream carton sits on the corner of my office credenza as a reminder of what is important during the job search process: relationships. As I was reading a *Los Angeles Times* article on how Halo Top founder and CEO Justin Woolverton took on Ben & Jerry's and Häagen-Dazs with his low-calorie ice cream, I couldn't help noticing how he started to build his Halo Top team. Woolverton met one of his top executives through an amateur basketball league and hired him as the company president and chief financial officer. He then hired the president's brother to manage social media, and the story goes on from there.[2]

Studies have shown that social networks and employee referrals are the top sources of quality hires.[3] These recruitment avenues are effective because employees who are hired through these channels tend to fit in better with the company values, stay with the company longer, reduce the time it takes to hire someone, and generate more profit for the company.[4, 5] No wonder 70 to 80 percent of available jobs are never advertised and more than 70 percent of job seekers land jobs through connections.[6]

Although social networks and employee referrals are top sources of quality hires, you won't find the word "networking" mentioned in any other paragraph in this book. When job seekers hear the word, most freeze and then run the other way. They don't know what it means, don't know how to do it, and don't feel comfortable attempting it. But the good news is that your job search isn't about networking; it's about developing and maintaining relationships—something you do every day.

> The good news is that your job search isn't about networking; it's about developing and maintaining relationships— something you do every day.

Unlike the Market Ready step where you learned more about your field by conducting online research, in the Relationship Team step, you will reach out to professionals and ask them for advice on the best ways to navigate your job search and prepare for your field. You are now seeking inside information while also getting your foot in the door at your target organizations and developing your relationship team. At this point, you are pursuing connections and opportunities, and the Relationship Team step will teach you how to do it.

Chapter 10

DEVELOP YOUR RELATIONSHIP TEAM

D) eveloping meaningful relationships is the core strategy used to get the jobs you want and advance in your career. It takes you from being seen as an outsider to being viewed as an insider, and most people who get hired are seen as insiders (either internal candidates or candidates the employer already knows or with whom they have a connection).

Your goal early in the process is to develop relationships while also getting yourself ready to compete. You want to become more appealing to employers while also expanding your relationship team and developing the contacts you need to get hired by your target organizations.

Get Back Door Access

Ideally, you will develop relationships with hiring managers and other key decision makers before jobs become available. You can meet decision makers early in the process by setting up informational meetings, attending conferences, connecting with people through professional associations, volunteering at your target companies, and completing internships. As jobs arise in your target organizations, you want hiring managers to think of you before they decide to post a position. Rather than try to get in the front door by applying to positions posted online, attempt to meet people in advance by going through the back door—the best door—and setting yourself up for positions that might arise down the line.

Getting in the back door is vital since many employers fill their positions through connections.[1] When several graduate students were pursuing a highly competitive position at a well-known apparel company, I was determined to find out what it took to land a job at the organization. I was particularly interested in knowing more because all the candidates were very qualified. When I asked why the company hired one candidate over the other very talented candidates, the hiring manager told me that it came down to who had connected with and expressed interest in the company before the position became available. The person they hired had reached out to the hiring manager before the job was posted and had shown an interest in the company, its mission, and its work. Ultimately, this was the one factor that sealed the deal for the top candidate.

If you can learn about a position before it's posted, this gives you another advantage: time. Once a department decides to hire a new employee, it could take two to four weeks (or longer) to work through the back-end administrative process to get the position posted. What do you think takes place during this time? The entire department is doing word-of-mouth recruiting before anyone else is aware of the position. This is truly the hidden job market. By the time the position is posted, the hiring manager may already have several potential hires in mind, and they may not even look at any of the applications submitted for the formal job announcement. If you are applying to the job posting, you may be two to four weeks behind. Connecting with decision makers or department team members before positions get posted is critically important, especially for highly coveted positions.

In some cases, companies will even create jobs for people because they were so impressed with them during preliminary informational meetings. This happened with Leylah, a 26-year-old job seeker from Walnut Creek, California, when she met with several people at a local consulting firm.[2] During Leylah's conversation with the first manager, the manager came right out and told her that the company didn't have any open positions. However, Leylah kept asking intelligent questions and presenting herself in a professional manner, and by the time she left the organization later in the day, she had received a verbal job offer.

Good things happen when you connect face-to-face with people and impress them with your knowledge and preparation. Always seek to get in front of people.

Diversify Your Relationship-Building Tactics

Whether you're just getting started building your relationship team or you already know many people in your industry, you should diversify your approach and use additional relationship-building avenues to connect with decision makers:

- Attend alumni events.
- Participate in professional association activities.
- Use platforms like LinkedIn and Facebook to connect with people.
- Attend trade shows to meet with professionals in your field.
- Speak at conferences and show your work.
- Blog and connect with people online.
- Take evening courses or workshops that bring you in contact with professionals who have similar interests.
- Tap into the local chamber of commerce to meet people within your field.
- Generate conversations with contacts at athletic clubs, coffee shops, pet outings, religious events, hobby groups, art or music clubs, charity events, and other settings.

Consider which of these avenues makes the most sense for your job search and works best for you. You only have so much time, and you don't want to spend too much time going down dead-end paths that never amount to anything. Be selective and use the avenues that help you connect the most with people within your field. Assess your progress along the way and adjust when necessary. Ideally, you will continue to connect with people throughout your career, so when you need to look for a new job, you already have a solid team of contacts who know you and your work.

You often don't need to look very far to find people who can help you. Many opportunities are sitting right in front of you if you put yourself out there. I was fortunate to attend a workshop facilitated by author and career coach Barbara Sher in which she took the participants through an activity that has stuck with me through the years. Sher had all attendees write down one or two career goals on a piece of paper. She then gave us about 10 minutes to walk around the room and find at least three people who could help us reach our goals. This activity was more than powerful—it was eye-opening and comforting. As she went around the room and had people share how the connections could help them, many were surprised by how useful the interactions had been and how helpful the connections would be in moving closer to their goals. It pays to share your goals and needs with others, even strangers.

If you don't open up and talk to people, you will never know what you might be missing. An executive once illustrated this point while telling me about his experience navigating the speaker sessions at a large conference in Atlanta.[3] While the executive was getting lunch at the conference buffet, one of the younger attendees turned to him and asked what session he planned to attend next. This question began a conversation that resulted in a connection and a referral. The executive was so impressed with the person that he referred him to someone he knew at a local consulting firm. If the young attendee hadn't asked a question, he wouldn't have sparked a conversation and acquired a referral to a potential employer. It pays to initiate conversations during your job search.

> When you strive to become the person you want to be and get yourself and your work in front of others, the people you want to come into your life will often find their way to you.

You would be amazed at what you get in return when you ask questions or say something to begin a conversation. Occasionally, you will get a cold shoulder, but when you are at an event that brings professionals together with similar interests, they are looking to connect. Take advantage of these opportunities and get out to events that bring you closer to the people you want to meet. The law of attraction is in full force during your career. When you strive to become the person you want to be and get yourself and your work in front of others, the people you want to come into your life will often find their way to you.

You also never know where a relationship may lead. One talented gallery curator got an excellent job because she asked a colleague at another gallery out for a cup of coffee.[4] The curator had worked indirectly with this person for close to seven years, and one day she asked if he would like to get a cup of coffee and chat. They finally met at the local coffee shop. As their coffee break came to an end and the curator took one last sip, her colleague asked, "Do you know about the position at the Frontline Contemporary Art Gallery?" The curator wasn't aware of the job, and she wouldn't have known about the position if she hadn't reached out to this person and had a cup of coffee with him. The curator went on to pursue and ultimately land the job that fit her background better and paid her significantly more money.

It's not difficult to find these types of stories and locate people who can help you, especially when the average American knows approximately 600 people.[5] But you do need to try to interact with people and share what you are passionate about and what you are trying to accomplish. Successful people understand the value of relationships, and they make it a point to connect with people regularly and nurture the relationships.

Never underestimate the value of all these relationship-building avenues. You never know who will end up opening the door to your next opportunity.

Use Brief Question-and-Answer Advising Sessions

While you should diversify your job search and use a variety of productive relationship-building avenues, in the following chapter, we'll focus on one of the most effective relationship-building tools you will use during your job search to get in the door and develop lifelong relationships: Brief Question-and-Answer Advising (BQAA) Sessions. Together with the methods outlined in this chapter, they will help you prepare well for the job market, locate hidden jobs, land excellent positions in either weak or strong job markets, and develop a strong relationship team for your entire career.

SET UP BRIEF QUESTION-AND-ANSWER ADVISING SESSIONS

rief Question-and-Answer Advising (BQAA) Sessions are relatively short meetings that take place between you (the job seeker) and someone (ideally a decision maker) who can answer a few questions and provide advice. The meetings aren't dedicated to learning all about the industry or hearing about someone's entire career. They are focused on getting targeted advice while acknowledging that people are busy and have limited time to talk to you. The BQAA Sessions allow you to

- Feel comfortable getting in the door at your target organizations.
- Begin to develop a lifelong professional relationship team.
- Get advice on how to become more marketable.
- Seek input on how best to break into a field or company.
- Expand your target organization and contact list.

BQAA Sessions will be a significant part of your relationship-building strategy. They will be the number one approach you use to identify, prepare for, and open the door to your ideal jobs.

Understanding How BQAA Sessions Work

Hiring managers often see "informational interviews" as time-consuming tactics used by job seekers to learn about the field when they are only interested in getting a job. BQAA Sessions are more efficient and effective, and they remove the negative stigma associated with the informational interview name.

You can no longer expect managers to have the time to provide in-depth information on careers, companies, industries, or fields. These types of meetings may be feasible and appropriate with someone you know reasonably well, but they will not be with someone you've never met. Many managers dread getting requests for informational interviews since they know they will often be in for a long session. It has nothing to do with their lack of desire to help people. Instead, they don't have the time to sit down with someone for a long period (more than 30 minutes) and talk about broad topics. Given managers' busy schedules, job seekers should use the shorter and more focused BQAA Sessions.

BQAA Sessions can take place through a variety of means (email, phone, in person, videoconference, or online chat meeting), and they can be as short as 10 minutes and go as long as 30 minutes, occasionally longer. If you have set up a 30-minute meeting, stick close to that time frame. If your contact appears to be busy and rushed, shorten the meeting and don't go beyond 20 minutes. If the BQAA Session takes place over the phone and the person seems brief or in a hurry, you may want to end the meeting in 10 to 15 minutes.

You will also find that some people will warm up to you during BQAA Sessions and want to chat a little longer. Concluding the meeting at 30 minutes might be inappropriate and rude. Some BQAA Sessions could go longer when your contact wants to walk you around the office to showcase the operations and introduce you to the staff. Other BQAA Sessions could be extended when a decision maker wants to conduct an informal interview because the person is impressed with you and has a position available or anticipates an opening down the line. In these cases, it would be inappropriate to stop everything and run out the door. Once again, use your best judgment and always look to respond to the needs and wants of the other person.

Getting Started

To begin the Relationship Team step, look at your list of target organizations and contacts. If you haven't already assigned a contact to each organization, use the following avenues to identify contacts for each company:

- LinkedIn
- Other social media sites
- Professional associations
- Professors
- Family and friends
- Past supervisors and coworkers
- Volunteer contacts
- Civic organizations
- Advanced internet searches
- Company website staff listings
- Business journals and directories
- University career centers
- Alumni associations and community platforms
- Conference connections

You can also look for articles written by professionals in your target organizations or articles about people in the companies. If you can't find someone who is working in one of your target organizations, you will often find that the other people you talk to will have contacts in the company or can connect you to someone who does have connections within the organization.

The contacts you assign to each organization are the people you will reach out to for advice. If you want to get interviews, especially in highly competitive industries, you need to establish a connection. And, ideally, your connection will be at the decision-making level or with someone who would feel comfortable referring you to the hiring manager or putting in a good word for you.

You often don't need your initial connection to be a contact in a relevant department or even in the same company. Based on my years of recruiting and placement experience, I have found that the connections that lead to jobs are often one or two degrees removed from the initial contact. There are plenty of people who can end up leading you to key decision makers in your target organizations, but you need to start connecting with people in your field to begin the process.

Since time is valuable, ensure each connection will be productive by targeting people who will be more receptive to your messages and more knowledgeable about your field of interest. Any connection is better than none, but some connections are much more productive than others.

I worked with a job seeker named Maryam who spent 90 percent of her initial job search conducting informational meetings with relatives and friends in the Portland, Oregon, area.[1] She thought she was approaching the job search the right way by connecting with as many people as possible. But even after two months, none of the contacts had resulted in any relevant leads, and she was exhausted. Rather than keep going down the same path, she reached out for help.

Maryam's initial approach was fine (reaching out to family and friends), but when she realized it wasn't working, she needed to assess and adjust. Maryam did just that. After my conversation with her, I referred her to a contact in the Portland area who was working in her field, and within less than a month, that one connection resulted in Maryam landing her ideal job. Why did it work? Because the approach was more targeted to her area of interest. By stepping back, assessing her situation, adjusting, and being more strategic, Maryam reached her goals much faster.

Alumni, professional association members, and colleagues will probably make up most of your contacts, but you could have a friend or family member who has relevant connections as well. Sometimes you will need to test the waters before knowing how fruitful each avenue will be. Use your best judgment and tap into the people who can help you the most. But always assess and then adjust if necessary.

Asking for a BQAA Session

Rather than contacting someone and saying, "I was wondering if I can conduct an informational interview with you to hear about your career," you will be more specific with BQAA Session requests. You will mention an existing connection you have with the person, share what specific information you are seeking, and include a little about yourself to add credibility and uniqueness. Here's one example:

Hi Marisol,

Bill Smith suggested I contact you. I met Bill at a UCLA football game, and he thought you would be an excellent person to contact about some questions I have regarding the advertising field. I am specifically interested in any advice you have on the best ways to break into the field within the Los Angeles area. I would also value your suggestions on ways to supplement my current experience, training, and skills to make me more marketable.

I noticed on LinkedIn that you also graduated from UCLA with a degree in psychology, so you will have a fairly good understanding of my background and university experience. I received my degree in June, and I also recently completed an internship with Carrera Branding.

I don't need to take much of your time, and I would be happy to call you or meet with you in person. If you are available to talk, my schedule is open on Tuesdays and Wednesdays, and I can also adjust my calendar on other days to accommodate your availability.

Thank you in advance for your help. I have attached my résumé to provide you with more information on my background, and you can also access my LinkedIn profile through my signature line.

I look forward to connecting with you, and I hope you have a great day.

Sincerely,
Bob Lloyd

Notice that this example focuses on the points of connection between the job seeker and the contact. The more you can link to something you have in common, the more you will engage your audience and get a response. You will develop even deeper relationships when you research your contacts in advance and focus your messages on them and their interests. Here is an example:

I noticed on LinkedIn that you switched from engineering to investment management. I am curious about what motivated you to make the change and how you successfully transitioned to your current position. Would you happen to have 15 minutes to talk about your career path?

When you show knowledge about a person, that makes them feel good and demonstrates interest in a "give and take" relationship. Do your research and find the best way to develop a bond and connection. You can always work your way into other questions once you connect with people through topics that pique their interests. This general approach will be your tactic for getting in the door at your target organizations and developing lifelong relationships with key people in your field.

Crafting Effective BQAA Session Email Requests

During your job search, you will contact people you know and people you don't know. To reach out successfully to a variety of audiences, you need to know how to write effective email messages that get responses. Below are some email guidelines to help you create compelling BQAA Session request messages.

1. Keep the email messages short—no more than 225 words; between 150 and 200 words is even better, depending on your audience.
2. Mention a referral name (if you have one) in the subject line (more on subject lines below).
3. Make a connection in the first paragraph or in another strategic location within the message. The connection can be through a referral or through something else that bonds you to the person or the organization. LinkedIn can help uncover areas where there may be commonalities. Are you a fellow professional association member or a graduate of the same school? If you don't have a connection, show that you have done your research by stating precisely what it is about this person that made you want to reach out.
4. Let the person know what you are after and be specific. If you are too vague, the person will get concerned that you will take up a lot of time. Rather than say, "I would like to learn more about the engineering field," seek targeted advice. When you are too broad with your "ask," most people don't have the time to figure out what you need or spend much time describing the field in general. Occasionally, you will find these people, but they are becoming

harder to locate in such a fast-paced work environment. The key is to know your audience and adjust your message and meeting format accordingly.

5. Praise the person or acknowledge the person's level of expertise or knowledge.

6. Add a little bit of information about yourself to bring you to life, add credibility, and connect you with the person.

7. Consider attaching your résumé to help facilitate the discussion and show your credentials. The more someone knows about your background, the better. Use your best judgment here, and don't include an attachment if you feel it is inappropriate. You can always send your résumé later.

8. Include a hyperlink to your LinkedIn profile or your professional career website.

9. Acknowledge that you are aware of the person's time and only need a short period to ask some questions. You can also ask for a specific amount of time (15 to 30 minutes).

10. Leave the door open for the person to contact you or for you to reach out again if the two of you don't connect via email (see example below). This is optional, but it is helpful to have a plan if you don't get an email response.

11. Offer specific days and times to connect (add a time zone if needed) or provide a calendar link.

12. Thank the person.

These guidelines will serve you well as you craft your own email messages. However, they are only guidelines. You have permission to break the rules in order to correspond effectively with your audience and get your desired results. Here is an email example of a BQAA Session request that meets the guidelines:

Dear Axel,

Sally Wright suggested I reach out to you. I used to work with Sally at Nautilus Products, and she said you would be an excellent person to contact to get some advice on landing a marketing position within a larger consumer products company in Ohio.

I recently received my graduate degree in marketing from Palisade College, and I have two years of marketing experience working for a small consumer products company in Connecticut.

I was wondering if you might have 15 to 20 minutes to talk. I am currently in the Cincinnati area, and I would be happy to meet with you in person, connect through video, or talk over the phone. I would also be happy to buy you a cup of coffee if you would like to meet at a local coffee shop.

I am available on Tuesday and Wednesday afternoons, and I can also adjust my schedule to accommodate your availability. Assuming you have some time to talk, please let me know what works best for you. If for some reason we don't connect by email, I will give you a call next week to see if we can set up a meeting time.

I have attached my résumé to provide you with a little more information on my background. You can also access my LinkedIn profile in my signature line.

Thank you very much for your time!

Have a great day,
Santiago Perez

Leave out the "I will give you a call" sentence if you feel it would be inappropriate to call the person or feel it is too assertive. However, there may be times when you will want to be more proactive. Giving a person advanced notice of a possible phone call is always recommended. Use your best judgment on how assertive you should be.

If you don't have a referral to add to your opening line, here are a few other ways to begin your message and make a connection:

As a fellow member of the Event Planning Association, I thought you would be an excellent person to reach out to for . . .

I noticed on LinkedIn that you are connected to Angela. Angela and I . . .

I came across your name through the Washington and Lee University alumni directory.

How you reach out to people will depend on your level of connection. If you know your contacts reasonably well, you can be more direct and ask for their help getting in the door. If you don't have a strong relationship with the people you are contacting, take a slower approach. Here is an example of how you could reach out to someone you know but with whom you have not communicated in a long time:

Hi Mark!

It seems like a long time since we corresponded. I hope everything is going well for you. I see that you are now working overseas for a technology company. I'm sure living and working internationally is an amazing experience.

I am reaching out because I recently came across a Finance Manager position at Google that interests me, and I thought you might have some suggestions for getting in the door at the organization. I know you used to work for Google, so I thought you would be the perfect person to contact.

Since our time together at Greensmith Corporation, I have gained additional experience working in finance for a large software company, and I recently received my MBA from New York University with a specialization in finance. I have attached my updated résumé to provide you with a little more information.

I have always been interested in working at Google, and I would appreciate any help you can provide. I would only need a few minutes to ask you some questions and seek your advice. Would there be a time we could connect via Zoom? I know you are in a different time zone, but I would be happy to accommodate your schedule. We can also correspond by email if that would be easier for you.

Thank you in advance for your help! I look forward to hearing from you.

Sincerely,
Lucia Durnin

If you are a student and would like to contact one of your instructors, here is an example of how a BQAA Session request might look:

Dear Professor Gutierrez,

Thank you for the excellent Marketing Strategy course you taught last spring. I learned so much from your course (I received an "A" in your class), and I was able to put the knowledge to good use during my recent internship at the Greyton Consulting Group.

I am now pursuing job opportunities as I get ready to graduate in May, and I know you have a close connection with AGT Management Consulting. I have a keen interest in this organization, and I was wondering if you might have time to answer a few questions about the company, especially since you have raved about the firm's work environment and services.

If you do have the time to talk, I am available on Monday and Wednesday afternoons, and I would be happy to adjust my schedule to accommodate your availability. Please let me know what would work best for you.

To provide you with a little more information on my background, I have attached my résumé along with a competitive advantage paper I wrote for your class. You can also access my LinkedIn profile and professional career website through my signature line.

I look forward to hearing from you. Thank you in advance for your help!

Sincerely,
Joe Bean

No matter how you write your messages, they shouldn't contain any errors or inconsistencies. Use the Antique Store Editing Approach to finalize all your documents and correspondence, and always have another set of eyes look at them as well.

Crafting Email Subject Lines

Effective subject lines do make a difference. Spend time coming up with a subject line that grabs attention and gets the contact to open your email message. For the text of the subject lines, capitalize the first letter of every word except for prepositions under five letters, conjunctions, and articles (known as title case capitalization) to make it more eye-catching. (If you're uncertain, you can easily find free tools online by searching for "title case converter.") Below are some subject line examples to consider when requesting BQAA Sessions.

If someone is referring you, consider using the following:

- Bob Smith Referral
- Referred by Bob Smith
- Seeking Advice—Sally Wright Referral
- Referred by Sally Wright—Quick Question

If you are reaching out to professional association members or alumni, consider these options:

- Fellow ATD Member Seeks Your Advice
- Fellow UC Santa Barbara Alum Seeks Advice
- Fellow Alum from University of Hawaii Loves Your Work
- Quick Question from a UCLA Graduate
- University of Vermont Graduate Could Use Your Help

If you are reaching out to someone after hearing the person's presentation, reading an article written by the person, or visiting the person's website, you could consider these options:

- Your Event Planning Talk Impressed Me
- Your Article on Sustainability Inspired Me
- Aspiring Financial Analyst Seeking Advice
- Loved Your Marketing Presentation at the Branding Summit
- Quick Question About Your Microfiber Research

If you met someone and want to follow up to initiate a BQAA Session, consider these options:

- Met You at the BSC Marketing Conference
- Nice Meeting You at the AEP Mixer!
- Reaching Out After the IT/Tech Conference
- Monica from the Energy Efficiency Conference Following Up

Do you notice a common theme with these subject lines? With each, the person has highlighted the previously developed connection in the subject line using specific details. People love to hear from people who are interested in and intrigued by their work, and they often bond with people who have similar interests and backgrounds. If you don't already have a connection, research the person on LinkedIn, the internet, and the company website to find something specific about the person that you can bring out within your subject line and correspondence.

Following Up

If you don't get a response from your first message, change the subject line, forward the original message, and include a follow-up message. Here is an example:

> Hi Elizabeth,
>
> I hope your week is off to a great start!
>
> I noticed that you are connected with Alice Green on LinkedIn. Alice and I grew up together and have collaborated on several personal projects. She is a close friend. Given this connection, I thought you would be an excellent person to reach out to for some advice on landing a position at East Rim Inc.
>
> I am specifically interested in a software engineering position at an innovative organization within the outdoor apparel industry, and East Rim Inc. has always been at the top of my list. I would greatly appreciate any inside information you can offer.
>
> Please let me know if you may have time for a quick phone or video call. I sent a more detailed message about a week ago, and I have included it below for additional information.
>
> Thank you!
> Adrian Bray

You can be subtle about the original message or be more direct. Here is an example if you want to be more direct at the start of the message: "I know you are probably quite busy, so I wanted to circle back on my earlier message."

Often the second email message gets a response because the timing is better or the person you reached out to makes it a greater priority. Always send a follow-up message.

To help you avoid the email guessing game, use an email tracking tool to determine whether your email messages are received, opened, or forwarded to someone else. While some basic services are free, most charge a monthly or yearly fee. These services can be worth it because they will take the guessing game out of job search emails and help you gauge the success of your messages. They will also help you determine the right time to check back in with people because you will know if and when your message has been opened.

Scheduling the Session

When the person agrees to meet with you, follow the professional and customer service guiding principles by making sure you accommodate your contact's schedule and respond to the person promptly. Since the people you are reaching out to will eventually become part of your lifelong relationship team and are taking time out of their busy schedules to help you, go out of your way to make the process efficient and enjoyable for them. For example, send them your bio, LinkedIn profile address, and résumé in advance so you don't need to spend as much time describing your background during the BQAA Session. Be proactive with the logistics: Suggest or provide the time, place, phone number, videoconference link, and anything else that will make the meeting run efficiently and smoothly. Don't make your contact do the work. Offer to meet at your contact's place of business or nearby if possible. Your goal is to minimize hassle and create a positive experience.

Preparing for the Session

Since you have requested and set up the meeting, you should take the lead on running it. Bring an agenda and have a list of first- and second-tier questions ready to go. First-tier questions are those you absolutely want to ask. Second-tier are those you will ask if you have a little more time. You always want to have additional questions prepared just in case.

Be specific and targeted to show your preparation and make the questions easier to answer. Below are some questions you can use or adapt.

Questions that feed back into your marketing documents:

- What qualifications and skills are essential for a successful career in this field?
- What critical skills should I highlight on my résumé and cover letter to help me stand out?
- Do you recommend getting any certifications for this field?
- Given my current credentials, do you see any gaps I should fill?
- Are there any strengths I should emphasize?
- What personal qualities are important for this field or this position?
- Do you have any suggestions on how I might improve my résumé?

Questions to learn more about the industry, field, and job search process:

- What are the best ways to break into this type of position or field?
- What are some challenges to breaking into this field, and what do you recommend for overcoming the challenges?
- What helped you break into this field and industry?
- What are some trends taking place within this field?
- What trade publications do you read, and what are the best ways to stay current on the latest trends, innovations, and news within this industry?
- What do you feel is the best career path to take to get to where you are in your career?
- What position should I pursue now to create a solid foundation for a career in this field?

Questions about your contact and the contact's company:

- What do you like best about working for your company?
- What do you like most about your work?
- What are your main responsibilities?
- What are the biggest challenges you face in your job?
- What is the structure of your department, and how does the department support the company's mission?
- If you could have made different choices early in your career, what would you have done differently, and how do you think it would have changed things?
- How do you set career goals and manage your career?

Questions you could ask at the end to help build your relationship team:

- Given my interests, are there any other companies you would recommend I explore?
- Is there anyone else you would recommend I talk to in this field?
- Are there groups or professional associations I should join to meet more professionals in this field?
- Are there people or companies I should follow online (or publications to explore) to learn more about this industry and field?
- Who are the leaders in this field?

These questions are particularly helpful early in the process when you are developing a relationship team and seeking help on becoming more marketable for your field. Feel free to add to the list as you work through the job search process and identify other useful questions. Also, revisit the questions outlined in the Market Ready step to see if you may want to ask any of them during your BQAA Sessions.

To make your questions specific and targeted, you'll need to know as much as possible about your contact. This is also essential in order to make a more personal connection on which you can build a relationship. Before each BQAA Session, spend at least 30 minutes refreshing your memory on your contact's background and interests. Determine what you have in common and see how you can make an emotional connection during your interactions. Maybe you will find that both of you coached a youth softball team or enjoy traveling.

Talking about these kinds of nonwork topics shows you are interested in your contacts—not just in what the contacts can do for you. The more you can bring out commonalities or touch on the person's interests, the more you will bond with your contact, and the more time the person will spend helping you. Conducting advanced research will also allow you to come up with icebreaker questions or comments you can make to help you develop instant rapport. Make a list of these questions or points of commonality and pick two or three that you plan to use. Never go into a meeting without knowing something about the attendees. Preparation always sells.

You should also plan what you will wear. Business casual will probably be the best attire for most BQAA Sessions. However, if you are meeting somewhere that suggests more formal attire, go with what feels right or ask what attire would be most appropriate. Formal attire, for example, may be more appropriate if you are meeting in Washington, DC, New York City, or another large city, or if you are meeting in a formal office setting. Spend some time learning about the setting and your audience so you dress the right way and don't appear out of place. However, if you're unsure, always err on the side of more professional rather than less. A good first impression is just as important during a BQAA Session as it is in an interview.

Plan to arrive early so that you don't waste any of the person's time waiting for you. And make sure you leave extra time to get to your destination. Ideally, you will arrive 20 to 30 minutes early at the general meeting location, depending on your transportation, parking logistics, and the meeting site. If you're meeting at the person's office, plan on getting into the company reception area around 10 minutes before your scheduled meeting, but don't check in more than 15 minutes early. If you are meeting someone in a public setting, arrive at least 10 minutes early and try to grab two chairs if the meeting site is crowded. Being early makes a good first impression and shows that you value the person's time.

If you want to stand out, be proactive about logistics, come prepared to lead the conversation, dress appropriately, and arrive early to the meeting location. Always show you care about the other person, both with your words and your actions.

Being Memorable

Every contact is a potential employer or a connection to a potential employer. If it makes sense given the contact and circumstances, find ways to stand out during the BQAA Sessions.

Can you imagine the impression you would make if you set up a BQAA Session and then called the person 20 minutes before the meeting and said the following?

> "Hi Dave! This is Laina. I am right across the street and headed your way. I noticed that there is a Starbucks around the corner, and since I have a few minutes before our meeting, I thought I would see if you would like something to eat or drink during our meeting. I would be happy to get you something."[2]

You can use this same approach in an email the day before the meeting: "I plan to arrive early to our meeting location, and I would be happy to pick up something for you at the Starbucks across the street. Would you like anything?" You will, of course, need to do some advanced research to know if you can pull it off based on what is available around the meeting location.

You could also bring something for your contact without saying anything in advance. What if you came to the BQAA Session with information that could help your contact? You could impress the person by researching the company and department and then putting together a report to improve a process, elevate customer service, run a campaign, or sell more products or services.

Spend time coming up with something different, personable, and relevant. When you go the extra mile, you will get much more in return.

Starting the Meeting

While you will need to be efficient during the meeting, seek to develop rapport first by saying something nice about the person in the meeting or the company. Your goal in the BQAA Sessions (and in your interviews) is to develop long-term relationships. Don't think of any contact as someone you use and then never talk to again. Think about developing a long-term relationship with the person first and foremost, long before you think about performing a job search or business transaction. Make sure you "give first" (show you care about the person) and "take second." Here is an example of how you might start the BQAA Session:

> "Thank you for meeting with me. Bill Smith spoke very highly of you, and
> I appreciate you taking the time to talk. I would first like to say how much
> I admire your company and the story behind the innovative product line.
> It is truly inspirational."

Or you could start by asking a simple question about something you have in common or something else you learned through your research.

Next, share your plan for the meeting to give the person an idea of what to expect. You might say,

> "Since I said I would only take a little bit of your time, I thought I would
> start by giving you a brief overview of my background and career goals.

Then, I would love to ask you a few questions about preparing for a career in this field. I hope this works for you."

Before you jump into your questions, create some interest by sharing your goals and reminding the person of the key parts of your background. Your purpose is to get information you need, so you don't want to take up too much time talking about yourself. However, given that the person you are talking to could end up hiring you or referring you to someone, you do want to promote yourself a little and be clear about your goals. Work on a one- to one-and-a-half-minute introduction using the Ice Cream Cone Approach. Avoid going on and on about yourself at the start of the BQAA Session and instead provide a brief, targeted summary of who you are and what you hope to get out of the meeting.

Asking Your Questions

After briefly introducing yourself and your goals, start working through the first-tier questions on your list, adjusting the order and content based on your contact's answers.

Make sure you take notes during the BQAA Session. Note-taking isn't just for you. While it helps you retain the information and access it later, it also shows the people you talk to that you value their advice and want to capture it. Don't try to write down everything the person says, but do jot down key phrases, names, and concepts.

If the contact is dominating the meeting, asking you many questions, and you're finding it challenging to ask your own questions, you can tie a question on at the end of your answer: "And this brings up another question I have." This approach will help you ask your questions without having to interrupt the person. Remember, the primary goal is to develop a relationship, so being kind and polite is more important than getting through your list of questions.

If the meeting goes well, you can be more proactive and ask a question about opportunities: "I'm impressed with the work you do and the department's mission and services. Do positions ever come up in your department? And, if so, what are the best ways to pursue opportunities in the organization?" In the next sections, you will learn more about how to ask about opportunities.

Keep an eye on the time so that you don't run longer than you stated, and try to gauge your contact's level of engagement based on body language and length of responses. If you feel you have covered the content of your first-tier questions and you still have some time left, that's when you can pull a couple from your second-tier list. Just make sure you leave about five minutes for asking the "chess game" questions and closing the meeting.

Asking "Chess Game" Questions

The job search process is one big chess game where you need to think at least one to two steps ahead if you want to win the game. Each stage provides you with an opportunity to set yourself up to perform better in the next stage. When you think one or two steps ahead and make a move that will help you later in the process, you will quickly stand out and start to separate yourself from your competitors.

Always come up with a few questions that will allow you to stand out in the future. Toward the end of the BQAA Session, ask at least one of the following "chess game" questions:

> **The job search process is one big chess game where you need to think at least one to two steps ahead if you want to win the game.**

- What do you wish you had more time to read about or explore that would help you and your business?
- What one or two books have had the greatest impact on your career?

And ask one of the following challenge or goal questions:

- What are some of the challenges you currently face in your department? What is the most significant one? Do any barriers exist to overcoming the challenge?
- What main departmental goals do you have in place for the coming year? What is the most significant goal you want to achieve? Are there any obstacles standing in the way of reaching the goal?

With the answers to the questions above, you can take the information, do some research, and then provide your contacts with something that can help them or their operations (more about this in chapter 12).

You should also feel free to come up with your own chess game questions. Based on your research, inquire about anything that will give you information to use later to help your contact. You could, for instance, inquire about one of the department's initiatives, campaigns, or programs and then later present ideas on how to advance the effort. Do whatever feels natural and adds the most value.

Asking About Opportunities

Most of your BQAA Sessions should focus on asking questions and getting advice, not asking for favors. Don't ask for too much too soon. Once you develop a relationship, you can ask for more help. If people don't know you initially, they are less likely to go the extra mile to recommend you for a job or refer you to someone in the company. They also may not think very highly of you for expecting them to give you preferential treatment so early in the relationship. But once they get to know you and begin to like you, they will be much more willing to make an effort to help you.

Your goal is to get in the door and have a pleasant conversation with someone working in your target organization, division, or department and then develop a relationship over time. You can ask about job opportunities at the end of the meeting or at a later date once your contact warms up to you. You will need to use your best judgment about the appropriate time and place to ask for more help.

In most cases, you don't need to ask for much. As long as you connect with decision makers (people who can hire you or be an advocate for you) and share what you can offer and what you're looking for, you will often get the help you need. If you impress your contacts with your preparation during the BQAA Sessions, they will say to themselves, "This is the type of person we could use in our company!" As a result, there is no reason to be too assertive at the start. Good things will happen if you stand out with targeted questions, intelligent answers, strong communication skills, emotional intelligence, a professional approach, and the right mindset. The best-run companies are always looking for sharp people regardless of whether they have an available position, and they will keep you in mind long after the meeting if they are impressed with you. Good things happen when you do your research and connect with people.

If you sense that your contact is warming up to you (through positive comments and body language) and is willing to help, don't be afraid to express interest in the company and ask about opportunities. Here is another example of what you could ask at the end of a BQAA Session when you know the two of you have bonded:

> "I am impressed with the work you do and the company's vision and services. What are the best ways to keep an eye on potential opportunities at the company? Is there anything I should build up in my background to become a stronger candidate and a more productive employee for this type of work?"

Toward the end of the meeting, you should be able to determine whether it is appropriate to ask about opportunities in the contact's company or seek additional help. If in doubt, you can always wait and ask for further assistance later.

Closing the Session

Be considerate of your contact's time and don't run over the duration you mentioned. If the person seems engaged and your time is almost up, you can test the waters: "I told you I would only take 30 minutes of your time, so I want to wrap this up, but I am really enjoying talking to you." You can then see what the person says. If given the okay to proceed, you can continue for about five more minutes. But you still need to be aware of the person's tone, body language, and willingness to share information. As much as 93 percent of communication takes place through body language and tone.[3] If people appear relaxed and make a lot of eye contact, those are good signs. If people begin looking around a lot or start picking up their things, these are signs that they're ready to be done. Don't go beyond the initial 30 minutes unless you are confident your contact has the time or wants you to continue to engage.

Close with something that leaves a positive and lasting impression. Conclude your meeting with two questions and a thank you:

> "I know you're busy, and I don't want to take up much more of your time, but I do have two final quick questions. First, is there anything else you feel would be critical for me to know when entering this field?"

> (pause for an answer)

> "Second, is there anything I can do to help you?"

> (pause for an answer)

"Thank you so much for taking the time to provide such valuable advice. It is very nice of you to spend this much time with me, and I know your advice will make a big difference in my job search and career."

Show that you are willing to go above and beyond expectations and provide extraordinary customer service. What do you think the "How can I help you?" question does for you?[4] It makes you likable and memorable. The question shows your contacts that you care about them and are the type of person who gives as well as takes. You become the person that people want to go out of their way to help.

Developing and maintaining lifelong relationships is about getting help and helping others. Be proactive, offer to help, and you will stand out and be memorable.

Following Up After the Session

Following up with the people who help you is very important because it sets the stage for the next time you reach out to your contacts. Make sure you send a thank-you note within 24 hours following a BQAA Session. Sending an electronic message is fine, but a handwritten note may stand out more. To cover all your bases, send a quicker electronic thank-you message and then follow it up with a handwritten note for a more personal touch.

Always seek to go the extra mile and send your contacts something they would value and appreciate. Remember the chess game questions you asked at the end of the meeting? Those questions will provide you with information you can use to comment on something or locate articles or tips related to the person's needs and interests. You could then attach the article or include the article link in your email. If you can't come up with anything practical to share, you can always comment on one of the recommended books. You will learn more about these approaches in the upcoming sections.

In your correspondence, comment on something you talked about in your meeting (business, sports, art, travel, etc.) or something the person accomplished recently that was highlighted on the company website, social media sites, or through a press release.

That first thank-you note is essential, but don't stop there. Use the Flower Bulb Follow-Up Approach illustrated in Figure D to continue thanking the people who have helped you during your job search and career. The illustration helps you envision three logical moments to offer thanks by comparing the advice you were given to a flower bulb:

Imagine a friend gives you an amaryllis flower bulb for a special occasion. You would initially thank your friend for the gift. As the flower bulb grows and starts to bloom, you could send your friend a photo of the flower to update the person on the flower's progress and beauty, and in the process, you would thank your friend again. And then, right when the flower has fully bloomed, you could send your friend a final thank you along with a photo of the final result. Now imagine how appreciated that friend would feel.

This thank-you approach can be used just as effectively when someone takes the time to help you. You are thankful for the information up front, but it becomes even more meaningful when you can apply it and see the benefits. Sharing the value you've seen from the advice makes the person feel genuinely appreciated. It also makes you memorable.

When people help you with your job search, plan to thank them three times.

1. Send an initial thank-you note (pre-bloom).
2. Update your contacts if something new or good happens and thank them again (partial-bloom).
3. Update your contacts once you reach your milestone and thank them one final time (full-bloom).

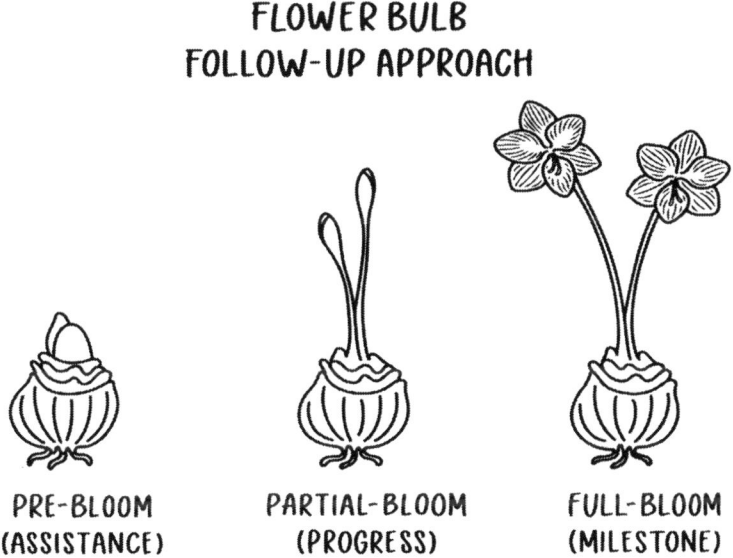

FLOWER BULB FOLLOW-UP APPROACH

PRE-BLOOM (ASSISTANCE)   PARTIAL-BLOOM (PROGRESS)   FULL-BLOOM (MILESTONE)

Figure D: Flower Bulb Follow-Up Approach

While the Flower Bulb Follow-Up Approach has three steps, use your best judgment. Once again, nothing is carved in stone. If the advice you received results in an immediate outcome, you may only thank the person once or twice. Consider your circumstances and audience, and then go with what you think will work best. But always thank people at least once. And never forget the power of a handwritten thank-you note for someone who would value a more personal touch.

Thank-you notes are a great way to keep your name in front of key people so they will think of you if a position opens up. If you continue to nurture your relationships, you will have an easy time working back through these people later. With your goal of establishing a solid job search foundation for your entire career, take the time to develop *and* maintain key relationships.

Laying a Foundation

Using BQAA Sessions will expand your relationship team, develop contacts within your target organizations, and get inside information that feeds back into your marketing documents and promotional platforms to make you more marketable for your field.

> "The best time to plant a tree was 20 years ago. The second-best time is now."
> —Chinese Proverb

If you stay in touch with your contacts and have thanked them along the way, you can often ask for specific job-related assistance further down the line. If people like you and feel you are qualified, they will do what they can to get your application materials in the right hands, especially if your contact is at the decision-making level. Don't be afraid to ask for what you need, but always work your way into the "ask." Developing authentic connections takes time, and this is why you need to build a relationship team before you actually need one.

While you want to have a relationship team in place early, you should never feel that you are in a bind if you don't have a large team at the start of your job search. You just need to understand that your job search is about your career, and you should focus on expanding your relationship team to set you up well for both the present and the future. Whenever you think about the right time to start developing your team, remember the following Chinese proverb: "The best time to plant a tree was 20 years ago. The second-best time is now."[5] Start building your relationship team *now* so you can get the help you need for your current job search and all your future career moves. Your goal is to look back in 20 years and thank yourself.

Chapter 12

CONNECT WITH HIRING MANAGERS

P eople hire people—they don't hire résumés and credentials. Of course, you need to have the right credentials, but ultimately the final decision is based on a candidate's ability to fit in well with all areas of the company. While people hire people, they don't just hire anyone. They tend to hire people they know or have had some contact with during the process. The more you can develop relationships with key people in your field and within your target organizations, the more you will become an insider and the more successful you will be at landing a position in one of your desired companies. When you start to pursue opportunities and compete for positions, you will need to make relationship building an even greater priority if you want to land your ideal job now or in the near future.

Ideally, early in your job search, you will conduct BQAA Sessions with decision makers virtually or in person to seek advice. Through these early meetings, you will expand your relationship team, learn more about your field, and seek input on how to become more marketable. Then, as your job search progresses and you actively pursue opportunities, you will leverage your existing contacts for additional help and continue utilizing BQAA Sessions to meet new people and open the door to your ideal jobs. As you get deeper into your search, you will focus more on connecting with hiring managers and potential hiring managers, uncovering hidden opportunities, and gathering inside information. These actions will allow you to customize your marketing documents and online promotional platforms, enabling you to market yourself more effectively for specific roles. You will be more targeted, strategic, and assertive as you make it a priority to connect with hiring managers and get in the door at your target organizations.

Hiring Managers

As you pursue opportunities, always seek to get yourself in front of the hiring manager or at least in front of someone who is involved in the hiring process. And, unless explicitly told not to, always send your application materials directly to the hiring manager even after you submit your materials through the online portal. You need to find ways to go beyond what others will do and bypass human resources and the formal online application process. Online avenues often turn into deep black holes where applications never surface. You can't risk having this happen if you want to land your ideal job.

In most cases, only a handful of online applications make it to the hiring manager, and sometimes none of the online applications get into the manager's hands. Unless you match up perfectly with the position requirements, you may find it difficult to get around the firewall that exists between the human resources department and most hiring managers. And the scary part is that very few applicants align perfectly with any job.

Human resources personnel are great, but they are very busy and don't know the positions nearly as well as hiring managers. As a result, they will often go by the book when reviewing your application. If you don't fit the rigid qualification guidelines, they will eliminate you. And if they are using an ATS, the same rigid evaluation process will be used, only this time it will be done by a computer.

Hiring managers are much more flexible because they know what is valuable in the job. They know what has worked well in the past, and they know what they like. If a hiring manager had a high-performing employee come out of a particular school and you attended the same school and program, the manager may overlook some of your weaknesses and invite you for an interview. Additionally, if you have already met with hiring managers through earlier BQAA Sessions and they have warmed up to you, they may overlook some minor deficiencies in your background because they know you and are impressed with you. You are considered an insider, and as mentioned before, employers tend to hire insiders.

Hiring managers often have the power to bring you in for an interview and hire you even when human resources may have rejected you. Given a hiring manager's level of influence, do whatever you can to get yourself and your materials in front of the manager. You never know what will grab the hiring manager's eye, and it could be something totally unexpected like your extracurricular activities, a sport you played in college, your membership in a professional association, a company where you worked, your customer service background, an award, or one or two courses you took in your major.

When you connect directly with hiring managers or other people on the hiring team, you have someone on the inside who can be an advocate for you during the hiring process. If you only connect with recruiters or people in other departments, you don't have someone on the inside who can influence the hiring decision as much. Ideally, you want to connect with people on the hiring team, especially the hiring manager who often has the final say.

There is another important reason to take the extra time to get your materials to the hiring manager: It works! And very few applicants do it. A study by Jobvite showed that hiring managers are one of the most effective sources of new hires.[1] However, very few applicants connect with hiring managers during the application stage, and most don't send their résumés and cover letters directly to them.

While attending a conference, I spoke with one hiring manager at a midsize consulting firm who told me that his company received more than 150 applications for two of their coveted positions. The two people they hired were the only two who reached out and contacted the hiring manager after submitting their applications through the formal online portal.[2]

Make it a priority to get yourself and your documents in front of the hiring manager. When you do, you will often jump to the head of the line. If you are concerned about locating the manager, you will find key tactics at slamdunkjobsearch.com on how to identify the hiring manager and locate the manager's contact information.

Here is an important note: Some companies, including government agencies, will not consider candidates for positions unless they submit their application materials through the formal online application portal by the required deadline. You never want to submit your materials to the hiring manager and then lose out on the opportunity because you didn't send your materials through the formal online channel. Cover all your bases by sending your marketing materials through the online application portal and directly to the hiring manager.

Connect with Hiring Managers

Depending on your circumstances, there are a number of ways to connect with hiring managers or potential hiring managers during the Relationship Team step:

1. Reach out to potential hiring managers and other contacts you have already met through earlier BQAA Sessions to provide them with an update, inquire about open positions, and get additional referrals to other people and companies.
2. If you already know of available job openings, reach out to the contacts (hiring managers, decision makers, or other employees) you have already met through earlier BQAA Sessions to learn more about the available positions, get advice on how to put your best foot forward for each position, and land an interview.
3. Connect with hiring managers to whom you have been referred for an open position.
4. Connect with potential hiring managers or other employees at your target organizations when no relevant jobs exist, you don't have any internal contacts, and you haven't been referred to anyone.
5. Reach out to hiring managers you don't know *before* you submit applications for available positions.
6. Contact other company employees you don't know *before* you submit applications for available positions.
7. Reach out to hiring managers you don't know *after* you submit your application materials through the formal online portal for available positions.

These seven approaches will allow you to stand out over a high percentage of applicants who only apply for jobs through the online portal. Let's take a look at how you can connect with hiring managers through each of these approaches.

1. **Reach out to potential hiring managers and other contacts you have already met through BQAA Sessions to provide them with an update, inquire about open positions, and get additional referrals to other people and companies.**

    When you start to compete for your ideal jobs, you will find that all your hard work conducting earlier BQAA Sessions will pay off for you. Reaching back out to people you already know will be much easier and more productive. During this stage, you should

    - Contact all or most of the people you already talked to during your earlier BQAA Sessions.
    - Update them on your situation.
    - Remind them about what you are interested in pursuing.
    - See if they have heard about any opportunities.
    - Seek further advice on ways to become more marketable.
    - If no positions are available, ask if they could recommend other companies to explore or people to contact.
    - Thank them again.

    If you're a student and have already conducted a BQAA Session with a potential hiring manager or another contact in one of your target companies, send another thank-you message prior to graduation, letting the person know how the advice has helped, and then asking for additional assistance. Here is an example:

    > Hi Maya,
    >
    > Thank you for all your help with my career. I am getting ready to graduate this May, and I want to let you know that I plan to pursue content management positions within the top ad agencies

in the Chicago area. Your guidance motivated me to move in this direction. Thank you!

Please let me know if you hear about any opportunities at Grey West Branding Inc. As you know, I am passionate about the company's vision and values, and I know I could make a strong contribution to the media department.

I have attached an updated version of my résumé. I think you will notice some differences, especially since I incorporated many of your suggestions. Please feel free to let me know if there is anything else you think I should do to become more marketable.

Thank you again for all your help.

Sincerely,
Finn

If you're further along in your career, follow the same basic structure by including what has changed since the last time you communicated with your contact. Here is an example for a more experienced job seeker:

Hi Julius,

Thank you again for meeting with me back in May. I greatly appreciate the time you took to answer all my questions and provide such valuable career advice. At your suggestion, I recently acquired two certifications—a digital event strategist certification and an event planning specialist certification—and I have expanded my contacts considerably during this time.

With these certifications now in hand, I have started to ramp up my job search and would like to land an event planning position in one of the large hotels in the Los Angeles area. If you happen to know of anyone who is working in this industry and geographic location, related or unrelated to event planning, please let me know.

I am trying to expand my contacts even more and would appreciate any help you can provide. Thank you!

I hope you had a nice time at the Event Planner Expo in New York City. I'm sure it was an amazing event.

Thank you very much for all your help. I'm excited to begin this new chapter in my career, and I owe much to you for helping me get started.

All the best,
Eva

You will, of course, need to tailor these messages to your specific situation. But these examples will give you a framework for reaching out to people during this stage of the process, particularly if you have already had contact with a potential hiring manager.

These types of messages can be helpful in getting people to assist you with your job search. You want your job search to be like investing in stocks and bonds or real estate. These investments work for you even when you don't have the time to manage them daily. You want your job search to function the same way. The more people you reach out to, impress, and inform about your job search and focus, the more people you will have working for you even when you can't spend time on your search. The more eyes on the market, the better. Expand your relationship team, and let people help you get where you want to go.

If you want to be more proactive with potential hiring managers after conducting BQAA Sessions with them, you can use the responses to your chess game questions to come up with ways to assist them in achieving their goals or overcoming their challenges. You can then ask for a meeting to discuss your recommendations (see approaches 4 and 5 for email examples of how to use this more assertive approach). At a minimum, consider sending the person some useful information: "While thinking about the _____ challenges you face within your department, I thought you might find the attached _____ article helpful."

2. **If you already know of available job openings, reach out to the contacts (hiring managers, decision makers, or other employees) you have already met through earlier BQAA Sessions to learn more about the available positions, get advice on how to put your best foot forward for each position, and land an interview.**

When a position becomes available in one of your target organizations where you have already conducted a BQAA Session (even with someone in a different department), you can reach out again to the person you talked to and see if your contact has any suggestions for breaking into the position and the company. The person may even offer to take your application materials to the hiring manager. If not, you should at least ask if your contact knows who the hiring manager is so you can send your documents directly to the manager. Here is an example of a follow-up message you can send to this type of contact:

Hi Layla,

Thank you again for all your help with my career. Through your advice, I worked with the marketing department at Golden North University to develop a highly effective program of study. The courses I took and the internship you recommended have prepared me well for an entry-level marketing position within a food and beverage company, particularly in market data analysis and management.

Besides thanking you again for all your assistance, I want to let you know that I was excited to see a Marketing Data Analyst position available in your company's marketing department. I graduate in two months, and the position matches up well with my background and would be a great opportunity to begin my marketing career.

I was wondering if you have some suggestions for making my application stand out. Any inside information would be appreciated. Additionally, I thought it would be a good idea to send my materials directly to the hiring manager. Would you happen to know the name and email address of the manager?

Thank you again for your help!

All the best,
Vea

Once you have reached out to your contact, received advice, and submitted your application materials, always send a follow-up thank-you note and get your materials into the contact's hands as well. If your contact hasn't already offered to deliver your résumé and cover letter to the hiring manager, the person may be willing to do so after seeing your documents. Here is a follow-up message example:

Hi Layla,

Thank you very much for your help in tailoring my application for the Marketing Data Analyst position. I also appreciate you providing me with Carli Wilson's name and email address. I plan to send her my résumé and cover letter later today.

I applied for the position this morning through the online application system. I also thought it would be a good idea to email my documents to you for your reference (see the attachments). Please let me know if I should do anything else to make a strong initial impression.

Your support has been invaluable, and I genuinely appreciate all your guidance. Thank you!

Have a great week,
Vea

Here is some more assertive wording you can incorporate into your message if you want to be proactive in getting your contact to put in a good word for you:

In case the company offers an employee referral fee, I also thought it would be a good idea to send my documents to you as well. No need to do anything, but I wanted to send them to you in case it could benefit you in some way.

If your contact happens to be the hiring manager or is on the hiring committee, you will probably not be able to get too much advice once the position posts. Many companies try to avoid having anyone on the hiring committee talk to candidates after the position is posted and before the interviews take place. They believe it could give one candidate an unfair advantage over others. This policy doesn't always exist, but if it does or you sense it will be difficult to meet with the hiring manager, you can send a message similar to the following to the manager:

Hi Sophia,

Thank you again for meeting with me back in October. Your advice was very helpful. At your suggestion, I enrolled in an energy efficiency certificate program through Southfield University Extension, and I have already completed three courses in the six-course certificate sequence. The courses have been excellent.

I am excited to let you know that I applied for the Energy Specialist position within your department. I sent my application materials through the online portal, but I thought it would be a good idea to send them directly to you too, especially since my qualifications match up so well with the position requirements.

Please let me know if you have any questions or would like additional information.

Thank you again for your help!

All the best,
Dustin

In many cases, when hiring managers already know you, they will reach out to encourage you to apply for their positions if they feel you would be a strong candidate. The magic of conducting BQAA Sessions early in the process is that they allow you to talk to people before companies post positions. And, as previously mentioned, employers are much more impressed when job seekers have expressed interest in the company before a position becomes available.

3. **Connect with hiring managers to whom you have been referred for an open position.**

    If you are fortunate to be referred to the hiring manager within one of your target organizations, include the referral name in the subject line (e.g., Bill Cartwright Referral) and in the opening line of your email message:

    > Hi Svana,
    >
    > Bill Cartwright recommended I reach out to you and let you know that I applied for the Sr. Human Resources Analyst position within your department at Berkshire Weston. Bill spoke very highly of you and your team, and I believe I can add considerable value to the position given my relevant education and experience.
    >
    > I received my graduate degree in organizational development from the University of San Francisco in May, and I also have four years of experience in training and development within the insurance industry.
    >
    > I applied through the formal online portal, but I also want to introduce myself directly since my background matches up so well with the position. I have attached my résumé and cover letter to provide you with a more thorough description of my background and qualifications.
    >
    > Please let me know if you have any questions or would like additional information. I look forward to hearing from you.
    >
    > By the way, Bill wanted me to tell you that he says hi. He also said he would be happy to talk to you about my qualifications.

I hope you have a great day.

Sincerely,
Natalie Adler

With this type of audience, you will need to promote yourself in the message since the person doesn't know you and might not open your documents unless you provide a good reason to look at them. The referral should generate enough interest, but as you know, not all referrals carry equal weight. Ensure your message can stand on its own by adding a few relevant and impactful qualifications or accomplishments.

4. **Connect with potential hiring managers or other employees at your target organizations when no relevant jobs exist, you don't have any internal contacts, and you haven't been referred to anyone.**

If you are starting to pursue opportunities and are reaching out to people for the first time when no positions exist, you will still use the BQAA Sessions. However, if you need to land a job quickly, you will want to be a little more assertive with your questions and approach. While you will still seek advice on how to become more marketable, you will ask more questions about job opportunities in the contact's company, potential target organizations, names of other people to talk to, and the best ways to break into the field and the company.

Begin by using the BQAA Session email guidelines laid out in chapter 11 to reach out to the potential hiring manager and ask for a brief meeting. Conduct the BQAA Session according to the instructions in that chapter. Then, you can use one of two main tactics to capitalize on your meeting: the reactive tactic or the proactive tactic.

If you want to be less assertive (reactive tactic), use the Flower Bulb Follow-Up Approach to remain in contact with the person. Continue to monitor the company's job announcements. Then, when a position comes up, you can apply through the online application portal and send an email cover letter message, along with your application materials, directly to the hiring manager (see Dustin's message to Sophia in approach 2 for an example). If you conducted a BQAA Session with someone other than the hiring manager, reach out and ask for advice on putting your best foot forward for the newly posted position (see Vea's messages in approach 2 for examples).

If you want to be more assertive (proactive tactic) after you have completed your BQAA Session, you can impress the potential hiring manager by capitalizing on the questions you asked. Use the responses from one of the "chess game" questions discussed in the previous chapter to provide the manager with helpful information. For example, if you can uncover the department's challenges, goals, and barriers, you can then come up with some ideas or recommendations on how the department can overcome its challenges or reach its goals.

You can search the internet, seek advice from experts, use chatbots (e.g., ChatGPT), read books, or access your own knowledge and expertise to come up with recommendations or ideas that could help the hiring manager. There are plenty of resources available that can help you develop solid recommendations and generate innovative ideas for almost anything. When you use this proactive tactic, not only do you impress employers, but you also advance your knowledge and skills within your field. Never let a job search go by without finding ways to become more knowledgeable and skillful. Once you have a proposal or a list of recommendations, reach back out to the manager and ask for another meeting:

Hi Hilario,

I hope everything is going well for you. Thank you again for meeting with me a few weeks ago. Through your advice, I was able to connect with five other leaders in the transportation industry. I really appreciate all the contacts. By the way, Frieda Bridge says hello.

Outside of thanking you again for your help, I want to let you know that I have been thinking about the challenges you face within your department, and I have come up with some possible solutions.

Please let me know if you might have 30 minutes or less to discuss my ideas. I think you will find them very useful, and I would enjoy discussing them with you.

All the best,
Bob

Do you think the potential hiring manager would pass up an opportunity to meet with you again to learn about possible solutions? Probably not. You can also use this same approach when you have already conducted BQAA Sessions with potential hiring managers early in the process and now want to get back in front of them to share how you can help them or their operations.

Ideally, you will not share your solutions or ideas in your email message. Your goal with your email is to create curiosity and get in the door. An interview or meeting is the best place to offer suggestions and present a proposal since you will be face-to-face with the hiring manager or potential hiring manager. Once in the door, anything is possible, especially since you will have the opportunity to ask additional questions to uncover information that will allow you to make even more targeted and appropriate recommendations. And don't be afraid to pitch a new position if you have something in mind and feel you can add long-term value to the department and the organization. Having these types of conversations with a hiring manager can often lead to future opportunities.

5. **Reach out to hiring managers you don't know *before* you submit applications for available positions.**

If everything goes according to plan, you will not have to use this approach because you have already secured a referral or connected with the hiring manager during an earlier BQAA Session. However, as we all know, it isn't always possible to connect with hiring managers or get referrals.

If you are interested in a job at one of your target organizations where you don't know anyone, use the company website, the internet, LinkedIn, other social media platforms, and employees or other contacts to find the hiring manager (visit slamdunkjobsearch.com for specific ways to identify hiring managers) and then reach out to express interest in the company and inquire about conducting a BQAA Session.

When reaching out to the hiring manager to schedule a meeting, you can use one of two approaches. With the first approach, you acknowledge that you know about the available position and ask if you can learn more about the opportunity. With the second approach, you express interest in the organization and the work they do, but you don't mention the position.

Mentioning the position and inquiring about a meeting sounds great, but it may not work. As mentioned before, many companies will discourage hiring managers from talking to applicants once the job announcement is posted because it gives one applicant an unfair advantage over another. With smaller companies this may not be an issue; however, with larger organizations and government agencies that have formal human resources policies and structured hiring practices, it could be a roadblock. Also, when you reach out to a hiring manager about an available job, your focus is on you and the position. You want to show that your attention is on the company and the work.

Employers will be more interested in meeting with you if you can show how you can help them. Here is an example:

Dear Kalani,

I came across your name through an article that was published in the Eagleton Press, and I was impressed with the work you are doing in the training and development department.

I have worked in the training and development field for the past six years. Recently, I moved 95 percent of my company's training online, saving more than $75,000. With the development of this new online system, I was honored with the company's Innovation and Customer Service awards. This achievement marks the first time an employee has received both awards in the same year.

The online training system and approach can be incorporated into any company, and I would be happy to talk with you about how I could help your department move in this direction.

I am specifically reaching out to you and your company because I have always admired Ninety Degree Athletics' product line and commitment to quality, and I would love to find a way to get involved with the organization.

Please let me know if you would be interested in hearing how I could help you and your company.

Thank you!

Sincerely,
Jackson Huse

As you can see, the message doesn't mention anything about the available position. You could also say that you have some recommendations for improving a process or service and would be happy to share them.

Here is an example of wording to use if you have never met the hiring manager, you have done your homework, and you want to reference the position:

I have spent time researching Ridgeline's competitors. In addition to discussing my qualifications for the Marketing Specialist position, I would love to share some innovative ideas I have for enhancing Ridgeline's current marketing campaign. Would you have 20 minutes to meet and discuss how my ideas could help?

Managers will be impressed that you have thought about their operations and have reached out to help. If the managers are interested, they will either ask you to come in for a meeting or ask you to send in your résumé and cover letter for the current opening. If a hiring manager tells you to send your documents through the formal online application portal, you should also email your materials directly to the manager and express your gratitude for alerting you to the position.

If you are uncomfortable coming up with recommendations with limited information, you can still show how you can have an impact by highlighting some other credentials that add value:

> I see that a significant component of the Call Center Manager position involves customer relations. When I worked for Horizon Entertainment, I went through a three-month award-winning customer relations training program and then trained and managed a customer service staff of 12 people over three years.

> In addition to discussing my qualifications for the position, I would be happy to share how my customer relations background could help you and your team continue to provide extraordinary customer service. Would you happen to have 20 minutes to meet and discuss how I could help?

Be creative and find ways to get in the door and meet with hiring managers before you submit your materials through the formal online application portal. Always use your best judgment on the right time to reach out to the hiring manager given the company, position, and hiring process.

If you don't feel comfortable reaching out to a hiring manager in advance or don't get a response from the manager, use the next two approaches to set yourself apart.

6. **Contact other company employees you don't know *before* you submit applications for available positions.**

No matter how hard you try, sometimes you can't identify the hiring manager, or the hiring manager never responds. In these situations, you will want to reach out to other company employees to locate the hiring manager's name or attempt to get a referral to the manager or department team members. This approach can be quite effective, and you may want to use it even when you have already identified the hiring manager. Having informal or formal relationships with employees will set you apart from other job candidates. And having an employee referral will often get you invited in for an interview, particularly if the referral comes from an employee who is respected by the hiring manager or the department team. In some cases, employees may get a referral fee if one of their referrals is hired, so they may benefit directly from your contact.

One possible tactic is to explore LinkedIn (company employee list) to find someone who works at the organization and is connected to you in some way. Once you identify the best person, reach out and ask for some assistance. Here is an example:

> Hi Liam,
>
> My name is Samantha Garcia, and I noticed on LinkedIn that we both know Monica Blackburn. Monica and I used to work in the permitting department at Western Wind Power, and we have stayed in contact through the years.
>
> I am very interested in a Senior Project Manager position at your company in the Asset Management Department, and I was wondering if you would be willing to share your thoughts about the company culture and your experience working at the organization. I would only need 15 [or, a few] minutes of your time, and I would be happy to chat with you over the phone or through a video session—whichever is more convenient for you.
>
> If you have time for a brief meeting, please feel free to schedule a time on my calendar here [hyperlink your calendar] or simply respond to this email with your availability.
>
> Thank you for your time! I look forward to hearing from you.
>
> All the best,
> Samantha

If possible, share what you have in common with your contact. Commonalities help you create an instant bond and often open the door to a deeper conversation. In the above example, Samantha could have also reached out to her friend Monica to seek a referral to Liam. Do whatever helps you connect with the person the most and works best with your timeline.

When you talk to company employees about a particular position, seek to uncover inside information on the position and the company by asking some of the following questions:

- How would you describe the company culture?
- Are there any important company values, core competencies, or professional standards that drive the company culture?
- What isn't typically included in job announcements that the company values in new employees?
- Are there any company values that are important to the organization but aren't widely known to the public?
- What types of employees fit in best within the company culture?
- What qualities and attributes does the company value the most?
- What do successful employees have in common?
- What do most employees wear to work?
- What is the best interview attire?
- Do you have any additional suggestions for putting my best foot forward for the position?
- Do you know who the hiring manager is, and would you happen to have the person's email address?

The answers to these questions will allow you to customize your marketing documents and promotional platforms to make you look more like an insider and get the hiring manager to start visualizing you in the company. They will also allow you to determine whether the company is right for your values, goals, and personality.

If the person you talk to is in the hiring department or knowledgeable about the available position, you could ask more targeted questions. For example, you could ask the person the same types of questions you would ask the hiring manager or potential hiring manager during a BQAA Session:

- What are some challenges the department faces?
- What are the most important goals within the department?

- What barriers exist to addressing the challenges or reaching the goals?
- What are some customer pain points?
- What is the department looking for in a strong candidate?
- Do you know why the position is available?
- Is there any other important information I should know about the position and the organization?

With the answers to some of these questions, you can then be more strategic when you send the hiring manager a message. Your message could contain recommendations for overcoming the department challenges or helping the department reach its goals. However, as previously suggested, you will ask for a meeting to share your recommendations. But occasionally, when a position becomes available, you might want to consider including one or two recommendations or ideas directly in your message as a teaser to entice the hiring manager to bring you in for an interview or a meeting. Use your best judgment on what approach to take based on your unique situation.

Once you talk with the company employee, send a follow-up thank-you message after your conversation:

> Hi Liam,
>
> Thank you so much for chatting with me about Horizontal Wind Power Inc. I enjoyed our conversation and was happy to hear about how close you are to Monica. It was interesting to learn that the two of you grew up together in Breckenridge, Colorado.
>
> Given your endorsement of the company and your description of the organization's culture, I'm excited to submit my application for the Senior Project Manager position. And, at your suggestion, I will emphasize my real estate background in my cover letter. Thank you for the tip!
>
> Since I always like to get my application materials into the hiring manager's hands and not rely on the formal online portal, would you happen to know who the hiring manager is in the Asset Man-

agement Department? Also, if the company offers an employee referral fee, I would be happy to send my documents to you as well, particularly if there's a chance you could benefit in some way.

Once again, I really appreciate you taking the time to talk. Please say hi to Monica for me.

Kind regards,
Samantha

Your follow-up message may be very different depending on what you talk about during your meeting. For instance, if you had already asked for the hiring manager's name, you won't ask for it again in your thank-you message. Also, ideally, you will say something related to the connection you have with the person (e.g., "I look forward to seeing you at the next IT/Tech Conference" or "Please say hi to Chris for me."). Remember, your goal is to develop relationships, not just to get specific information.

7. **Reach out to hiring managers you don't know *after* you submit your application materials through the formal online portal for available positions.**

Unfortunately, sometimes you don't get the opportunity to connect with hiring managers or anyone else before the application deadline approaches. This might happen because the manager never responds to you, the manager can't meet with you prior to the formal interview process, you came across the job posting right before the application deadline, or you don't feel comfortable reaching out to the manager until you have formally submitted your application materials. In these situations, work hard to identify the hiring manager, which you have probably already done for your cover letter, and get your application materials in front of the manager.

Sending your marketing documents to the hiring manager isn't a choice—it's a necessity. If you want to land your ideal job, send your materials directly to the hiring manager for each position you pursue unless explicitly told not to contact the manager.

Once you have identified the hiring manager and have submitted your formal application materials through the online portal, send the manager a shorter email cover letter message:

Dear Julieta,

I have a proven record of reengineering inefficient processes and running efficient and safe operations. I am confident my four years of production and operations management experience, combined with my manufacturing management education, would allow me to excel in the Production Manager position within your department.

While working full-time at Round Peg Manufacturing, I completed a graduate degree in manufacturing management from the University of Toledo. And, in the past year, I participated in a six-week intensive lean manufacturing and quality improvement training program.

I immediately applied for the Production Manager position through the online portal, but I also want to introduce myself directly since my background matches up so well with the job. I have attached my résumé and cover letter, and I would be happy to answer any questions or provide additional information.

As a side note, I am known for my safety expertise. In all my jobs, my supervisors have given me high-performance marks related to safety and compliance and have specifically complimented me on my work in this area. I would bring this same safety and housekeeping expertise and mindset to the Production Manager position.

Please feel free to access my LinkedIn profile and the attachments for more information on my background.

Thank you!

Sincerely,
Blake Johnson

If you have already met the manager, you can add a more personal introduction. Either way, you will want to promote yourself and show why you are an excellent candidate and potential employee.

Avoid going on and on with your messages. They need to be short, targeted, and effective. The goal is to generate curiosity and get the hiring manager to invite you in for an interview. Hiring managers only have time to read brief messages, and since you are breaking the script by sending your information directly to them, ensure you grab their attention quickly. Here is an example of how Blake could make the email cover letter message less formal and more impactful:

Hi Julieta,

I hope your day is going well!

I was excited to hear about the Production Manager position within your department. I applied through the online portal, but I also want to introduce myself directly since my background matches up so well with the role.

I know you are seeking an innovative and experienced professional who can optimize your production line. At Round Peg Manufacturing, I was hired to revamp the production process, improve quality control, and decrease shipment times. In the first sixteen months, I achieved the following results:

- Reduced cycle time by 22% through material usage, scheduling, and assembly line improvements.
- Implemented a quality control program that reduced product defects by 33% and minimized customer complaints.
- Identified $75,000+ in overstock by conducting a comprehensive warehouse inventory audit.
- Used data analytics to improve inventory control, decreasing carrying costs by 29%.
- Trained 60+ employees on new systems and safety guidelines, following all OSHA standards.

I believe my experience and skills align well with Northrod's mission and goals, and I would love to contribute to your team's success. Thank you for taking the time to review my application. I am excited about the prospect of joining the Northrod team and helping the company grow and excel.

All the best,
Blake Johnson

Blake could also use this bullet format and weave in some credentials, including his graduate degree and lean manufacturing and quality improvement training. The goal is to do whatever works best to capture the attention of hiring managers and persuade them to invite you in for an interview.

You may also consider using shorter "email" cover letters for the letters you send through the online application portals, particularly if you are pursuing positions with fast-paced companies, such as start-up organizations, where brevity and informality are often valued. However, as always, consider your audience and choose the most suitable approach for each situation. If you are uncertain about what to do, reach out to someone within the organization who can provide guidance. If you are still unsure how to proceed, send a traditional cover letter (described in the appendix) through the online portal, followed by a shorter email cover letter (described in this section) to the hiring manager. Regardless of your approach, do your best to get yourself and your documents in front of the hiring manager.

While you will try your best to send your documents to the hiring manager, there are some sectors—the government sector in particular—where managers are told not to look at applications unless they are received through the formal application channel. If you are pursuing positions in federal or state agencies, you will need to use your best judgment and weigh whether it's worth the effort to send your materials directly to the hiring manager. Getting advice from internal contacts will help you make these types of decisions.

Fine-Tune Your Messages

Since you will have drafted your messages in advance in the Market Ready step, you will now be able to focus on customizing each message to your target audience. You need to view your messages through their eyes. Read your drafts again as if you were a hiring manager receiving the messages. How do they feel for the type of audience? Are they too forward? Are they too formal or too casual? How do they visually look? Are they too long? Do they show that you care about the person on the other end? Do they create curiosity? If the messages look good and sound good, send them. If they need work, put in the extra time to make them professional and competitive. Spending 15 to 30 additional minutes now can take your messages from noncompetitive to competitive. And, if you want to land your ideal job, your messages need to be competitive.

While you want to get a shorter "email" cover letter message in front of the hiring manager, many employers will still require applicants to submit a more traditional cover letter through the company's online application portal. These cover letters are typically one page in length and between 250 and 400 words. In the appendix, you will find a traditional cover letter example along with comprehensive guidelines on how to write this type of letter.

Become an Insider

Whether before you identify available positions or after, contacting hiring managers and other decision makers should be your highest priority during the job search process. There is no better way to wow people than to get in front of them, talk about your work, show how you can contribute, and exhibit the right mindset. Since you know that most employers hire insiders, you need to become an insider. The BQAA Sessions will be your primary approach to connecting with hiring managers and becoming an insider.

As advances in artificial intelligence (AI) lead to greater automation in the hiring process, you will need to make it an even greater priority to get yourself and your documents in front of hiring managers. Connecting with hiring managers isn't an option; it's the price of admission to your ideal job. You will find that good things happen when you meet with decision makers and share your passions, talents, and goals.

Do you want
to know
how to be
ahead of your
competitors
both right out
of the starting
gate and
all the way
through the
finish line?

Step 5

COMPETITIVE COMMITMENT

Champions are brilliant at the basics.[1]

—JOHN WOODEN

The introduction to the Competitive Commitment step could be one sentence long: "Always be competitive throughout the entire job search process." Unfortunately, many job seekers make mistakes throughout the process, and I want to ensure you don't follow in their footsteps. This step is about making sure you do the basics well across the board. If you do, you'll position yourself ahead of most of your competitors even before the Slam Dunk step.

Imagine you completed the final interview, and you think it was a slam dunk. You have a good feeling about landing the job. You keep checking your email and voicemail messages, hoping to get the job offer, but there is no call or email. You don't understand why there is such a delay. How could they not want you with all your experience and skills? You thought you had it all wrapped up. However, it looks like you were wrong as the following message arrives in your email inbox 10 days after the final interview: "It was a difficult decision, but we have decided to hire another candidate. We wish you the best with your future endeavors." Devastated, you wonder what went wrong.

A few weeks later, you talk to someone who works at the company and find out that the decision came down to you and another strong candidate, and the hiring committee had a hard time deciding. But then, the contact explains, the decision became much easier when the hiring manager received a well-written thank-you note from the other candidate. The other candidate also sent a tactful follow-up email message a week after the interview, expressing her continued interest in the position. The hiring manager decided to go with the person who showed the most interest and approached the process in a professional manner across the board. Unfortunately, you didn't feel that either of these actions—sending a thank-you note or following up—were necessary given your experience and strong interview performance.

Don't let that be your story. Remember, you never have total control over the job search outcome, but you do have control over what you do in the present. Make this commitment right now: "I will never pursue a position I want unless I am willing to make a commitment to conduct a quality job search across the board and compete effectively for every position." This is the fifth step: the Competitive Commitment step.

Chapter 13

COMMIT TO QUALITY

In the Competitive Commitment step, you don't necessarily need to be concerned about standing out from your competitors at each stage. Instead, this step gets you focused on doing the basics well and exhibiting quality and consistency across the board. Quality comes down to giving the customer what they want at or above the expected level and continuing to provide the same level of quality or service over time. When an employer is taking a close look at everything you do during the job search process, you will stand out if you consistently do the basics well. Based on my experience, this step could help you beat out 90 to 100 percent of your competitors even before getting to the Slam Dunk step.

When you perform at a competitive level across the board, you often come out ahead of your competitors in the end. Why? Because all or most of your competitors will not perform at a competitive level throughout the entire process. Most job candidates make mistakes that cause them to fall into the noncompetitive pool quickly. They think they have everything ready and polished until they get professional feedback on their brand, promotional platforms (LinkedIn profile, professional career website, and other relevant platforms), documents (résumé, cover letter, work samples, reference sheet, and thank-you notes), and job search approach and strategies.

Many job seekers fail to put in the extra time and attention needed to avoid mistakes or learn about what they should be doing during their job searches to land their ideal jobs. They develop an image in their minds of what they want (the outcome), but they don't do what they need to do to make it happen. The following paraphrased story cleverly illustrates the importance of taking action to get what you want:

A young man had lost his job, was about to lose his house, and could not seem to make ends meet. Soon, the other parts of his life started to fall apart as well. He thought the only way out of his situation was a miracle, so he walked down to the local church, sat in the front pew, and prayed: "Dear God, I need help with my financial situation. Please help me win the lottery." He continued praying every day for a month, and yet nothing happened. Finally, when the young man was about to despair, he heard a voice say, "My son, please, please help me out and buy a lottery ticket."[1]

Hopefully, this story will stick in your mind and help you remember the importance of doing what you need to do to get what you want. Not sending a thank-you note and not following up after an interview are good examples of failing to do what you need to do to get the results you desire. You can dream all day long about landing your ideal job, but you will not make it happen unless you take all the necessary steps to conduct a quality job search. Continue to remind yourself that hoping for something is not a game plan. If you want to get your ideal job, commit to doing whatever is necessary to land it, and always take action that moves you in that direction.

Submit Competitive Marketing Documents

Based on my hiring experience, up to 90 percent of résumés and cover letters can be eliminated within six to twelve seconds for one reason or another. This is even before reviewing candidates' online presence. Most documents have at least one of the following flaws:

- Spelling errors
- Grammatical mistakes
- "What's in it for me?" tone
- Wrong company name listed
- Generic content (not targeted to the job and the company)
- Hiring manager or company name spelled wrong or missing
- Poorly balanced (text-heavy at the top and light at the bottom or vice versa)
- Too much text and not enough white space
- Not enough text
- Too wordy

- Too many big words
- Paragraphs too long
- Weak cover letter opening ("To Whom It May Concern")
- No bullets
- Lack of hooks (e.g., numbers, percentages, relevant acronyms, keywords, or company names) to back up accomplishments
- Inconsistencies
- Negative or arrogant tone

More than 75 percent of recruiters will reject an applicant if a résumé or cover letter has a typo.[2] To be competitive, you need to avoid making errors and mistakes.

I worked with a 33-year-old job seeker from Boise, Idaho, named Thom who asked me to review his cover letter.[3] Thom had already applied for the position but was worried about the quality of his cover letter because he hadn't heard back from the employer for several weeks. I liked the design of the one-page letter. It had plenty of white space and an excellent combination of paragraphs and bullets. Additionally, it was professionally laid out and well-balanced. The visual aspects were all great; however, the minute I started to read it, I could tell that Thom wasn't a competitive applicant. He addressed the letter "To Whom It May Concern," which showed me that he didn't take the time to find the hiring manager's name, which also meant he didn't send his documents directly to the hiring manager.

Additionally, Thom's opening paragraph didn't entice me to read more. His opening focused more on his needs than the employer's needs: "I am excited to apply for the Claims Manager position. I am looking for a rewarding position where I can utilize my claims and insurance skills." Employers want to know how you will help them reach their goals and overcome their challenges. That is why they are filling the position, and that is what is important to them. Expressing interest or passion is fine if it also creates some curiosity and pulls

> More than 75 percent of recruiters will reject an applicant if a résumé or cover letter has a typo.

the reader into the letter. But, in Thom's case, the opening didn't grab any attention. There was nothing new or different, and I wasn't enticed to read his résumé or proceed further with his cover letter. If a hiring manager did read further, the manager would have found that the word "compliment" was misused. The applicant should have used the word "complement" because the sentence was stating how his background complemented the position.

When you follow the right process and commit to quality across the board, you often get the results you desire, and you become a better person along the way.

When you add up these five missteps—generic "To Whom It May Concern" salutation, no hiring manager name, weak opening paragraph, a "What's in it for me?" focus, and the misuse of a word—Thom had no chance of getting invited in for an interview. And he wasn't. The most disappointing part was that the hiring manager or recruiter probably had eliminated Thom even before reading his qualifications. Thom could have been the most qualified candidate for the position, but he never gave the recruiter an opportunity to see his qualifications. He had eliminated himself too early by neglecting to make his documents competitive.

It would have only taken 15 to 30 minutes more to turn the application materials into eye-catching, highly competitive sales materials. Instead, all the effort invested in preparing the documents resulted in a negative outcome. When you follow the right process and commit to quality across the board, you often get the results you desire, and you become a better person along the way. Nothing is a waste.

Interview at a Competitive Level

When it comes to the interview stage, many job seekers go down the same noncompetitive path as they do with their marketing documents. Most job candidates make at least one of the following mistakes during the interview process that drops them out of the running:

Prior to the interview, candidates

- Fail to research the company and the interviewers.
- Forget to review the job announcement.
- Neglect to prepare for a variety of interview questions.
- Spend little time working on ways to develop instant rapport and show fit.
- Fail to double-check the interview time and the location the night before the interview.

Right before the interview, candidates

- Leave too little time for travel and parking, and arrive late for the interview.
- Treat the parking attendant and receptionist poorly.
- Wear inappropriate interview attire.
- Look at texts while waiting in the reception area (or pull out a phone in the interview!).
- Forget to turn off their cell phone before the interview and receive a call or notification.
- Shake hands poorly (flimsy or sweaty handshake).
- Appear unprofessional (e.g., disengaged body language, poor hygiene, bad manners, or a negative attitude).

During the interview, candidates

- Appear nervous (e.g., talking quickly, making little eye contact, fidgeting, adjusting clothing, speaking too slowly, rambling, or sweating).
- Arrive at the interview without a padfolio in hand and without a pad of paper, pen, and extra résumés. (A padfolio is a leather or synthetic leather folder that contains slots for a pad of paper, pens, business cards, and writing samples. Padfolios can also be closed and secured with either a zipper, snap, or buckle.)
- Don't understand employers' needs and therefore neglect to focus interview responses on what is important to employers.
- Respond to interview questions with common and generic answers.

- Fail to exhibit a sense of humor.
- Speak poorly of others.
- Show no long-term commitment to the company and the field.
- Fail to make eye contact and smile.
- Say things that don't align with what is presented in their marketing documents and promotional platforms (demonstrating a disconnect and lack of consistency).

At the end of the interview, candidates

- Neglect to ask questions.
- Ask predictable and standard questions.
- Ask questions about benefits, time off, salary, and other "What's in it for me?" questions (before an offer is on the table).
- Ask too many questions (three to six is about right, depending on the questions asked, time allowed, and the field and the job).
- Fail to close the interview by saying something positive about wanting to move on to the next stage.

After the interview, candidates

- Neglect to send a thank-you note.
- Forget to check in to see what can be done to help the employer.
- Follow up too much and are seen as high-maintenance.
- Fail to have a reference sheet ready to go.

If you want to be competitive and perform well, you can't make these kinds of mistakes. Small oversights can often compound into big problems.

In one situation, a job candidate created a stressful situation for himself when he didn't build in enough time to accommodate the unexpected during the interview stage. The 24-year-old candidate had an interview with a large insurance company in downtown Los Angeles.[4] On the day of the interview, the traffic was much worse than expected. By the time he reached his interview destination, he was cutting it close to the interview time. But the candidate felt like he could make it if he found a parking spot quickly.

The candidate immediately entered the building's parking structure, grabbed a parking ticket from the meter, and started to drive from floor to floor, looking for an open parking space. When he reached the top and couldn't find a spot, he quickly headed back down, hoping someone would be leaving. Unfortunately, it was morning, and no one was on the way out. When nothing was available, he drove up to the exit kiosk to leave and find another parking structure.

As you can imagine, the candidate's stress level was elevated. It was 9:49 a.m., and the interview was to commence at 10 a.m. He only had 11 minutes to find a parking space and get into the building and up to the interview on the 22nd floor. He handed the attendant the parking ticket and told him that he was unable to find a spot. The attendant informed the candidate that he still needed to pay the minimum required fee and had to pay with a credit card. The candidate refused. After about a minute of back and forth with the parking attendant to get the gate open without having to give out his credit card number, the candidate reached his stress limit. He just wanted to park and get to the interview.

Unable to accept that he was going to be late and acknowledge that he didn't build in enough extra travel time, the candidate told the parking attendant to put his own credit card number on the ticket. He then shifted into reverse, backed up about 30 feet, shifted into first gear, hit the gas pedal, and drove right through the exit bar. The wooden bar broke off in one piece and flew across the exit drive.

Still thinking he might be able to get to the interview on time, the candidate accelerated down the street and parked in the first available parking structure. He then quickly made his way back to the building and entered the nearest elevator to get to the 22nd floor. Unfortunately, in his flustered state, he entered an elevator that only serviced the 25th to 50th floors. Already a few minutes late, the candidate pushed the 25th-floor button, thinking he would exit the elevator, use the stairwell, and walk down the stairs to the 22nd floor.

As the candidate entered the stairwell on the 25th floor and heard the door close behind him, he realized he had entered a fire escape stairwell that didn't have any entry handles on the doors. Without much thought, he quickly worked his way down the stairs. Luckily, the job candidate found the 20th-floor door ajar. He flung the door open, entered the correct elevator, got to the 22nd floor, checked in with the receptionist, and sat down, now seven minutes late, with sweat dripping from his face.

How well do you think the candidate performed in the interview? Do you think he was at his best and better than everyone else?

While this story is extreme, these types of situations happen more than you think, especially when job seekers don't put in the time to be competitive at every single step. Since you know that most candidates will make mistakes, you have a great opportunity to stand out if you do all the basics well across the board.

Be Brilliant at the Basics

When Hall of Fame football coach Vince Lombardi moved from the New York Giants to the Green Bay Packers, the media asked what he planned to do to elevate the Packers to a championship level. He provided the following answer: "We are not going to try anything fancy; we are just going to become the best team in the National Football League at kicking, running, passing, and catching. We're going to become brilliant on the basics."[5] Lombardi was smart. He knew he could win with this strategy because no other team was brilliant at the basics from start to finish. Lombardi went on to win two Super Bowls with the Green Bay Packers.

Now you are starting to understand how the person who interviewed for 300 positions as a hobby received more than 60 percent of the job offers.[6] The person was not the most qualified candidate for most of the positions, but he knew the value of strong job search skills, and he became brilliant at the basics. As long as he handled all stages of the job search process well, he knew he didn't need to be the most qualified person for the position. All he had to do was play the job search game well. Just imagine how well you would do if you were one of the most qualified candidates for the job and you also conducted a competitive job search across the board.

Becoming brilliant at the basics means more than sending clean documents and interviewing well. It means being professional in every setting, exhibiting quality and consistency in everything you do, demonstrating a customer service approach, and being well prepared for your job search. It also means being ready for anything and everything and performing well regardless of the circumstances.

Be Prepared for Anything and Everything

The unexpected and peripheral moments are often the defining moments for many job seekers, either making or breaking their candidacy. Everything during the job search process is a test.

As a recruiter and hiring manager, I have discovered that candidates often reveal the most when they don't feel like they're being evaluated. Given the importance of peripheral moments, recruiters and hiring managers keep a close eye on everything you do during the recruitment process. They want to know what candidates are really like, and often candidates act very differently when they are out of the interview or job search setting. Many people can present themselves well in a one-hour interview. However, it doesn't necessarily allow employers to get to know the true nature of a person. That's why well-run companies spend many hours meeting with job candidates. They want to determine who the real person is before extending an offer. Why do you think some hiring managers take candidates to lunch during the interview process? They try to get the candidates to let down their job search "walls" so they can see the real person. The behind-the-scenes assessments do work, and you need to assume they are in play during your job search.

You are always being evaluated even when you think you aren't. Employers are looking at everything you do to ensure you are the right person for the position and the company. Most job seekers understand they are "on" when they are interacting directly with employers. However, you need to realize that you are on even when you aren't face-to-face with the employer. You are on when you are in the parking lot before an interview, when you post something on social media, when you are driving away from the company after your interview, and when someone searches for your name on the internet. Everything is a test. How you treat the receptionist in the lobby prior to an interview is a test. How you present yourself on the phone when setting up an interview is a test. And even your email correspondence is a test. Always assume you are being evaluated, and never leave anything to chance.

Many job candidates hurt their job candidacy when they let down their guard and don't realize that the evaluation process is taking place all the time. Candidates are less competitive when they

- Are hard to reach.
- Have an unprofessional voicemail message or email address.

- Ask questions they should have been able to find the answers to on their own.
- Don't respond in a timely manner.
- Fail to list contact information in their email signature line, including a phone number.
- Don't come across as professional during the interview (e.g., lack appropriate attire, good manners, and a positive attitude).
- Lack emotional intelligence throughout the process (e.g., talk too much, don't listen, check in frequently, lack awareness of the time, or fail to understand nonverbal communication signals).
- Are demanding (e.g., immediately want to know the status of their candidacy, are adamant about getting reimbursed for local parking, or demand a different interview time).
- Don't follow directions.
- Continue to check in repeatedly and excessively (more than a couple of times over three weeks—typically, you will wait a full week between correspondences).
- Lack passion for the work, field, or organization.
- Have a "What's in it for me?" attitude.
- Are inconsistent (appear one way in their documents and another way on social media sites or during interviews).
- Exhibit poor communication skills.
- Make the hiring manager's job more difficult.
- Aren't very flexible and accommodating.
- Don't have an online presence.
- Haven't cleaned up their online presence.
- Don't take the time to set up a professional LinkedIn profile.

When job seekers don't understand that everything they do has an impact on how employers view them, they often fail to treat the *entire* job search process the same way. Instead, commit to quality at every step, even when you think it might not matter, and you will never be caught on your heels. Act like everything you do is an opportunity to close the deal because, for all you know, it might be.

Commit to the Process

If you want to land your ideal job, make a competitive commitment now, and seek to use the Slam Dunk Guiding Principles to guide your performance at every turn. Making a competitive commitment also means not skipping any of the steps involved in the 6-Step Slam Dunk Job Search Process.

To help you live up to this commitment, create checklists to guide you through the process. Checklists, like the one used in the Antique Store Editing Approach, are a fantastic tool for staying on track and developing a competitive edge. Instead of negative "what not to do" statements, make a list of positive "what I will do" statements:

- I will provide my contact information (email address and phone number) in my email signature line.
- I will set up a professional voicemail message and run it by someone to confirm that it is professional and welcoming.
- I will try to answer my questions before reaching out to company representatives for the information.
- I will do whatever I can to make the hiring manager's job easier.

Make a list of constructive statements for each of the Slam Dunk Job Search steps. Do whatever works best and use whatever tools will help you conduct a quality job search from start to finish.

You need to be good before you can be great. To reach both levels, you need to begin by doing the basics well across the board. If you do, you will often be great in the end because few job candidates do the basics well from start to finish. The Competitive Commitment step was put in place to help you avoid all the mistakes

You need to be good before you can be great.

and missteps that 90 percent or more of job seekers make right out of the starting gate. In the next step, the Slam Dunk step, your goal is to go beyond the basics and be one step ahead of your competitors at each stage of the process, and definitely during the interview stage. You will seek to be remarkable.

Do you want to know how to elevate your job search performance above that of your competitors, seal the deal, and land your ideal job?

Step 6

SLAM DUNK

*If you are always trying to be normal, you will
never know how amazing you can be.*[1]

—MAYA ANGELOU

When I coached my daughter's softball team, I had a difficult time getting the young, talented players to run as hard as they could down the line through first base. No matter what I said, it was a struggle for them to accelerate consistently for 60-plus feet. The girls kept hearing "run faster," "run harder," "run all the way through the base," or "run, run, run." Nothing seemed to work. They would still slow down before reaching the base.

With my recollection of coaches also having a difficult time getting me to run all the way through first base, I knew I needed to do something different. As a result, I broke the script by using reverse psychology and saying something the players had never heard before. I shouted, "Run like a baby!" as each girl ran down the line. I knew they would get a kick out of visualizing a baby running to first base, and I also knew it would take their minds off the mundane task of running hard down the baseline.

What do you think happened? It woke them up. The girls suddenly started flying down the line and running as hard as they could right through the base. The statement changed everything because it broke the typical script. It was different, and it worked.

The same idea applies when you're trying to get an employer to like, remember, and hire you: You must do something different to wake them up.

When I used to interview students one after another during university recruitment days, I had a difficult time paying attention to everything the candidates said in the interviews. Like the softball players, I heard the same thing repeatedly. In my situation, it was the same small talk, the same interview responses, the same questions at the end of the interview, and the same closing remarks.

When I was asked to provide written feedback for the students at the end of the day, I couldn't remember many of them without referring to my notes. The students I did remember were the ones who used the "run like a baby" tactic—the ones who mixed things up, told memorable stories, demonstrated their work, shared relevant examples, communicated tactfully why they were special and unique, responded to interview questions in a different way, asked thoughtful and interesting questions during the interview, brought up unique and relevant questions at the end of the interview, and closed the interview differently. Somewhere along the way, they broke the script, did something different, and stretched higher.

In the Slam Dunk step, you will look for ways to stand out and seal the deal. You will use the "run like a baby" tactic whenever you need to grab attention and get employers to act. The Slam Dunk step is about pushing further and stretching higher to make yourself different and memorable—to leave it all on the court and come away with a win.

Chapter 14

STRETCH HIGHER

If a position is your ideal job, there is a high probability it is someone else's ideal job as well. Always assume you are competing with at least one job candidate who is passionate about the position and more qualified than you. Given this assumption, you can't afford to think that a competitive job search alone is enough to land you the job. Doing the basics well across the board from start to finish is important and necessary, but it may not be enough, and you never want to leave anything to chance. In the Slam Dunk step, you will go the extra mile and stretch higher than any other candidate. You need to make moving along in the process a slam dunk no matter who you are competing against.

Try this exercise: Face a wall, raise your hand straight up, reach up as high as you can on the wall, and mark the highest point.[1] This is your competitive commitment—the commitment that keeps you competitive with the other job candidates. Now see if you can beat that mark. Do you think you can reach higher? Yes, of course you can. By stretching even higher, you are making a Slam Dunk commitment—a commitment to go beyond everyone else. Mark that point on the wall as a visual reminder of what you need to do to land your ideal job.

If you want to make landing your ideal job a slam dunk, approach each stage with the creativity and confidence displayed by the girl in the following story:

A young girl asks the CEO of a large corporation for a charity donation. The CEO puts both a quarter and dollar bill on the table and says, "Take your pick." The girl looks at what is in front of her, glances up at the executive, and says, "My mother always taught me to take the smaller piece, so I will take this one, but I will wrap it in this piece of paper to keep it safe."[2]

Try to be like this girl. How can you find creative ways to come away with the entire prize? The piece of paper you want is the offer letter pinned high on the wall, waiting for you to grab it by reaching higher than everyone else.

We can all push ourselves more when we have the right motivation, follow the right process, develop the right mindset, commit the time, and put the right tactics in place to make it happen. Your goal is to go beyond the other candidates. If you do, you will often get what you want in the end, and you will have conducted a Slam Dunk Job Search!

Differentiate Yourself

The question is, how do you stretch higher and make it a slam dunk at each stage of the job search process? How can you be remarkable? You do something memorable, differentiate yourself, and show employers why they should hire you over other job candidates.

As I was sitting in the waiting room at the dentist's office one day, I had a few minutes to peruse a publication called *The Guide: A Greater Palm Springs Magazine*.[3] Within this edition, there was a short write-up on each of the nine resort cities that make up the greater Palm Springs region. Each city sold itself quickly through a unique image and a short opening-line description of the area that defined each city's identity and differentiated it from the other cities. I've included four of them below. As you read through the opening lines, notice how each differentiates itself.

Palm Springs
"The name 'Palm Springs' is globally recognized, and its mere mention evokes playful vibes, a chic lifestyle, and endless sunshine."[4]

Palm Desert
"Home to verdant parks, scenic hiking trails, award-winning golf resorts, exhilarating art walks, eclectic retail, and the region's only zoo and botanical gardens, Palm Desert offers nearly unlimited opportunities to discover and explore new wonders."[5]

Indian Wells

"Internationally recognized as the host of tennis's 'fifth Grand Slam,' this country club city is also home to some of the area's most private estates."[6]

Indio

"Home to events like the Coachella Valley Music and Arts Festival and the International Tamale Festival, Indio has carved out its niche as the desert's City of Festivals."[7]

The sections within the magazine go on to describe each city more thoroughly. The opening lines and images, however, define each city's unique value proposition; they communicate each city's brand and unique qualities. Why should someone visit and stay in one city over another? Each city is trying to differentiate itself from its competitors.

You can use this same differentiation or branding tactic throughout your job search. Why should someone invite you in for an interview or offer you the job over another candidate? Find what is essential to the employer and then identify what unique talents, credentials, or special qualities you can bring to the job to address the employer's needs. If you don't differentiate yourself, you will get lost in the shuffle while other candidates pass you by and get the job. You need to be qualified, professional, different, and better!

> "Being different wakes people up."
> —Vanessa Van Edwards

Vanessa Van Edwards, in her book *Captivate*, highlights an experiment that demonstrates how being different can benefit people. For the experiment, researchers hired an actor to play the role of a street-corner panhandler. The results showed that the actor collected more money when he asked for 37 cents than when he asked for money in a more traditional manner, such as "Can you spare any change?" or "Can you spare a quarter?" Van Edwards concludes, "Unique questions, unexpected stories, and uncommon occurrences keep us alert in conversation. In other words, being different wakes people up." She goes on to say, "When you try to be the same as everyone else, it's boring. When you try to fit into a mold, you become forgettable.

When you try to be 'normal,' you become dull."[8] The last thing you want to be during your job search is boring, forgettable, and dull.

Your goal is to wake up employers in a positive and professional manner during the job search process. Fortunately for your job search, most job seekers do the opposite. They look at books or online examples of résumés and cover letters, and they go with the same look and wording as most of the examples. As a result, many cover letters start and end with similar sentences, and most résumés have exactly the same section headings and aren't focused on each target audience. Copying other résumé and cover letter designs and using the same structure and wording is safe and easy, but what good is safe and easy if it doesn't work? It will not wake up employers when they are reviewing 100 to 250 (or more) applications.

If you use a standard design and then give yourself permission to move content around and change the wording and headings to better fit your audience, you will grab attention and stand out. But if you fail to adjust, you will risk having your documents look like all the other résumés and cover letters, which will be forgettable and boring.

I was working with a 24-year-old job seeker from Dayton, Ohio, named Amy who had started her cover letter with a typical opening: "I am excited to apply for the Programme Analyst position with the United Nations." During one of our meetings, I realized that Amy needed to grab more attention if she wanted to get an interview. As a result, I asked her why she was interested in working at the United Nations (UN), and here was her response:

> When I was 16 years old, I told my parents I wanted to work for the United Nations. My family was interested in international issues, and they always listened to international programs on the radio and television. Growing up in this environment, I developed a strong desire to help countries work together to solve complex problems. With my long-standing interest in the UN and all my preparation for this type of work, I was thrilled to see the opening for the Programme Analyst position.[9]

Bingo! This was the material for the opening line of her cover letter: "Ever since I was 16 years old, I have wanted to work for the United Nations." It would create curiosity and pull the reader in for a journey through her letter. It could also be used as a more elaborate story for the "Tell me about yourself" question during her interview.

At each stage of the job search process, think about what makes you different, and then find interesting ways to share this information with the employer. If you do, you will start to take your job search to a whole new level.

Ask Yourself the Slam Dunk Question

When you enter each stage of the job search process, ask yourself the Slam Dunk Question: How will I make this stage a slam dunk to moving on to the next stage? When you ask yourself this question, you will often find ways to add a little novelty to each stage of the process and bring yourself and your qualifications to life. Never let a stage go by without asking yourself the question and implementing Slam Dunk tactics at key times. What can you do to turn ordinary moments into exceptional moments that will be remembered throughout the entire job search process? How can you be the one the interview committee members are impressed with at the end of each stage, and how do you ensure you are the top candidate at the end of the final interview? These are the questions you want to ask each time you have the opportunity to separate yourself from your competitors.

Capitalize on Moments of Separation

Think of the job search process as a series of moments where you can separate yourself from the competition. You can refer to these as moments of separation. If you excel at key moments and magnify them, you will stand out from the crowd, and you will have a greater opportunity to separate yourself from the competition and land your ideal job. The job search process also becomes much more manageable and strategic if broken down into short "stand out" opportunities. Many moments of separation exist during each job search. Here are the main ones:

- Communicating your brand through your promotional avenues (LinkedIn, professional career website, voicemail recordings, business cards, and other social media platforms).
- Reaching out to the hiring manager and other contacts within the company.
- Submitting your application materials for a job.
- Sending your application materials directly to the hiring manager.
- Following up on your application materials.

- Setting up the interview via email or phone.
- Communicating with the hiring manager before the interview.
- Arriving at the interview.
- Talking with company employees around the building before the interview.
- Developing rapport at the start of the interview.
- Answering each interview question.
- Asking questions during the interview.
- Asking questions at the end of the interview.
- Closing the interview.
- Leaving the interview.
- Sending a thank-you note.
- Following up on the status of your candidacy.
- Handling the job offer stage.

Other moments exist and may be unique to your job search, but you will find these key moments during most searches. Your initial goal should be to break the job search process into these smaller, compartmentalized moments and prepare to do the basics well within each. Your second goal should be to develop tactics for standing out if it makes sense for you to capitalize on a particular moment of separation.

View Every Interaction as a Possible Closing Opportunity

Some job seekers think all they need to do to land the job offer is match up with the position requirements, get the interview, and then answer the interview questions well. They believe the interactions before and after the interview don't mean much. Beware of this type of thinking. The peripheral moments and all moments of separation are just as important as the interview itself and can even be more important. Throughout the job search process, keep in mind that you can stand out and seal the deal at any time.

The following story offers an excellent example of why it's essential to see every interaction as a closing opportunity. Adam interviewed for a finance position in Hartford, Connecticut, right out of college.[10] He ended up getting the job and working for the same insurance company for 40 years until his retirement. In Adam's case, it wasn't simply the interview that helped him get the job. Shortly after Adam was hired, he was told that the hiring decision had come down to two highly qualified candidates—Adam and one other strong candidate. Since the hiring committee members were having a hard time deciding between the two, they left the decision up to the front office assistant. The assistant was the one who sat next to the candidates while each waited to be called in for the interview. Adam did a better job developing rapport with the assistant, and he landed a lifelong career out of capitalizing on an important moment of separation that most job seekers ignore or consider insignificant.

You may even be able to seal the deal during the application stage by taking advantage of the halo effect (using an initial positive impression to influence how someone views you throughout the entire process) and impressing employers early in the process. For example, LeAnn, a job seeker in Nashville, Tennessee, knew she didn't have the experience to compete with other applicants for a position at a prominent hotel, so she decided to impress the hotel with how well she knew the business and how much she cared about learning the business. She did her research on the industry, hotel, division, position, and clients, and she made sure her cover letter showed that she knew the business better than any other candidate. She stretched higher, and her approach landed her an interview, which eventually led to a job offer.

After LeAnn started her new job, her manager shared the following with her: "You didn't have the experience level of the other candidates, but you got it; you got what we are all about and what we are trying to accomplish. That set you apart from the others." One statement in her cover letter meant so much to the manager and the business that the manager enlarged, printed, framed, and hung it in LeAnn's office so she could see it the second she walked in on the first day: "Marketing is the art of directing the public through pleasant diversions, in any media—printed or performed—for a specific intent: their fun and our profit."[11] LeAnn's story demonstrates that you can differentiate yourself through your cover letter and set yourself up for a job offer down the line. Every interaction is a closing opportunity.

If you don't have the time to do what LeAnn did, you can come up with an interesting story about what attracts you to the company or grab the hiring manager's attention by sharing what separates you from your competitors. You don't always need to put hours and hours into your research to stand out. For example, even how you answer the phone can set you apart, and it only takes seconds.

When one Fortune 500 hiring manager had to decide who to hire between three talented candidates, she said it came down to how each candidate answered the phone during the call to set up the final interview. [12] The manager said she could immediately tell who was the most customer service-oriented person, and that made one candidate stand out over the other top candidates. Instead of just saying "Hello," the top candidate answered the call by saying, "Hello, this is Mia. How can I help you?" That was it! All Mia did was add her name and a short, customer-focused question. What did she accomplish with her simple greeting? Mia showed that she was friendly and approachable and cared about the person on the other end. The hiring manager didn't have to ask for Mia. She knew she had called the right number and had the right person. The manager was also excited to talk with Mia because Mia's message communicated interest and enthusiasm.

Often, the little things are the big things

Here is a job search tip you should never forget: Often, the little things are the big things. Mia was the only candidate who answered the phone this way. It separated her from her competitors, and it made the employer's job easier. Don't underestimate the importance of the little things—they make a big difference, and they will often help you seal the deal.

Ask Yourself the Right Follow-up Questions

Once you have asked yourself the Slam Dunk Question, you need to dig a little deeper with your questions. To help you understand what types of questions you could ask, let's assume you are pursuing a finance position in Seattle, Washington, and you live in Southern California. Let's also assume you match up well with the critical job requirements and don't know anyone in the Seattle area. Given this scenario, here are some questions to consider asking yourself:

- How will I make getting an interview a slam dunk?
- How do I plan to separate myself from the Seattle job applicants? Why should the company take a risk on someone outside the Seattle area and especially someone from sunny Southern California?
- What is my experience with Seattle? How can I show that I am knowledgeable or familiar with the city and the state?

- Do I know anyone who is connected to Seattle in some way? Can I identify someone who can refer me to the hiring manager? Have I looked on LinkedIn to see if I am connected to anyone in the company? Have I contacted my alumni association to find contacts?

- Have I explored the company employee list on LinkedIn to locate people I can connect with through a shared interest or other commonality?

- How can I have the employer see me "in person" when I am physically in a different state? Can I share a video of myself or my work? Is my work published? Are my accomplishments highlighted on a company website or my professional career website? Have I received any awards that I can refer the employer to online? How can I become more tangible and personable when I live a thousand miles away?

- How can I get inside information on the organization, position, and hiring process?

- Can I show a connection to the organization through my contacts, the type of work I have done, the training I have received, the knowledge I have of the organization, or a combination of these?

- Have I addressed all the essential job requirements in my cover letter and described why I am the best candidate? Have I weaved key terminology into my marketing documents and promotional platforms?

- What is unique about me and valued by the employer? What do I have that 99 to 100 percent of my competitors will probably not have? How will I communicate this information directly to the hiring manager?

- Do I have a compelling story of why I am interested in the position and the company? Have I grabbed attention at the top of my résumé and cover letter?

- Do my online platforms communicate a consistent brand that is focused on the position and the field?

- Have I identified who the hiring manager is so I can send my marketing documents through the formal online application portal (with my cover letter addressed to the hiring manager) and then send the documents directly to the hiring manager with a shorter, more hard-hitting email cover letter message?

- Is there anything else I can do to make getting an interview a slam dunk? Can I include a relevant report, a glowing letter of recommendation, an article

I wrote, a related thesis or project, a list of key achievements, or a link to an eye-catching professional career website or LinkedIn profile? Can I address a problem the department has by suggesting some solutions? Will testimonials help? (There is often a fine line between providing too little and too much information at this stage. Some of the tactics within this bullet may be more appropriate to use at later stages of the process. But, of course, you can't do anything if you don't get to the next stage.)

- How will I follow up in case I don't hear anything? How can I reach back out in a way that helps me stand out rather than makes me look desperate?

These types of questions will force you to think differently. How many Slam Dunk tactics you use will depend on what makes sense for the job, how qualified you are for the position, and how much you want the job. If you lack key qualifications, you may need to implement more tactics or at least make sure you do the basics extremely well from start to finish.

While you should look for and capitalize on moments where you can stand out and separate yourself from the competition, use your best judgment on when you should attempt to stretch beyond everyone else and when you should merely rely on doing the basics well. Sometimes doing the basics well is all you need at a particular stage, and doing something extra might be inappropriate. Pick the moments where you feel most comfortable adding a little novelty, and always do what works best for your audience.

With government agencies and companies with very structured work environments and rigid policies, you will need to follow all instructions carefully. If you decide to break the rules by going against the application or interview requirements, the agency or organization will probably eliminate you. Within more structured work settings, focus on doing the basics well across the board and adhere to all requirements and steps. If you do decide to elevate your job search performance, focus on using the first five Slam Dunk Guiding Principles to stand out:

- Exhibit Quality and Consistency
- Present Yourself in a Professional Manner
- Provide Extraordinary Customer Service
- Think Like a Salesperson and Act Like an Artist
- Go Above and Beyond Expectations

The sixth principle, being different and memorable, often comes down to applying the first five principles. And, as discussed earlier, there isn't much risk involved in any of them. They allow you to stand out and fit in at the same time. Good companies are always looking for people who fit into the company culture and also bring something different to the organization. Apply these principles throughout your job search, and you will fit in and stand out without taking on big risks.

Look for Ways to Break the Script at Each Stage

As you move through the job search process, think about how you can break the typical job search script (with little risk) at each stage and at each moment of separation. As Oscar-winning composer Hans Zimmer said, "If somebody tells you a rule, break it. That's the only way to move things forward."[13] What can you add or change during the job search process to grab hiring managers' attention and wake them up? What can you do to add a little novelty and be memorable?

While you have already read about various Slam Dunk tactics throughout this book, here are examples of some additional tactics you can use during different moments of separation that involve little to no risk:

> What can you add or change during the job search process to grab hiring managers' attention and wake them up?

- Create an outgoing voicemail message that is different, useful, and customer service-focused: "Hello, you have reached John Hilton. I'm sorry I can't talk right now. Please leave a message, and I will return your call within one to two hours. If you need a more immediate response, please feel free to text me in case I can respond sooner through text. Thank you, and have a great day!"

- Add a testimonial to the top of your two-page résumé if you have a relevant and impactful one- or two-line quote that communicates to the employer why you would be an excellent candidate for the position and the company. It acts as a stamp of approval and lets employers know that other people are impressed with you and your performance. Here is an example taken from the Career Profile in chapter 5: "Emilia goes above and beyond expectations to create events that leave people in awe."

- Be proactive during your interactions. Whenever you connect with an employer, you have an opportunity to acquire inside information and set yourself apart. For example, when you set up the interview with the hiring manager via phone or email, you can ask the following: "To help me focus my answers on your needs, would you be willing to share one or two challenges you would like the new hire to address?"

- Bring your business cards to life. Treat your business card as a small marketing brochure and design it with your photo on the front and a tagline (your unique value proposition) on the front or back. Your business card will sit on a potential hiring manager's desk as a reminder of you and your professional approach. Having your photo on your business card will also help people remember you after conferences, mixers, or other social events.

- Use your actual signature (scanned into your computer) at the end of your electronic cover letters, and add a postscript (P.S.) at the bottom of your letter to draw the employer's attention to something that is important and relevant: "P.S. I have also received 'Exceeds' ratings on all my performance evaluations, and I would bring the same level of performance to the Financial Manager position." Or add a postscript to provide employers with some critical information: "P.S. I will be on a business trip from November 12 through November 22. The best way to reach me is by text at 714-555-1234. Thank you!" Both tactics will allow your cover letter to stand out over other cover letters and immediately separate you from your competitors.

- Leave a little "glitter" in unexpected places. Add a testimonial below each name on your professional reference sheet: "Layla is one of the best employees I have ever had. I was able to empower her with full responsibility for overseeing every large event, and she always did an outstanding job." – Sylvia Dashti

Stand Out

When employers see that you are both different and exceptional throughout the process, they will be impressed with you and will start to visualize you in the position.

Use the job search process to show employers how you will function if hired. Showing is much more impactful than telling, so find ways to demonstrate your value at every turn, and you will stand out and be memorable. Nowhere is this more important than during the interview, the subject of the next two chapters.

Chapter 15

PREPARE FOR A SLAM DUNK INTERVIEW

The interview is the most important time to break the script because this is often when you have the best opportunity to land the job offer. The job search process is too long to get toward the end and not seal the deal. When you reach the interview stage, your game needs to be at its best and better than everyone else's.

The way Michael Phelps won his seventh 2008 Olympic gold medal provides a useful analogy. During the 100-meter butterfly, Phelps trailed for the entire race, and everyone thought he had lost. Even his mother was holding up two fingers, thinking he had come in second. But, with his extra effort at the end, Phelps touched the wall first, beating his Serbian competitor by one-hundredth of a second. As the replay showed, the difference between first and second came down to who finished the strongest. Phelps stretched while Milorad Čavić coasted.[1]

Job seekers often get to the final stage of the process and coast to the finish line. They don't up their game and finish strong. When you get to the end of the job search process and don't close the deal, you may start to question your worth, become mentally drained, and begin to doubt your ability to reach your goals. The 6-Step Slam Dunk Job Search Process was created to help ensure this doesn't happen by getting you to stretch higher and finish stronger within the Slam Dunk step.

When you reach the interview stage, tell yourself that the dues just got more expensive, and the price of admission to your ideal job has increased. You never want to get this far along in the process and then let the job slip away. And, if it does land in someone else's hands, you want to be able to say,

"I followed the right job search process, had the right mindset, prepared the right way, used all possible tactics to close the deal and get the job offer, put in the extra effort, and I still didn't get the job. Undoubtedly, the job wasn't right for me at this time. I now need to follow up with a nice thank-you note and then reflect, adjust, improve, and move on. There are other ideal jobs out there for me, and I need to get ready to compete for them."

When you can say you did your very best at the end of the hiring process, you can feel proud of your effort and certain that the job wasn't right for you at that time. If you were that strong and it didn't work out, you must not have been the right match for the position or the company. But in order to say that, you have to know that you stretched and finished strong.

Break the Interview Script

The interview is the most critical moment of separation. To make your job search a slam dunk, you must stand out and be remarkable during the interview stage.

To help you break the script and leave a positive lasting impression, let's look at how most hiring managers and recruiters see an in-person interview script:

Greet the job candidate in the reception area, listen to standard small talk, walk the candidate to the interview room, sit down and talk about the organization and the position, ask the candidate a variety of questions, listen to standard interview responses, see if the candidate has any questions, respond to standard end-of-the-interview questions, walk the job candidate out to the lobby, say goodbye, and hopefully receive a thank-you note a day or two later.

As an interviewee, you can be memorable by changing this script. Rather than giving the same interview responses as everyone else, come up with responses or stories that will wake up employers, or be proactive and share an example of your work or present a report highlighting ways you could help address the employer's needs.

To be memorable, you need to add a little novelty. Think about it: How many people do you think use common adjectives or typical strengths to describe themselves in an interview? Probably 95 percent of job candidates. When you're predictable, you risk being boring and forgettable.

When Sara Blakely, founder and CEO of Spanx, was asked during a *SUCCESS* magazine business interview what four words would best describe her, she responded with "driven, courageous, innovative, and tired."[2] Out of these four words, which word stands out to you? Tired, right? Blakely went on to say that earlier in her career, the fourth word would have been "funny" instead of "tired." But now she was too tired to be funny. Either word (tired or funny) would have stood out to most people. Why? Because they were different. If you were to think back to Blakely's response a couple of days later, you wouldn't remember driven, courageous, or innovative, but you would remember tired or funny. They create curiosity because they are unique, and that makes them memorable. Saying that you are tired is probably not the best way to describe yourself during a job interview, but if you can find the right word that leads to an interesting story and adds value, it could be well worth it.

During your interview, you want to break the script in strategic ways. It can be as simple as preparing to share one adjective or strength that creates interest, generates curiosity, leads to a relevant story, and is memorable. If you do, you will stand out over the other candidates. Remember, the little things are the big things. Even one word can make a big difference.

Prepare to Stand Out

To break the interview script effectively and make your interview a slam dunk, you must prepare well for each stage of the process.

When you are prepared for the interview, you will be more relaxed and will become a better interviewee. Rather than being concerned about what to say and do,

> "One important key to success is self-confidence. An important key to self-confidence is preparation ."
>
> —Arthur Ashe

you will be more in tune with your surroundings and more focused on employers' needs. You will listen for the meaning behind employers' words and look for themes that can give you hints about what is important to them.

Preparing well has another benefit: It boosts your confidence. As International Hall of Fame tennis star Arthur Ash stated, "One important key to success is self-confidence. An important key to self-confidence is preparation."[3] Knowing that you are qualified for a position, understanding how to demonstrate your qualifications, having a plan for how to answer difficult questions, and practicing the skills that will create a positive and relaxed atmosphere will help reduce fear and enable you to be yourself—your best self—during the interview. Who knows? You might even have fun!

The more inside information you have about the job interview, the better you can prepare for it. Always seek inside information to make your preparation more efficient and effective. Use online platforms like Glassdoor and your connections to uncover possible interview questions. You can also search the internet for other resources. Sometimes companies post information on their websites or other online avenues to assist job candidates with interview preparation. Spend time searching for anything that will provide you with additional information, and don't be afraid to ask recruiters for details on the interview structure. You can also ask if they are willing to share who is on the interview committee. Having the committee member names will allow you to learn more about them before the interview.

No matter what information you collect, prepare for questions that revolve around four main areas: interest, core credentials, uniqueness, and fit. Most interview questions will fall within one of these areas. And, as you probably noticed, these are the four parts of the SD Triangle Offense.

To help you get ready for any interview, use your Career Profile to provide you with your interview material (most relevant qualifications, accomplishments, training, certifications, skills, affiliations, and activities) for each position. With the information you acquire from your Career Profile, company research, and BQAA Sessions, use the SD Triangle Offense (see chapter 6) to put the content into an effective framework for communicating your interests, core credentials (knowledge, skills, experience, education, and training), uniqueness, and fit. As you may recall, you can use the entire SD Triangle Offense framework to answer a variety of interview questions, including "Why should we hire you?" and "Why do you think you are the most qualified candidate for the position?"

Each individual part of the SD Triangle Offense also offers unique opportunities to stand out if you prepare adequately. Let's now look at how each part can help you prepare for the interview process, elevate your confidence, impress the hiring committee members, and seal the deal.

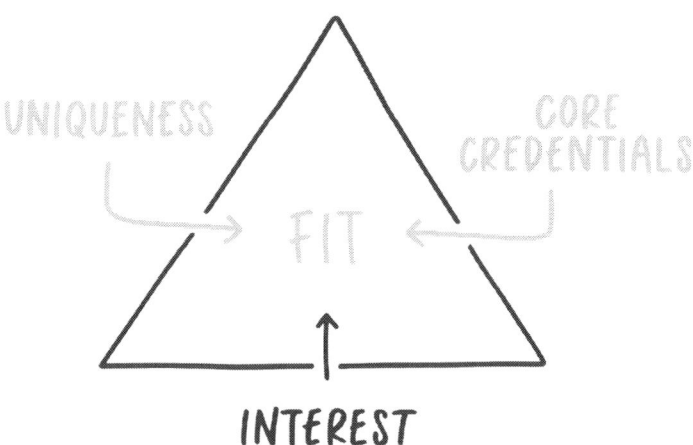

SLAM DUNK
TRIANGLE OFFENSE

UNIQUENESS   CORE CREDENTIALS
                FIT
            INTEREST

Interest

To effectively communicate interest, anticipate interest-related questions and then prepare to answer them. For example, what would you say if the hiring manager asked you,

"Why are you interested in the company?"
"What interests you most about the position?"
"What do you know about the company?"
"Why did you select this field as a career?"
"What motivates you to work?"
"What inspires you and why?"
"What did you like most and least about your last position?"
"If we were to offer you the job, how long do you think you would work here?"

Would you be ready to answer these questions? Be prepared to articulate why you are interested in the company, department, position, and field. To help you come across in an authentic manner when expressing interest, use stories or examples to communicate your interest and passion (see chapter 6 for specific examples).

To further demonstrate interest, be proactive and use the following Slam Dunk tactics to ensure the hiring committee members know you have a strong interest in the company and the position.

Show Your Interest and Engagement from the Start

Most job seekers think the interview is primarily about responding to the questions they are asked. In reality, it's equally important to ask your own questions to show curiosity and engagement.

Come up with a question or two in advance that you can ask before the interview begins to break the ice, generate small talk, and show interest and engagement: "How long have you worked for XYZ Corporation?" "Can you believe the amount of snow we are getting?" "How has your day been going?" "How long has the company been in this location? The building is beautiful." You can also use these types of questions with the receptionist or anyone else you meet if it makes sense given the situation and setting. When you get to the interview site, you might find something more appropriate and unique to ask about or comment on (e.g., "I love the café in your lobby. What is your favorite item on the menu?"), but having a few questions prepared in advance will be a good backup and help put you at ease. And, as you will see in the next chapter, you can also ask questions during and after the interview to continue to show curiosity and engagement.

Show You Did Your Research

By doing your research and learning as much as you can about the organization, you will understand the company better, which will allow you to focus your interview answers on what is most important to the company and the department. And your extensive research will show the employer that you are interested in the job and willing to spend time learning as much as you can about it. Additionally, by researching the organization, you will never get caught off guard when asked common questions like "What do you know about the company?" or "Tell us why you would like to work for the organization."

If you have not had an opportunity to exhibit your knowledge of the company, be proactive and show your interest and preparation by asking a question or two during the interview or at the end of the interview. Here is an example: "I noticed on the website that the company is focused on expanding its client services, and I was wondering how this position and department contribute to this endeavor." Try to ask at least one question to show you did your homework. You will find a list of end-of-the-interview questions in the "Stand Out at the End of the Interview" section within chapter 16.

Show You Follow the Company News

You can also show interest and stand out by demonstrating up-to-date knowledge of the company and the industry. The more specific your information is to the company, the better.

Research the company on social media sites one or two days before your interview. See if anything new and relevant has happened that you can bring up or ask about in the interview to show how you are on top of the company news and activities. To find information, search the internet for Google Alerts, follow the setup instructions, and then add the names of the organizations you want to track. Google Alerts will then provide you with the most current information (e.g., news, web pages, articles, and blogs) for each company. You may want to explore other monitoring platforms as well, but most will charge a monthly fee.

Show Your Interest Through a Story

Stories are powerful and memorable. If you can come up with an authentic story of why you are interested in the company, you will go a long way in convincing the employer that you match up well with the company and will probably have a long-term commitment to the organization if hired.

Showing commitment is important because many employers hire the least risky candidate—the person the hiring committee believes will stay with the organization for the long haul. One thing I've found to be true throughout my decades of experience is that employees hired into a position without a meaningful attraction to the company are much more likely to jump to another company the minute a better opportunity presents itself. In contrast, when people have a good reason for wanting to work at a particular organization (e.g., interest in the company's vision, mission, people, location, culture, or products), they will often stay with the company even when more lucrative jobs come their way. Employers know this, so it's crucial to share a compelling reason why you want to work for the organization.

The best way to communicate this kind of deep commitment is with a story that frames the position or company as the logical next step for your career and life. Make sure you connect the dots for the employer by explaining how this job will be meaningful to you in light of the story you just told.

Show You Know the Obvious

Be prepared to get asked the obvious interview questions. The quickest way to communicate disengagement, lack of interest, and poor preparation is to answer obvious questions ineffectively. You will increase your confidence and reduce any fears by anticipating questions you are likely to get. Ask current and prior employees and search the internet to uncover the obvious questions you should be prepared to answer for each company.

What if you have an interview with an organization like The Walt Disney Company? Would the hiring committee members ask you about your favorite Disney character? Probably! Would you need to know your favorite bird for an interview with the National Audubon Society or your favorite river with American Rivers? What about your favorite Nike product if you have an interview with Nike? Do you know the story behind the Starbucks Corporation name or what IBM stands for? Do you know the meaning of each acronym listed in the job announcement?

You should also anticipate standard interview questions around common topics: Why are you interested in the position and the company? What are your greatest accomplishments? What are your strengths and weaknesses? What are your career goals? What are your salary expectations? Prepare answers to these questions and make certain your responses focus on what is meaningful to the employer. If you don't have complete information to provide a specific response, still prepare to answer the question in a way that shows commitment and interest.

What if the hiring manager asks you to share your short- and long-term career goals and you are unsure what career paths exist within the company? The more you understand why a question is asked, the more you can share a compelling answer even when you don't have complete information. For example, with the goal question, you can weave reassuring material (long-term commitment) into your response: "With my interest in _____, I would like to join a company like [company name here] that is committed to _____. And I would like to grow with the same company and move into a leadership role where I can _____ and ultimately make strategic decisions for the organization."

Always prepare for the obvious questions you might get related to the company, position, and field. Dig below the surface to know more than everyone else. See chapter 6 for more tips on how to demonstrate interest.

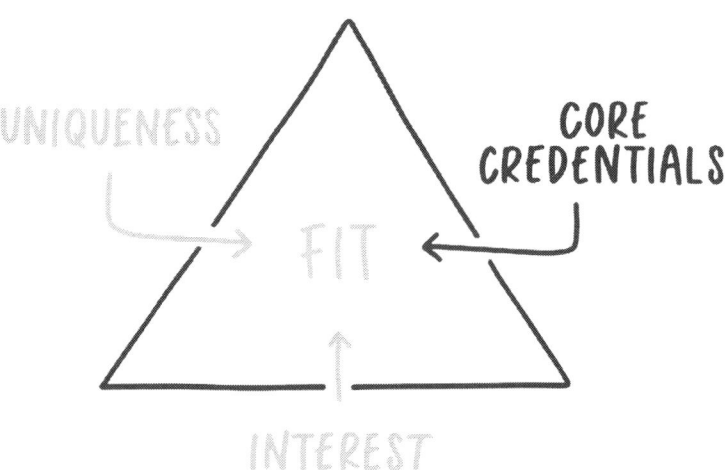

Core Credentials

To effectively communicate your core credentials, anticipate credential-related questions and then prepare to answer them. For example, what would you say if the hiring manager asked you,

"What qualifications do you have that relate to the position?"

"What training or experience do you have in _____?"

"What are your top three strengths?"

"What are your greatest accomplishments?"

"What makes you a strong candidate for this position?"

"How has your education prepared you for this job?"

"What responsibilities in the job announcement will challenge you the most?"

"What skills do you possess that will add the most value to this position?"

Would you be ready to answer these questions? Be prepared to articulate the credentials you bring to the position that tie directly into the required qualifications and responsibilities. Think about how your core credentials set you apart.

To further demonstrate your core credentials, be proactive and use the following Slam Dunk tactics to ensure the hiring committee members know you have the necessary credentials to do the job and do it well.

Review Your Qualifications

If you've been asked in for an interview, the hiring manager already thinks you're qualified for the position. Your job is to solidify that opinion by emphasizing and expanding upon your strengths as well as addressing and minimizing any weaknesses.

Before you enter an interview, make sure you can say something intelligent about all the responsibilities and qualifications related to the job. Pull out the job announcement during your interview preparation, and ask yourself what knowledge, skills, education, training, and experience you have related to each qualification and responsibility. Use your Career Profile to come up with your most relevant credentials, and write down your answers for each item contained in the job announcement.

If you don't have any knowledge, skills, education, training, or experience related to a qualification or responsibility, do your best to get up to speed on the area before the interview so you can share what you do know or what you did before the interview to learn more about the topic or skill. Through this preparation, you should feel confident answering any question related to the job announcement content, and you will have a convincing answer even when you lack a particular qualification.

If you don't have time to learn more about a deficient qualification, come up with an answer for a nonanswer. Here is an example:

"While I don't have experience in _____, I do have experience in _____, and I think I can get up to speed quickly on _____. Additionally, I'm a quick learner. When I was at _____, I was thrown into _____, and I was able to _____. I also thrive on learning new skills and advancing my knowledge, and I look forward to continuing to learn as much as I can about _____."

This response at least shows that you have thought about the gap in your qualifications and can get up to speed quickly. It also gives you an opportunity to stand out by handling a difficult question with poise.

Once you have made some notes about your knowledge, skills, education, training, and experience related to each qualification and responsibility, take it one step further and write down an example or story to illustrate each one. What have you done that will bring your background to life and demonstrate your potential?

Think of stories or examples that highlight the impact you have had. Then, when you are asked about anything related to the position, you will have a story or an example to share that emphasizes your impact and brings your credentials to life. You can also weave these impact stories into your responses to broader questions like "Why should we hire you?" or "Why do you feel you are the most qualified person for the position?"

Remember, stories, examples, and accomplishments showcase your talents and stick with employers. They will also show the impact you can have in this new role. Ideally, you will generate these impact stories or examples early in the process so that you can also incorporate them into your marketing materials and promotional platforms.

Pull from All Areas of Your Background

Everything in your background is fair game when it comes to promoting yourself. Use anything that helps you make a point about some important qualification the employer is seeking. "Everything" includes volunteer activities, travel, extracurricular accomplishments, school activities and clubs, board positions, professional association involvement, charity work, parenting, and any other significant experience or activity. Employers are often impressed when you can pull from different areas to show you have the skills to do the job and do it well.

I conducted a mock interview with a 36-year-old job seeker from Mill Valley, California, named Sidney.[4] Sidney was pivoting to a new career, and I asked her if she could share a time when she had to deal with a difficult customer. She struggled coming up with an answer because she said she didn't have much customer service or retail experience. To help Sidney, I quickly ran down her résumé to uncover areas she could pull from to develop a strong answer. I immediately spotted her teaching experience in the Additional Experience section and asked her if she considered students and parents to be her customers. She said, "Oh, I see. Yes, I have plenty of examples of times when I had to deal with challenging customers."

Don't limit yourself to information that only appears 100 percent related to the interview question. Everything you have done in your life and career is related in some way. If you look hard enough and think differently, you will always find a connection. Once you identify the link, describe how the unique experience will add value to the position, and try to share a story to bring your answer to life. Your unique experiences will make you memorable, especially if you can show how they add value to the position, department, or company.

If you have a hard time connecting your past to the present or seeing what value you bring to any position, seek help. When you are too close to something, you may not see what is right in front of you. As some people have said, it can be hard to read the label when you're inside the bottle.[5] You may need a career coach or a close friend to show you just how talented and gifted you are by providing an outside perspective and reading the label for you.

Demonstrate Your Value

Act like you already have the position and then show the employer what you can do to excel within the role and department. The more information you collect early in the interview process—either before or during the first interview—related to the company's goals, initiatives, challenges, barriers, or customer pain points, the more inside information you will have to develop a plan for helping the department.

Identify a relevant problem, initiative, or goal, and then develop a plan for moving things forward. In your plan (e.g., an electronic or printed slide deck), include a cover sheet, bio that lists your relevant qualifications, brief description of the issue or initiative, summary of your desired outcomes, and your recommendations, ideas, or action plans. You can then ask to share this information at an appropriate time.

If presenting your entire plan is unrealistic or inappropriate, look for ways to share a recommendation at some point during the interview. For example, you might say, "I can see how _____ has created a challenging situation for the depart-ment. Have you ever thought about _____?" or "While thinking about the challenges related to this area, I came up with a few strategies that might help. Would you like me to share my ideas?" You could also consider including a recommendation in your thank-you note or within one of your follow-up messages.

When you act like you are already in the position and then share how you can advance the work and department, you will impress employers by demonstrating your skills, knowledge, expertise, and value.

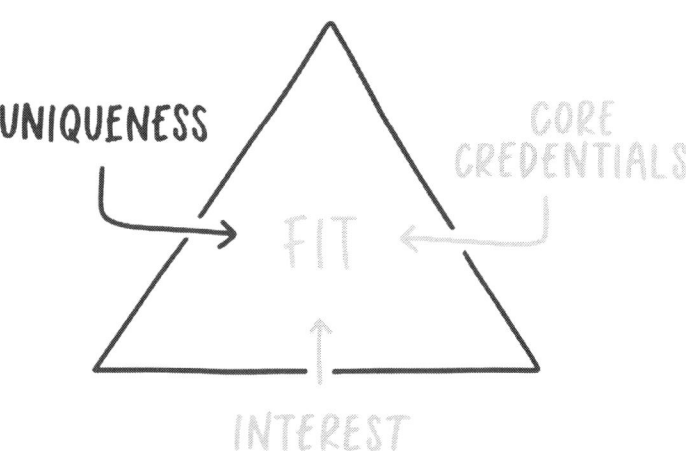

SLAM DUNK
TRIANGLE OFFENSE

UNIQUENESS   CORE CREDENTIALS

FIT

INTEREST

Uniqueness

To effectively communicate uniqueness, anticipate uniqueness-related questions and then prepare to answer them. For example, what would you say if the hiring manager asked you,

"Why should we hire you?"

"What will you bring to the position that no one else will bring?"

"Why do you think you are the most qualified candidate for the job?"

"What do you do in your spare time?"

"How could you add value to our department?"

"What do you consider your superpower?"

"What is your greatest strength?"

"What makes you unique?"

Would you be ready to answer these questions? Be prepared to articulate what you bring to the position that no one else will bring that adds value to the organization, department, and position. Think about how your uniqueness gives you a competitive advantage.

To further demonstrate uniqueness, be proactive and use the following Slam Dunk tactics to ensure the hiring committee members understand why they should hire you over other candidates.

Identify Your Unique Selling Points

To avoid leaving an interview without emphasizing your most valuable and unique credentials and qualities, go into each interview having written down three to five of the most important points you want to make during the interview. What is different and unique about you? What do you have that 99 to 100 percent of your competitors will not have that is valued by the hiring manager and the company? What will impress the employer and add the most value?

When you write down your key selling points, you will remember them and make it a point to share them. If you are involved in a video interview, place Post-it Notes around your computer screen (near the webcam) to remind yourself to cover your most important and unique selling points. See each interview question as an opportunity to weave one of the selling points into your answer.

Bring Yourself to Life

Have you excelled in sports, art, music, or some other extracurricular activity? Do you have a unique talent or quality? Find a way to share your most impressive or unique talent, quality, or extracurricular activity during the interview and tie it back to the position to tap into the hiring manager's emotions. Sharing something slightly personal that is unique and different will make you memorable, bond you with the hiring committee members, and make you more likable. People remember unique talents, personal qualities, and accomplishments more than they remember credentials (unless a credential is unique or impressive).

When I look back at all the people I have helped and hired, I don't remember their work-related skills and credentials nearly as much as their unique extracurricular talents and stories. I remember what was special about each person, such as that the job seeker

- Grew up in Alaska.
- Played the cello superbly.
- Spoke seven languages fluently.
- Visited all seven continents.
- Was attacked by a great white shark.
- Photographed birds around the world.
- Climbed Mt. Kilimanjaro.

- Hiked the entire Pacific Crest Trail during the winter.
- Drew incredible charcoal portraits.
- Lived and worked in Cameroon.
- Competed on an NCAA Division I National Championship Gymnastics team.

This list could go on and on. People remember others through their special and unique skills, traits, and extracurricular activities because these things make them human.

Think about the habits, soft skills, or other qualities that you developed through your activities. For example, a musician might have learned how to listen closely, work well with others, and practice every day for months to prepare for one big performance, all skills that would make the musician an excellent member of a marketing team.

Find what is unique and special about you, determine how it will make you a better fit for the job, and weave it into the narrative at some point during your interview. Of course, once again, use your best judgment. If you don't have something to share that makes sense, or it is inappropriate for the audience, don't use this tactic.

Demonstrate Uniqueness During the Interview

Prepare to show your uniqueness by planning to do something different during the interview. Use the interview itself to reinforce your brand and separate yourself from the competition. Here are some ways to be different:

- Bring something tangible to share with the interviewers during an in-person interview (e.g., a report, a list of key accomplishments, work samples, or a list of testimonials). Or ask to share a document during a virtual interview. Make sure that whatever you share is visually appealing and professional.
- Come up with questions to ask at the beginning of and during the interview to develop a more informal dialogue (more on this in the next section).
- Develop recommendations for how the department can overcome some challenges and then talk about your ideas during the interview.
- Prepare to close the final interview by asking for the job offer.

Whenever you are face-to-face with company representatives, you can separate yourself from your competitors. Take advantage of any interaction by coming up with unique ways to demonstrate how you are different.

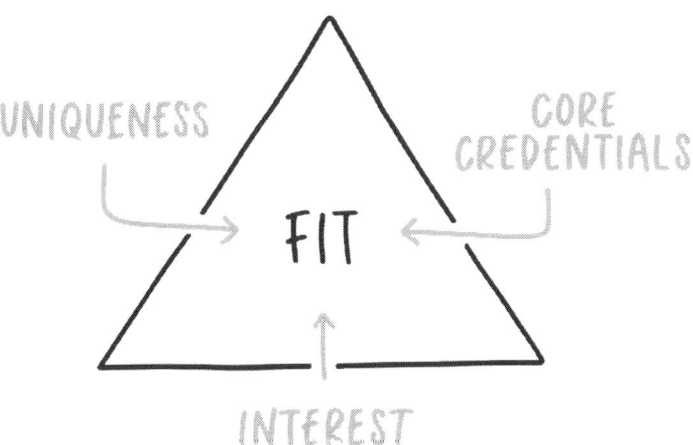

Fit

Using the first three parts of the SD Triangle Offense (interest, core credentials, and uniqueness) to stand out will go a long way toward helping you wow employers. But job candidates will rarely land a job offer unless they can also show they will fit in well with the work, people, and company culture—the fourth part of the SD Triangle Offense.

As explained in chapter 6, interest, uniqueness, and core credentials all feed into fit. If you are interested in the organization, have the credentials to do the job and do it well, and bring something different and valuable to the company, you will probably fit in well with the organization. However, if you don't connect with the hiring manager and employees (chemistry and rapport) and demonstrate fit across the board, you will probably not get the job.

To effectively communicate fit, anticipate fit-related questions and then prepare to answer them. For example, what would you say if the hiring manager asked you,

"What type of work culture do you prefer?"
"Would you rather work remotely or come into the office?"
"What type of work environment makes you most productive and happy?"
"When working on a team, what role would you naturally gravitate toward?"
"Tell us about the best job you have ever had."
"Describe your ideal job."

"How have you incorporated diversity, equity, and inclusion (DEI) into your work?"

"What are your short- and long-term goals?"

"What are your salary expectations?"

"Why do you think you are a good fit for the company?"

Would you be ready to answer these questions in a way that articulates how you fit into the company, department, and position? Think about how you align with each company's values, core competencies, and professional standards, and make sure you have examples and stories to share. The more you can show that you have worked with people in the industry and have done similar work, the more you will convince an employer that you will enjoy the job, excel in the position, and fit in well with the organization.

To further demonstrate fit, be proactive and use the following Slam Dunk tactics to ensure the hiring committee members understand how well you will fit into all areas of the company.

Show Fit Across the Board

Beyond interest, core credentials, and uniqueness, employers look at many other areas to determine a candidate's potential match with the position and the company. They want to ensure the top candidate aligns well with the company's

- Vision and mission.
- Culture (values, core competencies, and professional standards).
- Employees and clients.
- Company and department goals.
- Career advancement structure.
- Salary expectations.

You want to show you fit into the organization across the board. There are many ways to show you match up well with the company. You can demonstrate fit by what you wear and how you present yourself. You can also research the company and then adjust your online platforms to show you align well with the company vision, mission, goals, and culture. You can then prepare stories to weave into your interview responses that demonstrate how you would work well with employees and clients and thrive within the company culture. And you can prepare answers to goal- and salary-related questions that show you align well with the company's career advancement and salary expectations. You never want to share career advancement goals that are too ambitious (or not ambitious enough) or salary expectations that are too high (or too low). Everything needs to be in alignment with what is vital to the company.

Do your research on the company and then come up with creative ways to show the employer how well you match up with the company in all the areas listed above. You can even show fit before you arrive at the interview. For example, Molly, a 26-year-old job seeker from Portland, Oregon, came up with a creative way to show fit after she received an invitation to interview for a project manager position with a Portland-based start-up.[6] She did her homework and knew the organization was environmentally focused. As a result, before her interview, Molly called and asked if the company had a bicycle storage unit in the building in case she rode her bike to the interview. They did have a storage unit, and Molly rode her bike to the interview. The hiring committee members were impressed with her, thought she fit in well, and hired her.

Remember, your goal is to make it easy for the employer to like you and want to hire you. Since fit is one of the ways to seal the deal, always spend time thinking about how you can show you align well with all areas of the company.

Prepare to Make a Personal Connection

In addition to other factors, many hiring managers use chemistry and rapport to determine fit.[7] If a hiring manager doesn't connect with a job candidate, there is little chance the person will be hired. As a result, job candidates should spend time preparing to develop a greater bond with the hiring manager and hiring committee members.

When you focus more on making a human connection, you will break the formal question-and-answer script and develop a more relaxed dialogue. To help you create an informal dialogue, come up with questions you will ask before the interview begins that create a more relaxed interaction: "It's nice to meet you. How was your weekend?" "Did you do anything fun over the holidays?" "Did you have an enjoyable Thanksgiving?" You may take a risk by being too informal and forward, but it could also be well worth it. This type of approach could work well for an informal or creative company, a start-up organization, a nonprofit, or a smaller firm, but it may not work as well for an interview with a federal or state agency or a larger and more traditional corporation. Always know your audience.

You should also have a response in mind when the hiring manager asks you icebreaker questions. For instance, instead of the usual "I'm fine, thank you" reply to the "How are you?" question, consider sharing a common interest: "I'm doing well! It's great to connect with another AEP member. I noticed on LinkedIn that you have been a member since 2012. I've been active in the Channel Counties chapter since 2016." Think of possible icebreaker questions you might be asked and how you could connect with the hiring manager through your responses.

Never enter a conversation with a hiring manager without first learning something about the person. Explore the manager's LinkedIn profile before the interview and try to come up with something to say that will develop a deeper connection.

When you connect on a personal level, you will feel more relaxed, and the hiring manager will begin to feel more comfortable as well, almost like you're already part of the team.

Show Fit Through Your Research and Preparation

One effective way to show that you are a good match with the organization is to research the company thoroughly and then demonstrate how you can add significant value to the position, department, and organization. In-depth research enables you to position yourself as an insider by incorporating relevant keywords into your narrative, displaying an understanding of the company and business, addressing the needs of the organization and department, and asking insightful questions during the interview.

Before an interview, and ideally before you apply for the job, learn as much as possible about the company, department, and position. Here are some ways to gather information:

- Review all parts of the job posting to identify common themes, important keywords, essential qualifications, and hints about the company culture.
- Explore the organization's website and blog.
- Search online for current data on the company and the hiring manager.
- Visit platforms like Glassdoor and other relevant online resources to read about employee reviews, explore potential interview questions, and get salary information.

- Ask customers and current and former employees for information.
- Use online resources like Similarweb to identify the company's competitors and learn more about the organization.
- Search Google News to uncover recent company developments.
- Test the product or service and explore online client reviews.
- Review all sections of the organization's LinkedIn profile.
- Examine the LinkedIn profiles of all members of the hiring committee.
- Use LinkedIn and alumni community platforms to connect with people who both graduated from your university and work at the company.
- Reach out to your relationship team for information and referrals to other people who can help.
- Listen to podcasts and videos featuring the organization's top executives.
- See how the company portrays itself on social media.
- Search online for information on the organization's hiring practices.

Here are some additional ways to gather information on public companies:

- Use the Google Finance website to explore the company's financial data.
- Ask a financial advisor about the organization's financial health.
- Listen to the company's most recent earnings calls or read the transcripts.
- Review the organization's quarterly and annual earnings reports.
- Read the company's annual report.

Use whatever research methods add the most value to your job search. The more information you collect, the more proactive you can be at each stage of the process. For example, during the interview stage, collecting inside information will allow you to recommend solutions to departmental challenges, ask probing questions about initiatives and programs, provide feedback on the implementation of new systems or processes, offer suggestions to advance departmental goals, or demonstrate an understanding of the company's operations and business. Conducting research will also enable you to adjust your promotional platforms and marketing documents to reflect what is most important to the organization and the department.

Learning as much as you can about the company and then weaving keywords, advanced knowledge, and relevant experience into your interview answers and employer conversations will go a long way toward helping you fit in *and* stand out.

Wear the Right Interview Attire

Know the culture of the company and the office environment and then choose attire that will make you look like an insider. Spend time exploring the company website to see if you can uncover clues to what would be appropriate to wear. Ask current or previous employees what they would suggest. Or ask the employer what you should wear if you know the interview will take place in a different setting. It can be awkward if the hiring manager takes you into the field or has you complete a physical assessment and you aren't wearing appropriate attire.

Color and style do make a difference. Unless your research points you in a different direction, wear neutral colors (charcoal, navy blue, gray, or beige). Most people's favorite color is blue. As a result, you may be able to create an instant connection with the hiring committee members if you wear blue to the interview. Additionally, blue tends to project calm, trust, and confidence—all qualities you want to communicate during most interviews. You will find plenty of information on the internet about what each color communicates. For example, black communicates authority and is a nice choice for leadership positions.

Style choices also send a message, so think about how you can communicate fit through the style of clothes you select. For example, trendy styles will seem more cutting-edge or hip, or certain fabrics might demonstrate a commitment to sustainability. Spend some time exploring ways you can use your interview attire and colors to send the right message during your interviews.

If in doubt about what to wear, err on the formal side out of respect for the company and the position, especially since employers expect you to be at your best during the interview. If you find you are overdressed, take off your jacket, blazer, or tie during the session if it seems proper to do so.

Ideally, you will determine the most appropriate way to dress before your first interview. However, sometimes it isn't obvious what to wear. If you go to the first interview and realize you are dressed inappropriately, you should adjust for the second interview. Fortunately, most companies will give you a pass on the first interview if you impress them in other ways. But they will rarely be as forgiving during the second interview. If you wear formal attire twice to a company with an informal culture, you are probably not the right person for the job, particularly with companies that have well-defined company cultures.

Also make sure your clothes demonstrate care and attention to detail. Polish your shoes. Iron your shirt. Check for stains. Comb or otherwise style your hair. If you wear a professional suit but have scuffed shoes, a wrinkled shirt, and food stains on your tie or scarf, what kind of impression do you think you'll make?

By paying attention to detail and selecting your attire with an eye to fitting in with the company culture, you'll prepare yourself to stand out.

Prepare to Win

By doing your research and preparing well, you set yourself up to walk into your interview with confidence. When you put in the effort beforehand, you can relax and enjoy the interview, which will improve your performance even more.

Steve Nash, former professional basketball player, explains it this way: "You have to rely on your preparation. You got to really be passionate and try to prepare more than anyone else, and put yourself in a position to succeed, and when the moment comes you got to enjoy, relax, breathe and rely on your preparation so that you can perform and not be anxious or filled with doubt." [8] When you prepare for interviews using the SD Triangle Offense as outlined in this chapter, you can feel confident that you have prepared more than everyone else. And when you're confident, you can relax, be yourself, and focus on presenting your qualifications effectively and naturally while making a genuine connection with the hiring manager.

Use the Career Profile to get your relevant selling points ready, and then use the SD Triangle Offense as a framework for communicating your value. And don't forget to use the Ice Cream Cone Approach to help you prepare for the "Tell me about yourself" question. If you use these tools and tactics, you will be well on your way to standing out in interviews and moving on in the process.

Chapter 16

CONDUCT A SLAM DUNK INTERVIEW

nce you've prepared for the interview, it's time to put it all together and use that hard work to impress employers. Your goal is to create a connection with interviewers that makes you memorable and likable while effectively demonstrating you are the best person for the position.

While first impressions are important, you must make a strong impression throughout the entire interview. Look for effective ways to break the interview script and be different and memorable right from the start. While trained interviewers know they should reserve judgment about a job candidate until they are at least 15 to 20 minutes into the interview, most interviewers aren't trained, and as many as 30 percent make the mistake of deciding whether they like candidates within the first 5 minutes.[1] And some studies have shown that people will develop an impression of others in the first few seconds after meeting them.[2] The good news is that you can take advantage of situations where people make quick decisions. Since interviewers might judge candidates early, you may be able to come out ahead if you can impress the hiring committee members from the very start.

Although trained interviewers are taught to reserve judgment until later in the interview, they can also be influenced by first impressions. The difference is that trained interviewers will take the time to verify their initial observations. They don't make decisions based on limited information. They dig deeper. Given that you don't know what type of interviewer you are meeting with, your goal is to impress early and often so both trained and untrained interviewers will be impressed with you throughout the entire interview.

The sections that follow highlight key Slam Dunk tactics you can implement throughout the interview process. As you read through these tactics, use your best judgment on what is appropriate for your unique situation. Sometimes, you may only use a few of the tactics to help you stand out; other times you may use more. You should be honest with yourself about your ability to implement tactics in an effective way. And remember, if you stick with the Slam Dunk Guiding Principles and prepare well for each stage of the process, you will be well on your way to standing out and landing your ideal job now or in the near future.

Stand Out from the Start

Everything you do is being observed, and you need to be "on" well before the interview officially starts. There are many ways to make a good impression and set yourself up for success before you even begin the formal interview. The following sections will provide you with plenty of tips for making a positive first impression.

Don't Be Late or Too Early

Arriving too early (more than 15 minutes early) or arriving late will get things off on the wrong foot and kill rapport from the start. Arriving around 10 minutes early in the reception area is about right for an in-person interview. If you have a virtual interview, enter the session about 3 to 5 minutes early so you arrive before the interviewers and give yourself a little extra time to address any technical issues. You also have a greater opportunity to create an informal dialogue when you talk to each person as they arrive, assuming you aren't put in a virtual waiting room. If you arrive when all the interview committee members are already present, you immediately enter a more formal interview setting.

Be Consistent and Kind

Treat everyone in the company well, and remember the "down" times are as important as the "on" times. As previously mentioned, developing a good rapport with everyone in the organization is essential. Connecting with the receptionist, for example, can be just as important as building rapport with the hiring manager. We saw this with the person who landed a 40-year career when the final hiring decision was left up to the office assistant.

Thank the people who help you along the way, including the receptionist and parking attendant, as studies have shown that a simple thank you can help bond people. Monica Bartlett, an assistant psychology professor at Gonzaga University, conducted a study that found that "an expression of gratitude [can] help initiate a new relationship." She went on to state, "Saying thank you—a simple thank you— leads people to view you as a warmer human being and consequently be more interested in socially engaging with you, continuing to get to know you, and [building] a relationship with you."[3] Never forget to thank the people who help you.

Develop Rapport

Know what you are really selling during your job search: "People buy from other people because of likability, chemistry, and people skills," states Harvey Mackay, author of *Swim with the Sharks*.[4] If you've made it to the interview stage, the hiring manager has already decided you meet the basic requirements of the position. Now, they are looking for something more.

Developing rapport during the job search process is critical, but the question is, how do you develop it and develop it quickly? How can you wow employers and stand out during the rapport-building stage? Below are some additional rapport-building tactics (also see chapter 15) that will allow you to create a halo effect and elevate you to the next level from the start.

As you read through the following list, please note that the tactics are not in place to force you to be someone you are not or get you to join a company that doesn't align well with who you are. If you don't feel comfortable using some of the tactics, don't use them. Not every tactic will work well for every job seeker.

Implement Rapport-Building Tactics

1. **Show your hands.**

   Make sure the hiring committee members can see your hands when you approach them. Having your hands visible reduces the subconscious fight or flight response that exists whenever you meet someone for the first time. There is a greater fear when people approach you with their hands in their pockets or out of view. The mind immediately alerts you that the person's hands may be hiding something that could harm you. Vanessa Van Edwards, in her book *Captivate*, has it right when she says that "pockets are murderers of rapport."[5] Try to keep your hands visible when you first meet people.

2.   Look interviewers in the eyes.

Eye contact is one of the fastest ways to develop a connection. By looking someone in the eyes, you immediately create a higher level of trust. To help you make eye contact each time you meet someone, pretend that one of your friends will ask you later about the color of the person's eyes. However, this doesn't mean you should stare at people. Instead, make eye contact about 60 to 70 percent of the time during the interview process (not 100 percent of the time).[6]

If you are in a virtual interview, make sure you look at the camera so you show interest, engagement, and confidence. You can glance away from time to time, but it is important that you appear to be looking at the interviewers during the session. Since you will naturally look at the interviewer's face on the screen and not directly at the camera, you should resize the window that shows the interviewers' faces and then move it up as close to the webcam as possible. Also, to have the greatest presence, make sure your head is toward the top of the screen (leave about 5-10 percent of the space above your head empty) and that you are the most prominent subject on the computer screen—not the background. By doing this, the interviewers will see your eyes and feel more engaged with you. You will also come across as more confident.

3.   Smile!

Many people think that smiling is the best way to develop instant rapport. Why? Because smiling can affect your mood and even the mood of the people you meet. Daniel Goleman, in his *New York Times* article "A Feel-Good Theory: A Smile Affects Mood," points out that studies have shown that "simply inducing people to place the muscles of their face in the pattern of a given emotional expression elicited that feeling."[7] Since smiling has an impact on how you feel while also potentially having an impact on how others feel (by getting them to smile in response), smile when you interact with people at the company, especially if it comes naturally to you and is not forced. When you smile, you also become more likable and approachable.

4. Shake hands properly.

If done correctly, a firm handshake expresses confidence and interest. Here are some tips to help you shake hands the right way: Extend your right hand with the palm to the side, grasp the person's hand, make sure the thumb flaps touch (the piece of loose skin between your thumb and forefinger),[8] and firmly shake hands (two or three pumps in a slight up-and-down motion for about two to four seconds). To help you understand what firm means, act like you are squeezing a semi-ripe peach. You want to apply some pressure, but if you squeeze too hard, you will make a mess.

5. Use the person's first name unless the person is introduced with a title.

Mentioning someone's name during a conversation can help create a greater bond between you and the person. Include the person's name when you first come in contact: "Hi, Becca. It is great to meet you." Then later, use the person's name again when you depart: "Thank you, Becca. I enjoyed meeting with you and hearing more about the designer position." Although some salespeople will tell you to use a person's name as often as possible, be careful with this advice. Using a name too often in conversation can be a turnoff. And the last thing you want during the interview is to come across as unlikable. But, once again, know your audience and your field, and do what feels natural.

6. Mention the person who referred you.

Referrals are a great way to establish instant credibility and initiate a conversation: "Kyle Smith was the one who referred me to the orga-

nization, and he spoke very highly of you and the company." If you
don't have a referral, introduce yourself and then use one of your icebreakers or positive statements to spark a conversation.

7. **Project an upbeat attitude by saying something positive.**

When you project an upbeat and friendly demeanor, you will often
create an upbeat and friendly attitude in the people around you.
You could make a positive comment about the building, weather,
artwork, or office decor. Try to find something to share or ask about
that creates a connection or exhibits the type of attitude you are trying
to project: "The landscaping around the building is beautiful. Was
the company involved in the landscape design?" "I love the atrium in
the entrance area. It is quite impressive." "The breezeway sculptures
are incredible. Were they created by a local artist?" It can even be as
simple as, "You can't beat this beautiful weather. I love this time of
year." When you make a positive statement, you are often seen as more
likable because the person hearing the remark sees the messenger in
a positive light.

If you have a virtual interview, you can use the same tactic by
keeping your eyes open for positive things to say about the virtual background or office decor (if appropriate). Always look for ways to say
something positive.

8. **Wait to be seated.**

Never sit before your interviewers unless invited to do so, and thank the
interviewers when they indicate where you should sit. And try to mirror
the posture of your interviewers—legs crossed, leaning forward, and so
on—while remaining professional.

These techniques will help you make a slam dunk first impression. However, for them
to work, you have to feel confident using them. Like any skill, these techniques are
improved through practice, and you want to be smooth, relaxed, and confident for
your interview, not worried that you will forget your icebreakers or fail to make strong
eye contact. Find someone to practice with who can provide honest feedback on your

level of likability. Depending on your general skill level in these areas, you may want to practice several times over the course of a week or two. At the very least, practice your ice-breaker "rapport-building moment" the morning of your interview or the night before.

Use Nonverbal Communication

One study indicated that nonverbal communication (body language and tone) can amount to 93 percent of all communication.[9] While this percentage has been disputed, most experts agree that the actual percentage falls somewhere above 70.[10] Whether you look at the low or high number, this percentage is significant. Employers believe what they see (body language) and hear (tone) more then what is actually said. Never forget this, and always strive to match your nonverbal communication with your words.

Your nonverbal and verbal communication must be in sync if you want to develop credibility and trust. If you say you are outgoing but can't look people in the eyes for very long, will you be very convincing? What if you say you are patient and calm but speak quickly and move your leg up and down in a nervous manner throughout the interview? If there is a disconnect at any point, employers will get concerned. Work on your nonverbal communication just as much or even more than your verbal communication.

Here are some tactics you can use to develop rapport nonverbally, both at the beginning of your interview and throughout it:

1. **Project confidence with your posture.**

    When you meet the interviewers, face them and show confidence by keeping your back straight, shoulders back, head up, and arms to your sides with space between your arms and torso. This opens your heart up and develops a higher level of trust and connection while also projecting confidence.[11]

2. **Subtly mimic or mirror the people you meet.**

    When you subtly mimic someone (subtly imitate the person's behavior), you often develop a greater connection with the person. While mimicking can happen unconsciously, it can also be used strategically to help you develop a closer bond with people. If you have the same mannerisms as the hiring manager, the manager will probably like you more even without thinking about it. Jonah Berger, in his book *Invisible Influence*, points out that one study showed that "people who mimicked their partner [during negotiation sessions] were five times as likely to find a successful outcome." He goes on to say that this happens because "mimicry bonds us together" and "when someone behaves the same way we do, we start to see ourselves as more interconnected. All without even realizing it."[12]

There are many ways to mimic people during the interview. What would you do if the hiring manager conducted the interview standing up and told you it was fine to sit or stand during the meeting? Given the importance of rapport, chemistry, and likability, you would continue to stand, mimicking the hiring manager. Always assess your situation, adjust, and seek to develop an authentic bond with the hiring manager or hiring committee members.

Here are some additional ways to subtly mimic people during the interview and throughout the job search process:

- Tone (If the interviewer has a certain tone, try to mimic it.)
- Volume (If the interviewer is talking loudly or softly, you may want to adjust your volume.)
- Tempo (If the interviewer is talking slowly or quickly, you may want to slow down or speed up the pace a little.)
- Keywords (If the interviewer keeps using the same word, you may want to use that word periodically.)
- Focus (If the interviewer is focused on numbers, you should put more emphasis on numbers.)
- Posture (If the interviewer is sitting upright, make sure you are sitting up straight. If the interviewer is leaning back, you may want to lean back every now and then.)
- Facial expressions (If the interviewer is animated, you may want to be more animated.)
- Gestures (If someone uses a particular hand gesture, try to weave the gesture subtly into your communication.)

- Eye contact (If someone stares at you, you could consider looking more directly at the person for a longer period.)[13]

Pick and choose what you feel most comfortable using and be subtle. Like anything, too much mimicking can be a negative. You may only use one or two of these tactics. Additionally, you don't need to mimic someone at the exact same time. If the interviewer leans forward, you could lean forward the next time you get the opportunity to talk. Making a move at a transition point will avoid having something appear too obvious or planned. And don't do anything that feels unnatural or inappropriate.

Mimicking doesn't need to take place only during the interview. You can also use it during the entire interview process when you are interacting with a variety of people in person, over the phone, and through email. For example, if someone corresponds with you by writing "Hi," "Hello," or "Dear," you can use a similar greeting on your return messages. You can do the same when you close your messages: "Sincerely," "Regards," "All the best," or "Thank you." You should also be aware of the length of the person's email messages or phone conversations. If they are short, you probably don't want to go on and on with your correspondence or conversations. When someone consistently communicates with you over the phone, you may want to continue communicating with the person through this same method. The more you get to know someone, the more you can tailor your communication to develop rapport and address the person's needs.

You can also mimic with name choices. If the person you are interacting with shortens the organization name, you can do the same to make it look more like you are an insider. You could start with the formal company name to let the employer know that you are aware of the official name, but then you could work the informal name into the rest of the narrative. For example, go from "Northbrook Partner's operations" to "Northbrook's operations." Similarly, you should also be aware of the hiring manager's or recruiter's name. If you initially send a message to me using "David," and I respond back with "Dave" at the bottom of my message, you should adjust and address your next message to Dave and not David.

Once you know what mimicking is and what it looks like, you can also use it to see if someone is bonding with you. If you see interviewers mimicking you, you have created a bond with them, and that is a good sign for you and your candidacy. It means you are on the right track, and your approach and tactics are working.

Since mimicking someone can increase affiliation and chemistry and help you seal the deal, think about how you can subtly mimic people within each stage of the process. You will be surprised how often you can use this tactic. But, once again, be selective and choose whatever form of mimicry makes the most sense for you and your situation. And remember, you will need to find the right balance between fitting in and standing out.

3. Listen carefully and attentively.

You are communicating even when you're not talking. When you show that you are listening by making eye contact, nodding, smiling when appropriate, and never interrupting, you communicate that you care about others and what they have to say. Good listening skills will help you establish rapport while also providing you with information about what is important to the company and the position. But there is a fine line here. Make sure you reach a balance between good listening skills and being part of the conversation.

If you want to land your ideal job, use nonverbal techniques to create a closer bond with the hiring manager. You will find that these skills will also help you on the job as you look to connect with people and get projects done.

Stand Out with Your Answers

The following tactics will help you break the script and be different and memorable while answering interview questions. Know yourself and your audience, and apply the tactics that are most relevant for your particular situation.

Connect the Dots

Connect the dots for the employer by relating your answers to the job qualifications and the company. When job candidates have similar credentials, the ones who do the best job connecting their qualifications to the position and showing the most value are often the ones who move on in the process. Don't let any question go by without providing an answer that demonstrates your interest in the company, your ability to excel in the job, your unique value, or your fit with the company culture and the people (the four parts of the SD Triangle Offense).

Here are some of the more common interview questions that you should be prepared to answer:

- Can you tell us about yourself?
- What are your strengths?
- What is your greatest weakness?
- What are your greatest accomplishments?
- Can you describe a challenge you faced and how you handled it?
- What are your career goals?

Each question is asked to see if you are a good match with the company and the position. Find a way to relate your answers to these and other questions back to the job qualifications and what is most important to the employer.

The Career Profile you create for each position will provide a one-page document you can refer to in your mind when you answer any interview question, including the most common questions. If you have not completed the Career Profile yet, take a close look at the position announcement, highlight the key skills, experience, and training required, and put the announcement content in a word cloud generator or chatbot (e.g., ChatGPT) to uncover the most important keywords. Most of your interview answers should focus on the core job qualifications and responsibilities and show you are on board with the company mission, vision, goals, and culture.

Many job seekers fail to connect their qualifications to the job requirements and instead make the following serious mistakes:

- Answer the "Tell us about yourself" question without showing they align well with the job and the organization.

- Share their greatest strengths without thinking about how their strengths link back to the position.
- Respond to the weakness question and feel good about their answer but don't realize that the weakness they shared shows they lack a core skill needed in the job.
- Talk about accomplishments that don't appear relevant to the position and fail to show how they are related.
- Describe a situation or challenge but don't tie the skills they used back to the position and show employers how the skills can help them.
- Discuss their goals but fail to align them with what is most important to the company and the department.

Connect the dots for the hiring committee members by focusing your answer on how you meet the job requirements. Specifically, you should think carefully about how you will answer the most common interview questions and

- Use the Ice Cream Cone Approach to answer the "Tell us about yourself" question and show the employer how your strategic actions have prepared you for the position and the field.
- Have six to nine strengths listed in your Career Profile and then share three of the most relevant ones for each unique job. If three strengths don't immediately stand out, you can use the SD Triangle Offense to help you decide, making sure that all four parts of the Triangle are covered by the strengths you select. For example, if you're seeking a position with an exercise apparel company, you might share your unique background as a competitive gymnast to illustrate your passion for fitness (interest, fit, and uniqueness). Then you could pick two other strengths that illustrate your core credentials.
- Stand out with the weakness question by the actions you have taken to overcome the weakness or by the way you frame your response. And avoid sharing a weakness related to the core job requirements.
- Access the content in your Career Profile to share your most relevant accomplishments for the position.
- Tap into an employer's emotions by talking about a challenging situation and then relating the skills used to address the challenge back to what is important to the company (more on this in the next section).

- Share career goals that relate to the company, position, and field to ensure the employer knows you will be committed to the organization over the long run.

You don't need to make a direct link with every single answer, but you do need to ensure the employer knows about your key qualifications and the unique value you bring to the position. To help keep your credentials in the employer's mind long after the interview, be prepared to share interesting examples and relevant stories related to your qualifications and accomplishments.

Use CARE Differently

As you may recall, the CARE acronym was used during the Success Mindset step to get you to focus on connections, advice, relationships, and emotions. Now, you can use the same acronym in a different way to answer behavioral or situational interview questions— to talk about challenges, actions, and results and continue to tap into employers' emotions.

Behavioral interview questions are used to see how job seekers behaved or performed in particular situations because there is a high probability they will behave or perform the same way later on in similar situations. In other words, past behavior is a predictor of future behavior. Here are two examples of behavioral interview questions:

"Tell me about a time when you had to deal with a difficult client. How did you handle the situation?"

"Describe a situation where you were working on an urgent project, your boss dropped another urgent project on your desk, and you had limited time to work on both. What did you do to navigate the situation?"

Use the CARE acronym to answer these types of questions effectively, connect the dots, and tap into the employer's emotions:

Challenge: Talk about the challenge you faced.
Actions: Discuss the actions you took to overcome the challenge.
Results: Share the (positive) results of your actions.
Emotions: Tap into the employer's emotions by connecting the skills you used to address the challenge back to the position and the company.

When you care about the people you are trying to help, you will seek to understand them and their challenges, and then you will focus on the "E" at the end of CARE—

emotions. For the most impact, share challenges that bring out the skills or traits that most closely align with the position and the company, and then tie your answer back to what is important to the job and the interview committee members. This will be different and will help you stand out.

To help you prepare for behavioral interview questions, come up with five to seven key accomplishment areas in your background (jobs, internships, education, charity work, extracurricular activities, parenting, projects, etc.) that you can pull from for most challenges. Access a variety of behavioral interview questions online and then practice answering them by pulling from your key accomplishment areas and using all four letters of the CARE acronym (Challenge, Actions, Results, Emotions).

You will incorporate the "E" (Emotions) by sharing challenges or actions that directly relate to one or more of the job requirements or sharing how the skills you used to handle a situation relate back to the specific job requirements. The more you can connect the dots, the more you will tap into employers' emotions. Here are a few ways to make it easy for the hiring committee members to see the connection at the end of your answer:

> "I thought about this particular challenge because I believe the actions I took demonstrate the skills I would use to help your department with its recruitment needs."

> "I chose this particular challenge because I believe my contract negotiations and theater production skills would allow me to help NorthPoint Inc. create events that come in under budget while still leaving people in awe."

> "I believe the management and data analysis skills I used in this situation, along with my regulatory compliance knowledge, would allow me to help you tackle some of the quality control challenges you face within your production line."

The formula is simple: "I chose this particular situation because I believe my skills in _____ and my experience in _____ would allow me to help you tackle _____." Feel free to modify the formula if you have a better way to connect your skills, experience, or knowledge to the position. You can also mix things up by adding the connection on the front end: "Given that a combination of project management and data analysis skills are critical within this role, I will share a recent situation that highlights these skills."

If the interview committee members ask many behavioral interview questions, you don't need to refer all your responses back to the job requirements. Instead, be strategic and relate a few answers back when you know you can make a significant connection to a particular job requirement and when the connection is not obvious from the other parts (C, A, R) of your answer.

If you want to stand out even more, go one step further and create a CARE document. Identify the most relevant challenges you have faced, and then write down each challenge, the actions you took, the results you achieved (impact you had), and the skills you used or learned that relate to the field or the position. If you keep it concise, this CARE document could also be given to the hiring committee during the interview process as a tangible example of what you have accomplished. You could also use this same exercise when developing content for your marketing documents.

You will find many approaches to answering behavioral interview questions, including STAR (Situation, Task, Action, Result), SOAR (Situation, Obstacle, Action, Result), CAR (Challenge, Action, Result), and SAR (Situation, Action, Result). However, none of these approaches focuses on tying the answer back to what is important to the job and tapping into the hiring manager's emotions. And remember that most people purchase something based on emotion rather than logic.[14] Maya Angelou had it right when she wrote, "At the end of the day people won't remember what you said or did, they will remember how you made them feel."[15] The more you can connect the dots and help employers see the real value you can bring to the position and the company, the more you will tap into their emotions, the more they will remember you, and the more successful you will be.

Share Commonalities

Weave commonalities into your interview responses to develop a greater bond with the interviewers. For example, if your research uncovers that you and the hiring manager both played a college sport, work this into one of your responses: "I would also bring strong multitasking and teamwork skills to the position. These skills were refined when I played on the intercollegiate tennis team at the University of Ridgeline. I maintained a 3.76 GPA while practicing three or more hours of tennis a day and competing in matches across the country. The entire team worked closely together, and we went on to win the Southern Conference Championship."

Find ways to connect with the hiring committee members. Based on your LinkedIn research, subtly try to engage the committee members in conversations around topics that are important and meaningful to them.

Bring Your Answers to Life

Another way to stand out and be memorable is to make your interview engaging for the hiring committee members. When people are having fun, their brains produce dopamine and norepinephrine, which increase alertness, improve concentration, and promote memory formation—exactly what you want to make your interview more memorable.[16] If you can make your interview not only informative but also entertaining, you'll be well on your way to a slam dunk interview.

There are many ways to bring your interview responses to life. You read about how Sara Blakely used one unusual word (tired) to bring her business interview to life and create curiosity and novelty. The following list will provide you with more tactics:

1. **Use vivid stories.**

    If you want employers to remember you and have fun, incorporate relevant stories into your answers. Chip Heath and Dan Heath, in their book *Made to Stick*, share a memory experiment where participants sat through a series of presentations. The researchers then asked the participants a variety of questions to see what information they retained. The study showed that 63 percent of the participants remembered the stories, while only 5 percent remembered the individual statistics.[17]

    Weaving stories into your answers is a powerful way to separate yourself from the competition and bond with the interviewers during the question-and-answer stage of the interview process. Stories cause the brain to produce a chemical called oxytocin that softens people and often makes them more open to your ideas and points.[18] Stories also spark curiosity. What happens when someone says, "When I was eight years old . . ."? You perk up and want to hear more. We all love stories, and good stories paint an image in our minds; they stick with us. The more you can share your qualifications through strategic stories, the more successful you will be throughout your job search.

Recruiters won't remember your credentials by themselves (unless they're unique), but they will remember your stories. And if your stories highlight your credentials, they will remember them through your stories. Incorporate stories about your work into your narrative at critical times throughout your job search, especially during the question-and-answer phase of the interview process. As you may recall, that is why a story is a key component of the Ice Cream Cone Approach used to answer the "Tell me about yourself" interview question. You want employers to remember you, your focus, and your skills from the very start. You want to bring your background to life.

Use specific, concrete details to paint a powerful image in the interviewers' minds. People remember about 80 percent of what they see, 20 percent of what they read, and only 10 percent of what they hear.[19] Your job is to use words to paint a vivid image in employers' minds so you raise the 10 percent closer to the 80 percent and get employers to remember what you said. Spend time focusing on the most vivid part of the story and include details that describe what you saw, heard, or felt.

Imagine that an employer asks a job candidate, Harper, why she is interested in sports management, and Harper responds with the following: "In addition to playing sports all my life, I helped my mother coach a high school basketball team when I was in fifth grade. The combination of these two things led me to pursue a career in sports management." Would this be enough to paint a vivid image in the employer's mind and make Harper memorable? Probably not. Harper would need to dig deeper and see if she could take the employer on a journey that painted a vivid picture, such as the following example:

"While I didn't know it at the time, I think my mother was preparing me for my career at a very young age. She taught high school math, but she also coached the girls' varsity basketball team. When I was 11 years old, she asked me if I would like to help with the team practices. Of course, I said yes, because I loved basketball. But I had no idea she would give me so much responsibility. I swept the floors before practice, tidied up the locker room, set up the court for practice by bringing out the basketballs and getting the water bottles ready, sat at the end of the bench and filled in the stats chart during practice games, offered the players water between quarters, and put everything away after practice.

"While I enjoyed playing three different sports for much of my childhood, I found myself enjoying the operational side of the game even more: planning, coordinating, and handling a broad range of behind-the-scenes duties. I loved being the team helper, and ever since that time, I wanted to be involved in some form of sports management."

This story is much more vivid and, therefore, more memorable. Harper uses specific details to take us on a journey through her experience. We were there. We were at the high school gym, on the basketball court, on the bench, and in the locker room. The story sticks.

When you paint a clear picture in employers' minds, you connect with them because you bring them into your world and develop a shared human experience. A vivid description or story also helps you control the narrative and avoid leaving any room for misinterpretation.

Peel the layers away and dig deep enough to find something relevant, vivid, and meaningful to share with the interviewers. If you do, you will stand out and be memorable, particularly if the story relates to your interest in and qualifications for the position.

2. **Add hooks to your narrative.**

Sprinkle in hooks along with your stories to grab attention, add credibility, and bring your work and accomplishments to life. Similar to what you used in your marketing documents, hooks can include awards, company names, numbers, percentages, keywords, names of relevant individuals (without name-dropping too much), specific examples, and clients. Don't overdo it, but adding specificity goes a long way in adding credibility, bringing your work to life, and helping you stand out and be memorable.

3. **Use Curiosity Statements.**

Creating curiosity is another effective way to grab employers' attention during all stages of the job search process and get them to listen and ask for more information. Here are a few examples of Curiosity Statements that spark interest and get employers to want to know more:

> "I planned and coordinated more than 30 events last year, and I received excellent ratings while finding unique ways to cut costs in half."

> "I increased energy efficiency by 30 percent through a new innovative program I designed, and I motivated all company employees to get involved in the program."

> "I completed an internship with a technology firm, and during the internship, I recommended some unusual strategies for breaking into a new overseas market. My recommendations were used, and by the end of my internship, the company was able to work its way into this new market."

These statements generate curiosity and lead employers to ask for more information. What methods did you use to cut costs? What was the innovative program? What unusual strategies did you recommend? Weave Curiosity Statements into your interview responses just as you did during your moments of contact (see chapter 9) and with your marketing documents (see the appendix).

When your answers connect the dots for the employer, paint vivid word pictures, and generate curiosity, you make your interview enjoyable and memorable for the hiring committee while ensuring they know you're the best person for the job.

Demonstrate Your Problem-Solving Skills

Within technical- and business-related fields, you may get brain teaser questions (e.g., Why are street maintenance hole covers round? How many ping pong balls can you fit in a 747 plane?), scenario questions (e.g., What would you do if your boss told you to do something a certain way and then your boss's boss told you to do it a different way?), and case interview questions (e.g., What is the size of the market for organic mouthwash in the United States?). With these types of questions, your goal is to demonstrate your communication and problem-solving skills. You also want to stand out.

To perform well in these difficult interviews, especially those with brain teaser and case interview questions, you should ask questions to determine the true problem and ensure you understand any confusing terms. The hiring committee members evaluate candidates on the questions asked. If you don't ask clarifying questions, you will have a hard time advancing to the next round, and you will definitely not stand out.

Once the problem is defined, summarize the issue, and then take the interviewers through your thought process, including assumptions you made that impact your solution, recommendation, or answer. In most cases, your thought process is more important than getting the correct answer.

With more in-depth case interviews or brain teaser questions that may take as long as 20 to 60 minutes, go one step further and develop a roadmap for solving the problem. Ask for some time to collect your thoughts and write down your problem-solving roadmap. Use a framework to break the case or problem down into smaller parts, and make sure you address all key issues. Next, with your visual roadmap in place, take the interviewers through your thought process and approach, sharing how you have broken down the problem and pulled everything together in the end to come up with your recommendation or answer. Depending on the case or problem, the interviewers will often assess your logical thinking, problem-solving, creativity, resourcefulness, communication, and analytical skills.

Prior to the interview, research the company and anticipate possible questions. Many large consulting firms provide case interview guidance on their websites or through other online avenues (e.g., YouTube). Follow the guidance and practice for the interview. You will find brain teaser questions and case interviews more prevalent in investment banking, management consulting, and engineering companies.

With any type of problem-solving question, demonstrate your composure, communication skills, and logical thinking. Try to relax, and then ask questions that will give you the information you need to put a clear framework in place to solve the problem or challenge.

Turn Negatives into Positives

No matter what comes your way during the interview, remain calm, take advantage of unique or unexpected circumstances, and frame everything in a positive light. If you do, you will often stand out. Below are a few ways to reframe the negative:

1. **Capitalize on the unexpected.**

   Even if you prepare for just about everything, the job search process probably will not go exactly as expected during the interview stage. There is no doubt about it—you will experience the unexpected, and you will need to zigzag along the way from time to time. Understand that the unexpected will happen; when it does, use the Slam Dunk Guiding Principles to handle these difficult moments effectively, demonstrating your ingenuity and poise. Here is an example that Claire Arnold, a recruiter at Kaiser Permanente, shared on a Glassdoor panel webinar:

   > Arnold stated that she was interviewing a candidate on the phone when the candidate's children interrupted to tell their father that their dog had pooped in the house. Rather than get off the phone and risk failing the interview, the father tactfully calmed his children down, cleaned up the mess, and continued with the interview throughout the entire process. Arnold was very impressed with how the candidate functioned under pressure, and the situation highlighted his strong multitasking skills and composure. This unexpected situation allowed the interviewee to demonstrate skills he wouldn't have been able to showcase had this problem not existed.[20]

   Expect the unexpected, remain calm, and always think about how you can turn problems into opportunities. If you do, you will often stand out and impress people.

2. Respond to negative questions with positive opening remarks.

Since employers want to hire positive people, they often ask interview questions to see if job candidates will speak poorly of others and go down a negative path. Don't fall into this trap. Find ways to say something positive even when confronted with negative questions. Here is an example:

Question:

"Tell us about a time when you worked with a supervisor who was difficult to get along with. How did you handle the situation?"

Response:

"Fortunately, I have always worked with amazing supervisors, and I got along well with all of them. However, if I need to come up with something, I can think back to the time when . . ."

If you can't think of an answer to a negative question, either ask to come back to it once you have had time to think a little more (e.g., "I know I have an example, but I can't think of one right now; I would love to come back to this question a little later.") or respond with a broader answer. For example, with the supervisor question, you might say something about a difficult or negative moment rather than a challenging supervisor. If you don't answer the question at all, employers will start to question your self-awareness, experience level, and honesty. Make sure you answer all questions, but don't be afraid to take a different course if you need to adjust. And always find ways to share positive remarks about people and situations no matter what question is asked. Positive equals positive!

3. Turn your weaknesses into strengths.

Most interviews include some version of the "What is your greatest weakness?" question. Many job seekers dread this question and have a difficult time answering it because they have the wrong mindset. When you view things differently and think differently, you will see the value in everything, and you will look forward to getting the tough questions because you know they will allow you to separate yourself from the other candidates and make your interview a slam dunk.

Let's use Carl, a 29-year-old job seeker from Los Angeles, California, as an example of how you can take advantage of the weakness question when you approach the process differently.[21] Carl was interviewing for a human resources position that required training and development, benefits, compensation, recruiting, and employee relations experience. He asked me to take him through a mock interview. When I asked Carl what his weakness was related to the job, he said he didn't have much experience in benefits administration but that he was a quick learner, and he thought he could get up to speed rapidly within this area given his other human resources experience.

While Carl's response may appear effective, he wasn't taking full advantage of the question, and I didn't want this obvious weakness to eliminate him. I wanted him to address it head-on and turn it into a strength by doing something different. Carl needed to think about how he could use his weakness response to stand out over the other candidates and authentically promote himself. He needed to go above and beyond expectations.

If you want to seal the deal, demonstrate that you are interested in the position enough to learn about it even before you land the job. The interview is also the time to show that your preparation is superb and that you will be a resourceful employee who comes to any project prepared and ready to work. I told Carl, "If you know your lack of benefits experience is your weakness, reach out to people before the interview and find out more about it. Then, during the interview, talk about what you did to learn more about this area of responsibility."

If Carl approached his preparation in this way, he could add some powerful content to the end of his initial response:

Initial response:

"After reviewing the job announcement and considering my qualifications, I would say that I don't have as much benefits administration experience. However, I believe I could get up to speed rather quickly in this area given my interest and expertise in all other areas of the human resources field."

Additional content:

"To learn more about benefits administration, I decided to reach out to several people working in human resources (HR) to learn more about it. I talked to an HR manager (a member of the Society of Professional Benefit Administrators), a vice president of human resources at a large Fortune 500 company, and an HR representative in a midsize corporation. Through this process, I learned about critical trends taking place in the industry, existing issues and barriers, strategies for running a successful benefits administration program, and ways I can get trained quickly in this area. I also believe my contacts within the human resources field will serve me well as I look to expand my knowledge within this area."

Think about how you can set yourself up to look forward to getting difficult questions and turning your weaknesses into strengths. If you do, you will often stand out because you will respond differently, and you will do it with confidence. Of course, you don't need to go to the extent that Carl did by contacting three people. You might only reach out to one or two people. But the more time you can put into your preparation, the more you will stand out, and the more knowledgeable you will become in your field.

If you are thinking this sounds like too much work, think again. Your job search is about your career, and expanding your relationship team within your field can only help. You would be hard-pressed to find a better way to connect with people than reaching out to them to gain knowledge about your field. As a matter of fact, you should contact people in your field prior to an interview to get inside information even if you aren't worried about any of the interview questions. Any time you can show you have prepared well for the interview, you will stand out above all the other candidates. Show the employer that you are willing to do more than anyone else to get the job.

Here is an important tip: In most cases, you should avoid drawing an employer's attention to any core deficiency (essential to the position) when you respond to a weakness question unless it is obvious that you lack a core skill and need to address it head-on. In Carl's case, it was obvious he was lacking relevant experience, and he needed to address it. Why give employers another weakness example when one is obvious? You should address the obvious weakness so you don't leave employers with any doubts about hiring you.

There are many other ways to stand out with the weakness question, including framing your answers differently or sharing a weakness that could bond you with the hiring manager. Which of the following answers to the "What is your greatest weakness?" question do you think markets the job candidate the most?

Option 1

"I get nervous when I give presentations, but I am always working on ways to improve my presentation skills. I am currently taking a Toastmasters International course, and my presentation skills continue to improve."

Option 2

"While I have given speeches to audiences ranging from 25 to 150 people and have received positive feedback on my talks, I still get nervous before each presentation. However, I know that the best speakers and performers get nervous as well. I believe the butter-flies show I care about what I am doing, and I want to do the best job I can for my audience. The nerves also force me to prepare well, so I leave nothing to chance. To maintain my presentation skills, I continue to take Toastmasters International courses through the local chapter, and I enjoy attending the sessions. I think communication skills—both presentation and writing—are critically important. As a result, I will continue to refine these skills throughout my entire career."

Both options mention working on presentation skills through Toastmasters International courses, but the second option begins by mentioning a strength and also demonstrates the person's self-awareness and long-term commitment to continuous improvement. Always start your response to a weakness question with a positive selling point. If you think enough about it, you can often find a positive way to begin.

While most job seekers should avoid saying anything negative about their communication skills, unless the weakness is obvious, you can see how framing a communication-related weakness in a positive manner can send a very different message to the employer. You can take something negative and turn it around to promote yourself.

You can also select a weakness that all the hiring committee members can relate to and then impress them with what you have done to overcome the weakness. For example, if you know everyone in a particular field is overworked, you can talk about how you found a way to be more efficient and productive:

"While I have strong multitasking skills and make sure my work is done in a quality manner, in the past, I didn't build in time to become more efficient and productive. In order to get more on my plate, I knew I needed to do things differently—I needed to find ways to become more efficient. Like many people, I was focused on what was urgent rather than what was important. To overcome this weakness, I started to schedule time on my calendar to improve the way I was functioning. I took training courses on Microsoft Word and Excel, and I doubled my productivity by identifying shortcuts and becoming more efficient. I am now much more focused on working smarter rather than just harder, and it has had a considerable impact on my productivity and overall performance."

Most people who hear this response will relate to it and wish they could do the same. It also shows that this person is always seeking ways to become more productive.

Take some time before your interview to plan how you will answer the "weakness" question in a way that emphasizes the positive, shows you are proactive, and turns the discussion of your weakness into another opportunity to stand out and seal the deal.

Take advantage of every negative question or situation to present yourself in a positive way. Prepare for those questions you should expect, like the "What's your biggest weakness?" question, and always frame your answer with positive statements. Stay calm when something unexpected occurs, and try to use the situation as an opportunity to demonstrate resilience, poise, and ingenuity. If you do, you will stand out, and employers will be impressed with you.

Control the Narrative

Remember that you are the CEO of your job search, and you have more control over the process than you think. You can't control what the interviewers decide, but you can control the narrative of your interview to a significant degree. There are ways to take control of the interview without making it seem like you are trying to run the session. When done well, this is another proactive means of demonstrating to a prospective employer why you are the ideal candidate for the job.

Here are some tactics to help you subtly and effectively control the narrative and the process:

1. **Provide an updated résumé.**

   Prior to the interview, update your résumé by adding something you've learned or accomplished since you submitted your application. Then, pull out your résumé at the start of the interview and say the following:

"Before we begin, I would like to give you the most recent version of my résumé. I included some additional skills and want to make sure you are aware of these changes. I specifically added _____."

Not only will you impress the hiring manager with your thoroughness, but you will also demonstrate that you are committed to learning more about your field and improving your skills. This approach will also create the halo effect from the very start, especially if the content you add and share stirs some interest and emotions. It could be a certificate you completed, a program you enrolled in, an award you received, a new software program you learned, an updated GPA, a short course you excelled in, or a project you finished. Even something small, as long as it is relevant to the position, will present you in a positive light.

2. **Create a situation that takes the discussion in an unexpected direction for the employer but a strategic direction for you.**

With so many companies now conducting virtual interviews, you can hang a quote on the back wall, set up an interesting virtual background, or use a bookshelf behind you to display something intriguing. For example, if you find through your research that the hiring committee members enjoy golf, and you play golf, put a golf ball on one of the bookshelves and have a story to share about that particular golf ball or your interest in golf. If your interview is in person, you can do something similar by wearing a unique pin on your suit lapel or adding an interesting design or logo on the front of your padfolio. Most interviewers will ask questions about items they are curious about or anything that taps into their interests. These tactics also break the ice and start the interview or the meeting in a more relaxed and informal manner.

There are other ways to reinforce a culture fit during a virtual interview. For instance, if you know the company is dog-friendly, have your dog walk in and say hi to you during your interview. You may need some help with this, but if pulled off the right way, you could develop a strong connection with the interview committee members and show fit with the company culture. But always use your best judgment when breaking the rules and doing something different.

If you think these are manipulation tactics, you should think again. Remember, your job is to help employers understand why they should hire you. If you think you can do the job better than anyone and you know you will fit in well with the company culture, you need to do whatever you can—using honest and authentic tactics—to make sure the employer knows this and will offer you the job. Don't let the employer hire someone who will not add as much value to the organization and will not fit in as well with the company culture.

3. **Ask questions during the interview, not just at the end.**

Don't hesitate to ask questions during the interview if you need to stall to give yourself more time to think of an answer, want to learn more about the company and create an informal dialogue, need additional information to help you share a more targeted response, or want the interviewers to clarify something.

When you ask relevant questions during the interview, it shows you are relaxed, engaged, and confident. It also shows you want to know more and care about helping the department and the company. And, even more importantly, it creates a less formal conversation that helps you stand out, fit in, and be memorable.

4. **Take control of the salary expectation question.**

What if the interviewer asks you about your salary expectations early in the interview process? This can be awkward if you are caught off guard and don't take control of the question. Practice how you will answer this question in a professional manner without eliminating yourself or committing to a particular salary so early in the process. Here is one approach:

> "I would be happy to talk about salary, but I would rather wait until we are further along in the process when I have more information

about the job and fully understand the value I will bring to the position and the company. I hope this makes sense."

No one should question this response because most jobs differ from what is presented in a job announcement and even outlined in a job description. What happens if you base your salary requirements on the job announcement and then later in the interview find out that the position involves much more responsibility? You will have a difficult time negotiating a higher salary because you already gave the hiring manager a lower salary figure or range early in the process.

If the hiring committee members push you for a figure, you can try another approach:

> "I did some research, but I was unable to come up with a salary range that aligns well with the _____ position. What would you consider a fair salary range for someone with my qualifications?" [Alternative: "What do you have budgeted for the position?"]

If you are uncomfortable asking the hiring manager for a salary range or you sense there is friction because you are not disclosing a specific number or range, you can say the following:

> "If you would like a salary figure now, here is what I can tell you: Of the positions I have been pursuing, the range has fallen between _____ and _____."

Here is some different wording:

> "If you would like a salary figure now, I can tell you that I am being considered for positions that range from _____ to _____."

The second option puts a stamp of approval on your candidacy by saying that others are interviewing you. Just be prepared if the recruiter or hiring manager asks what companies are interested in you. If you are interviewing with some other organizations, this can work to your advantage. If you aren't interviewing with anyone else, you will want to stick with the first option. However, anytime you can show that others are interested in you, you will create competition and gain some negotiating power.

The benefit of either of these options is that you don't say that the salary level is what you want from the company. Since the salary range is based on what you have been pursuing with other companies rather than what you are requesting for the current job, you should feel more comfortable moving past the range if you decide to negotiate.

Your goal is to delay the salary discussion until you are further into the hiring process. The more employers like you and understand how you can help them, the more likely they will be to elevate the starting salary. When you become their number one choice, the power shifts in your direction and employers are more willing to find creative ways to elevate the salary or total compensation package and get you on board.

5. Ask yourself a question by asking the interviewers a question.

If you've been unable to share one of your key qualities, you can ask a question that will hopefully provide a segue. This is usually done best at the end of the interview when you're asked if you have any questions. Here is an example:

> Your question at the end of the interview: "What qualities or skills would you like to see in the top candidate related to customer service that haven't already been discussed?"

> The interviewer's response: "We are also looking for strong writing, time management, and active listening skills."

> Your response to the interviewer's answer: "I'm happy to hear that these are some of the other skills you are looking for in a candidate. I believe I would come to the position with similar skills, especially with my training and experience in _____ and _____."

Come up with one question you can ask if you want to set yourself up for a follow-up response. You can use the question if you haven't yet emphasized one of your key selling points. Be careful with the time, though. At the end of the interview, keep your responses short if you decide to respond to one or two of the interviewer's answers.

Stand Out at the End of the Interview

Your interview doesn't end once interviewers are finished asking their questions. The time after the formal question-and-answer interview session is one more opportunity for you to promote yourself, gather valuable information, and set yourself apart from your competition.

Ask Strategic End-of-the-Interview Questions

One of the easiest and most powerful ways to impress employers and set yourself up well for the future is to ask the right types of questions at the end of each interview. You can show your interest and engagement by asking follow-up questions about projects, initiatives, goals, or challenges that build on what was discussed earlier in the interview. You should also have a list of questions written down in advance that you can pull from when the time comes to wake up the employer, elevate yourself above your competitors, and get useful information. Since many job candidates ask the same standard questions, you have a fantastic opportunity to stand out and separate yourself from your competitors by being different.

Rather than look up standard post-interview questions on the internet, ask yourself what information would be valuable to know for the next interview and what information will allow you to understand the employer's needs better. Your goal is to show employers you can help them more than anyone else when it comes to their challenges, priorities, and goals.

To think the right way and gather the most important information, act like you are a consultant who needs to put together recommendations to present to employers at a later date on how you will help them address their challenges and meet their goals. If you think this way, you will ask very different questions. You can then use the answers to these questions to prepare for future interviews.

While you will probably only ask three to six main questions at the end of most interviews (depending on the interview format, field, and the questions you ask), the examples below will provide you with plenty to select from for each unique job search and interview.

1.	**Questions to set you up better down the line:**

	•	What are the three most important qualities or skills you are looking for in the top candidate?
	•	What challenges exist within the position or the department?
	•	What is the company's biggest challenge, and how does this position play a role in addressing the challenge?
	•	If you were to think of someone who fits in well with the company culture, how would you describe that person?
	•	What major goals do you have in place for the unit/department this year?
	•	What barriers do you anticipate as you strive to meet or exceed your annual goals?
	•	For employees who have excelled in this position, what did they have in common?
	•	For employees who have not performed well in this position or the company, what held them back?
	•	What soft skills are valued most by the organization?

	You can use the answers to some of these questions to develop recommendations for how the company or department can improve its services, processes, initiatives, or products. Consider presenting your recommendations in subsequent interviews. You can also make recommendations on the spot if you feel comfortable addressing the employer's needs during the interview. At the very least, the answers to these types of questions will allow you to be more focused on what is important to the employer during future interviews.

2.	**Questions that get the interviewers to visualize you in the position:**

	•	If I were fortunate to be offered the job, how would my performance be measured relative to department goals?

- If I were fortunate to be hired into the position, what would you want me to focus on in the first three (or six) months?
- If I were fortunate to get hired, what would I need to do to receive an exceeds performance rating at the end of the year?
- If I were hired and could help you receive a stellar review at the end of the year, what would I need to do to make it happen?
- If I were fortunate to join your team, what would you like me to learn or further develop before I start working?
- If I were hired and excelled in the position, what more could I take on to help the department and the company?
- Two of my strengths are _____ and _____. If I were fortunate to receive the job offer, where do you see me adding value immediately with these skills? (Only ask this question if you know the skills you present are valued skills and you haven't already discussed them.)

3. **Questions to help you stand out and show you did your homework:**

   - I noticed on the website that _____. Can you tell me more about _____?
   - While talking to Bob Smith in the risk division, I heard _____ and I was wondering _____.
   - I had the opportunity to use the ____ product and talk to some customers about it, and I was interested in knowing _____.
   - I read an article on _____ by your CEO, _____, and I was wondering about _____.

   Plan to ask at least one question that will show you are well prepared. Employers always like job candidates who have done their research and are resourceful.

4. **Questions that address concerns:**

   If you sense there could be some concerns about you or your background, or you just want to get a better feel for where you stand in the hiring committee members' minds, you can ask these types of questions:

   - Is there anything in my background or related to my credentials that you would like me to elaborate on or clarify?

- Is there anything you would like to see in my background that I don't appear to have?
- Are there any additional credentials you wish I had that you feel would make me an even stronger candidate for the position?

Once the hiring committee members answer these types of questions, you should immediately address their responses so you can eliminate any concerns. If the committee members have any doubts about you when you leave the interview, there is a high probability you will not be asked back for another interview and will not get the job offer.

5. **Questions to help you learn more about the company culture and show fit:**

To learn more about the company and develop a closer bond with the interviewers, ask the interviewers to share their thoughts about the company or some program or initiative. You should ask these types of questions if the interview is with one or two people. If there are many hiring committee members, you will use the entire end-of-the-interview question-and-answer session on one question as all the interviewers go around and share their thoughts about the company. If the hiring committee comprises more than two people, avoid these types of questions or cap them: "If you could only use one word to describe the company culture, what one word would you each select?"

Here are some company-related questions you may want to ask if the hiring committee is relatively small:

- What do you like most about working for the company?
- How long have you been with the company, and how has it changed over the years?
- What surprises new hires the most about the company once they start working?
- What upcoming initiatives or projects are you most excited about?
- How would you describe the company culture, and what types of people fit best within the company?
- What office activities or traditions do you like the most?

- What does the team usually do during lunchtime?
- What professional standards define the company culture and help the company provide extraordinary service?
- What are the company values and how do they tie into this position? (Ask this only if you couldn't find the values on the website.)

The responses to these questions will provide you with inside information you can use later to come up with stories to weave into future interviews that will show you have a strong culture fit. And, as you may have noticed, some of these questions overlap with other categories and can serve more than one purpose.

6. **Questions to generate thank-you note content:**

- I would imagine it is difficult to stay up on everything within your field. What do you wish you had more time to read about or explore that would help you and your business?
- Given your success in this field, I was wondering what book has had the greatest impact on your career.

As you have seen in the Relationship Team step, you can use the responses to these questions to customize your thank-you notes or follow-up messages. (See the thank-you note examples in chapter 7.) These questions are also useful during the BQAA Sessions when you are finding ways to bond with and help your contacts. In a more formal job interview, use your best judgment about whether to ask these or similar types of questions. But they can be a great way to add a little novelty and provide you with useful information.

7. **Questions to clarify the process:**

Ask about the timeline so you know when you will want to check back in after the interview.

- What are your next steps in the interview process?
- I am excited about the position, and I was wondering when you plan to get back to candidates.

Or if you're in the final interview:

- I'm excited about the position, and I was wondering when you plan to make a decision.

The responses you get from the questions outlined above will provide you with plenty of information you can use to prepare for the next interview, get you ready to prepare for your close, and help you negotiate a higher salary. Select the questions that work best for you and your job search.

Have 12 potential end-of-the-interview questions written down on page two or three of the notepad in your padfolio. Break them into first- and second-tier questions: six possible questions to ask, and six questions to ask if you have more time. While you will typically only ask three to six questions (depending on your questions, the interview structure, and your field), you will want to have the second-tier questions ready in case some of your first-tier questions are answered during the first part of the interview. Additionally, you can always use your second-tier questions during subsequent interviews if you don't ask them in the initial interview.

Having 12 total questions prepared in advance is also important because you never know for sure what will happen in the interview. Some hiring managers conduct their interviews by having job candidates ask all the questions. The managers ask follow-up questions, but they base most of their evaluation on the quality of the questions asked and the candidate's composure during the process. By having a list of 12 questions, you will never be blindsided if a hiring manager uses this interviewing tactic.

Pick and choose your questions carefully. In most cases, asking a long list of questions can leave a negative impression at the end of an interview. Remember, once the offer is on the table, you can ask as many questions as you want. Before this time, be strategic and targeted.

Close the Interview

At the end of the interview, you can also stand out and be memorable by emphasizing your interest in the position and reminding the interviewers one more time of your most relevant qualifications. Most job candidates will say they don't have any other questions and then thank the interview committee members for the opportunity. That isn't enough. Go one step further and say something along these lines:

"I don't have any more questions at this time, but I would like to say that I hope our meeting convinced you that I am the right person for the position, and I hope you make me an offer. I know I would thoroughly enjoy working with you and the entire team."

As any successful salesperson will tell you, you should ask for the business (job). However, if the above approach is too aggressive for you, consider one of the following closing statements:

"I don't have any more questions at this time. However, I would like to say that I believe I match up well with the position, and I hope you feel that I am a strong fit as well. Thank you for meeting with me."

Or

"I don't have any more questions at this time; however, I would like to close by saying how much I enjoyed talking with you about the position. After our discussion, I am confident I can help you and your team reach your goals, especially with my skills in _____ and my experience in _____. Thank you for giving me the opportunity to share my qualifications with you today."

Or

"It was a pleasure meeting you and the other hiring committee members. I am very excited about the possibility of joining your team, and I hope you agree that I could make a strong contribution to your unit and the company. Thank you for taking the time to meet with me today."

You will need to practice your close to see what feels most natural, but these examples should give you some ideas to work with as you determine what is best for you and your situation. Feel free to mix and match the content to come up with the best close.

If you haven't addressed all four parts of the SD Triangle Offense during the interview (interest, core credentials, uniqueness, and fit), address the missing parts at the end of the interview. When you do share additional information, don't go too long. If you feel time is limited or it is inappropriate to say too much, particularly during an initial screening interview, you can add a little more to your thank-you note to reinforce some important qualifications.

Provide Something Tangible

Have the interviewers touch something you have created. When an attachment is part of an email message, it often remains an attachment and may never be opened. The end of the final interview could be a good time to leave something tangible with the hiring manager. For example, you might share a report you wrote, a one-page list of your most relevant accomplishments, or a portfolio you compiled. When you give the hiring manager a hard copy document, it will sit on the manager's desk as a reminder of you and your talents. It will make you memorable. Take the time to prepare something tangible to share with the hiring committee members, such as one or two of the following (see chapter 7 for more examples):

- A paper you wrote
- A blog you developed
- An article you published
- A lesson plan you created
- A list of client testimonials you acquired
- A description of a program you designed
- A printed PowerPoint presentation you made
- An outline of a professional training course you completed

Have a sample or two of your work in your padfolio that you can pull out if an opportune time arises to present it to the hiring manager. This tactic can be compelling because a physical product is different. It will set you apart in the interview, especially if the interviewers are impressed or happy with everything else about you. Very few people will bring something to share, so try to take advantage of this opportunity to stand out and add some novelty. But, once again, know your audience and your values. If you are pursuing an opportunity with an environmental company, you may want to send your documents through email to avoid using paper. Do what works best for you and the company. You can also display documents and other visuals during a virtual interview if the interviewers will allow you to share your screen. Merely offering to present a document will add a little novelty.

Of course, like with everything else, use your best judgment when it comes to timing. If pulling out a sample of your work early in the process is inappropriate, use this tactic at the end of the final interview to seal the deal.

Leave the Interview the Right Way

Similar to arriving at the interview, you can also stand out by how you leave the interview. As you depart, thank people and exchange business cards with the hiring committee members. If you have interviewed with people separately, exchange business cards at the end of each interview. Since you will need accurate email addresses and names when you customize and send thank-you notes, you will be glad you collected business cards along the way.

You can also add notes to the back of the business cards immediately following each interview or before you get home (in your car prior to leaving the parking lot) so you remember what was discussed. Write down what intrigued or impressed you the most about each interview and any points of commonality you uncovered, and then find a way to incorporate this information into each thank-you message. Having notes will allow you to customize your messages and help you stand out.

Stand Out After the Interview

What you do after the interview can significantly impact the hiring decision, particularly if the employer is undecided between the top candidates. Attention to detail and thoroughness are critical throughout the entire process, and they should not be forgotten after the interview. Now is the time to up your game even more and do whatever is necessary to close the deal.

Send Customized Thank-You Notes

If you are conducting a Slam Dunk Job Search, you always need to send a thank-you note after your interviews. There are many ways you can send thank-you notes to have a greater impact:

1. Send post-interview thank-you notes to each person who interviewed you. Send them within two to six hours and definitely the same day as the interview unless the interview takes place late in the day. Customize your message for each person based on something specific that was discussed. When employers have a difficult time deciding between two candidates, a personalized thank-you message can help seal the deal. The more you can

customize the message and even offer suggestions, the more you will tap into employers' emotions by showing you care about them and want to help them. Customizing your thank-you notes will elevate you above your competitors and get employers to start to visualize you in the position. You will find more information on thank-you notes in the Market Ready step.

2. Submit a post-interview thank-you packet if you have completed the final interview. A more comprehensive thank-you packet (electronic thank-you note, attached Career Profile, and attached reference sheet) will allow you to stand out when the employer is deciding between the top candidates. As discussed in the Market Ready step, the Career Profile is a one-page snapshot of your most relevant credentials and accomplishments, and it can be a powerful way to close the interview process and seal the deal. Your reference sheet can do the same, especially if you have an impressive list of references. You will find more thorough descriptions of each of these documents in the Market Ready step.

3. Do what others will not do and send a handwritten thank-you note in addition to your electronic thank-you message. Handwritten notes can be effective because they are different, and they will sit on a person's desk or bookshelf as a reminder of you and your follow-up skills, professional approach, and qualifications.

4. Consider sharing a thank-you video at the end of your final interview if you can pull this off in a professional manner and feel you need to close with something spectacular or creative. If this is too much but you still want to do something different, send a Paperless Post (paperlesspost.com) electronic thank-you note or something similar. Once again, use your best judgment and do what works well for each audience and situation.

Update Your Contacts

If you have contacts at the company or even outside the company who have helped you during a particular search, and you have a close relationship with them, update your contacts on your interview and ask if they would be willing to put in a good word for you one last time to help seal the deal. If they are willing to reach out to the hiring manager again, they will remind the manager of your internal connection (if the contacts work at the company), which will reinforce your fit for the position and the company. If the hiring committee is having a difficult time deciding between the top candidates or one candidate has a slight edge, your contacts may be able to shift the decision in your direction right before the hiring decision is made.

If you don't feel comfortable asking your contacts to put in a good word for you, you may find that they will offer to say something to the hiring manager without you having to ask. As a result, keep your contacts informed of your progress and continue to thank them for their assistance.

Follow Up on the Status of Your Candidacy

Employers like job candidates who are interested in the position enough to continue to express interest. As a result, you should check back in with the employer after your interview. The question is when and how.

At the end of the interview, inquire about the hiring process timeline. Knowing the employer's anticipated timeline will allow you to determine the best day to send a follow-up message. When the interviewers say they will get back to you in one week, then you know they plan to decide fairly quickly. If you have something relevant to share with them, such as a report, paper, article you wrote, or recommendations for addressing the department's challenges, consider sending a follow-up message with the attachment before the employer makes the hiring decision:

> Hi Catherine,
>
> Thank you again for meeting with me last week and discussing the Training Manager position. I am still very interested in the opportunity, and I am confident I can help you meet or exceed your department's training goals, especially with my skills and extensive experience in workshop design, coordination, and facilitation.
>
> Since it has been about a week since our meeting, I thought I would check in to see if I can provide additional information to help with the hiring decision. I would also be happy to answer any further questions you may have.
>
> While thinking about the challenges you face within your department, I thought you might enjoy reading the attached article written by one of my

professors. It provides several innovative suggestions for stretching a limited training and development budget. I would be interested in hearing what you think about her suggestions.

I hope you have a great week!

All the best,
Tyler

P.S. Thank you for suggesting Simon Sinek's book *Leaders Eat Last*. I enjoyed reading it and understand why it has had such an impact on your career.

Find ways to serve and wow employers and make their jobs easier while keeping your name at the very top of the hiring list. Checking in isn't about asking for a response for your benefit. Instead, it provides you with an opportunity to see how you can help the employer.

Although an employer-focused email message like the one above does not require a response, hiring managers will typically respond if they are interested in you. But if they run out of time and can't get back to you right away, they won't feel stressed and see you in a negative light as a result. Employers view this kind of approach in a positive light, and you will most likely get a response.

What happens if you have another offer on the table and need to know about the status of your candidacy? You can still use a customer service approach rather than a demanding, "What's in it for me?" tone:

Hi Baylon,

Thank you again for meeting with me last Tuesday. I want to let you know that I am still very interested in the Social Media Specialist position, and I am confident I can make a valuable contribution to your department.

I am reaching back out because I received a competitive job offer today, and the employer has given me until Friday to make a decision. I don't want to put any pressure on you to do anything. However, out of courtesy, I thought I should let you know about my situation.

The Social Media Specialist position at Layered Outerwear Inc. is my number one choice. If I am one of your top candidates, and I hope I am, please let me know if there is anything more I can do on my end to help with the hiring decision.

Thank you!

Sincerely,
Mary Beth

Effective communication and customer service will go a long way in helping you stand out and be remarkable. Why? Because few people approach the job search with this mindset. They don't see employers as customers, and they don't see every interaction as an opportunity to separate themselves from the competition. Employers value communication and customer service skills and understand the impact they can have on the company's performance and employee morale.

Conduct a Slam Dunk Interview

The interview is your best opportunity to wow employers and seal the deal. Stretch higher than your competitors by ensuring that you stand out at the start, develop and maintain strong rapport, connect with employers' emotions, and give stand-out answers that connect the dots and grab attention with vivid stories. Remember that you can control the narrative, and you should always seek to turn negatives into positives. Use your best judgment on what is appropriate and feasible for your unique job search and audience, but no matter what, always seek to do everything in your power to address the company's needs and close the deal.

Chapter 17

STAND OUT DURING THE JOB OFFER STAGE

Congratulations! You have followed the 6-Step Slam Dunk Job Search Process, and you have landed the job offer. Doesn't it feel great to get the offer? All your hard work has paid off for you. But you also know that your job search isn't over quite yet. You still need to navigate the job offer stage just as well as you did with all the other stages.

While it may take weeks or months to receive an offer, the job offer stage can move quickly (possibly two or three days). Without thinking through this stage in advance, you could get caught off guard and fail to ask for what you need and want.

Once you receive the job offer, you are viewed differently. You are no longer seen as a job candidate. Instead, you are now seen as a valuable employee of the company. The hiring manager likes you, wants to hire you, believes you can contribute, and doesn't want to lose you. The power has shifted in your direction. Now is the time to negotiate.

While some companies may take salary negotiations off the table, don't assume the salary is fixed unless explicitly told that the offer is nonnegotiable. And even when the salary is set, you might find that you can negotiate other parts of the offer. Employers will often try to come up with more money or creative arrangements when they realize you're the right person for the job and don't want to lose you.

How you navigate the job offer stage will determine how well you transition into your new job and excel throughout your career. This is not the time to coast.

Responding to the Job Offer

Although you will negotiate for a higher starting salary before you accept the offer, you don't need to hold back your enthusiasm and gratitude:

> "Thank you for the job offer. I am excited about the possibility of joining your team [or, company name]. I hope it is fine if I take a day or two to review the written offer once it arrives and then get back to you with my questions."

Get the job offer in writing so you understand the entire offer (total compensation package), and make sure you get the benefits information so you can review the various options and costs before making a decision. When the written offer arrives, never commit to anything until you have had time to review it, understand it, ask questions, consider the offer, negotiate, and receive a revised written offer. Don't feel pressured to make a quick decision. With most companies, you should be fine asking for a few days to decide.

Deciding to Negotiate

Believe it or not, most employers want you to negotiate even though they won't admit it or don't realize it. When employers offer you a job and you immediately accept the offer without negotiating, they wonder if their offer was too high, and they may question the value you will bring to the position. Employers could also get concerned that you may not fully understand what the job entails, especially since they offered less than they thought you were worth because they expected you to negotiate.

The following analogy should help you understand why it is important to negotiate for a higher salary. One time I was trying to negotiate a lower price on a painting, and I made what I thought was a very low offer compared to the asking price. I was expecting the gallery owner to negotiate. He didn't. Instead, he accepted my offer on the spot. I had mixed feelings. On the one hand, I was excited to get the painting for such a low price. On the other hand, it made me nervous. Was I missing something? Was it really an original painting? Was my research on the price and market accurate? Was the painting damaged? I started to question the painting's real value.

The same thought process takes place when you don't try to negotiate for a higher salary. Hiring managers might start to wonder if they made the right decision about your potential value, and you never want to leave the manager thinking this way about you. Here is the worst thing an employer will probably say if you ask if the salary is negotiable: "No, the salary is nonnegotiable; we have given you our best offer." If this happens, you at least know you didn't leave any money on the table. And then you can use the lack of movement on the salary as leverage to negotiate additional perks that will elevate other parts of the total compensation package.

There are two other important reasons to negotiate. First, studies have shown that it could cost you a million dollars or more in lost wages over your lifetime if you don't negotiate a higher salary throughout your career.[1] If your starting salary is higher, retirement contributions and merit increases throughout your career will mathematically amount to more money. Second, negotiating also sends a message to the hiring manager that you have strong negotiating skills and expect to get paid for the value you bring to the organization, and it therefore sets the stage for future negotiation sessions and merit increase decisions. With future performance evaluations, you never want your manager to think you will be fine with a lower merit increase. You want to get paid for what you are worth, and you want to make this clear from the very start.

Like all the other stages, use your best judgment during the salary negotiation stage. For example, there may be times when you decide not to negotiate for a higher salary. In some situations, the employer will offer you a very high salary or accommodate you significantly in other ways, and it would be inappropriate to ask the employer to increase the salary. While you will need to use your best judgment, always enter the job offer stage with the thought that you will negotiate, especially when many employers leave money on the table in anticipation that you will ask for a higher salary.

Negotiating the Offer

Before you receive a job offer, ensure you have an effective negotiation strategy in place. Your goal is to continue to stand out during the job search process by confidently and tactfully negotiating for a higher salary. The key to getting a higher initial salary is understanding your worth, researching the industry salary norms for the position, asking for a higher salary, and then justifying why you think you deserve more.

When you negotiate, have a win-win mindset. Don't come on too strong and demand everything in the world. Ask for what is important to you and then be willing to work with the employer to come up with a total compensation package that is satisfactory for you and the employer.

If the offer falls short of what you were expecting, you need to ask for what you need. Be up-front with the employer about your concerns. Sometimes it just doesn't work because the employer can't afford to offer more and you can't afford to accept less. If this is the case, you will need to part ways, but your goal is always to maintain a positive relationship and close everything out the right way. Who knows? Maybe the company will find more funding or open another position later and try to recruit you back to the company.

Your negotiation meeting should take place in person, via videoconference, or over the phone, not through email. Having direct contact with the hiring manager or recruiter allows you to mimic the person (to increase likability) and pay close attention to nonverbal communication (body language and tone), which can tell you a lot about how the session is progressing and how you should proceed.

There are two other important reasons why you should avoid negotiating through email. First, employers have a more difficult time saying no to someone in person than they do through email. You don't want to allow the employer to say no before you have the opportunity to justify your reasons for a higher salary. Second, during negotiations, you rarely want to reveal your entire strategy all at once. You want to ask one question, get a response, and then ask the next question based on the hiring manager's response. This question-and-answer negotiation approach is effective in person but awkward and inefficient over email. As a result, people who negotiate by email often present everything at once, and it doesn't allow for much strategic posturing. Do your best to negotiate in person, through videoconference, or over the phone.

When you meet or talk on the phone to discuss the offer, confirm that you have until a certain date to make a decision:

"Thank you again for the job offer. I also appreciate you taking the time to meet with me to answer my questions.

"I first want to confirm that I have until Monday to get back to you with my decision. I would like to get my questions answered today and then sit down over the weekend, take a close look at everything, and consider the offer [alternative: consider my options]. Does this time frame still work for you?"

Think back to the chess game strategy. Use the moves you make now to set yourself up better for moves later. With the time frame question, you want the hiring manager to know that you are not yet 100 percent on board with the position and the company. You still need to think about the offer, and the discussion that is about to take place (getting your questions answered) may have a considerable impact on your decision. By planting the seed that nothing has been finalized, you will get the hiring manager to take your negotiation requests more seriously. If you have some other opportunities in the works, use the "consider my options" wording to let the hiring manager know you have other options.

Your next question will focus on salary and might go something like this (use your Career Profile to fill in the blanks with your most relevant qualifications):

"I would also like to talk about the salary. I was wondering if the salary is negotiable [if there is flexibility with the salary]. [no pause] The reason why I ask is because I believe I can add considerable value to the department with my skills in _____, training in _____, and experience in _____. And I was hoping we could get the salary closer to _____ [or, I was hoping we could elevate the salary up to _____]."

Or

"Given how well my credentials align with the position, especially with my skills in _____, training in _____, and experience in _____, I was hoping we could explore a slightly higher salary of _____.[2] I know I can get off to a fast start and contribute immediately."

You don't have to follow these scripts exactly. Feel free to modify them to fit your particular situation.

Once you initiate the conversation, you can either be silent and wait to hear what the hiring manager says (although sometimes awkward, this can often be the best approach), or you can tack on one of the following questions:

"How can we elevate the salary up to [or, closer to] this level?"

"Is there a way to elevate the salary up to this level?"

If you are nervous about using this approach, you can merely ask if the salary is negotiable. If the answer is yes, you will then feel more comfortable asking for a higher salary because the hiring manager has opened the door for this conversation. You can then state your case by adding your justification and asking for what makes sense based on your research.

While the above salary negotiation tactics are highly effective, use your best judgment for your situation. If you have inside information that points toward a more effective and appropriate negotiation strategy, go with what you know will work best. In one case, a job candidate in the real estate development field negotiated a higher salary because she said she didn't want her husband making more than she made. The employer gave the candidate the increase and hired her. This isn't a recommended strategy, but it did work for this person and her unique situation. In most cases, your justification will focus on how well you can do the job and the qualifications you bring to the position. It could also focus on what the market is paying:

> "I would also like to talk about the salary. Based on my research, comparable companies are paying between _____ and _____ for Risk Specialist positions. The average falls around _____. Given this, and considering my skills and experience in _____, I was hoping to earn _____." [Alternatives: "I was wondering if we could explore a slightly higher starting salary of _____" or "I was hoping to get closer to _____."]

How high you elevate the salary will depend on the initial salary offered, the benefits package presented, other perks provided, the value you bring to the position and the company (training, experience, education, and skills), and the salary range for the type of position, company, and field. Do your research and then determine what makes the most sense for your situation. Use platforms like Glassdoor, Indeed, Levels.fyi, LinkedIn, Payscale, Salary.com, and The Salary Project to research salary ranges and determine an appropriate range for the current position. Additionally, ask members of your relationship team for input and guidance.

Most job candidates will seek a 10 to 15 percent salary increase over the initial offer, but as mentioned before, the percentage will depend on a number of factors, and it may be as high as 20 percent or as low as 5 percent.

If the employer doesn't move on your salary negotiation request or only accommodates you a little, you can find other ways to elevate the salary. Here is an example:

"I understand you can't increase the starting salary. However, given that I match up well with the position and believe I can hit the ground running and add considerable value, could we build in an earlier review—a six-month review—with a merit increase if I am meeting or exceeding expectations? This would allow you to observe my work during the first six months and then increase my salary based on my performance."

Here is another example:

"I understand you can't increase the salary. However, since there is a gap between the value I believe I bring to the position and the current offer, I was wondering if there is a way we could make up the difference in other areas [or, could we make up the difference by adding _____ and _____?]."

For the greatest payoff, you should focus on areas that will provide you with more annual compensation. Besides salary, this would include annual performance bonuses and stock options, assuming they are available. Negotiating a signing bonus or relocation package can also add money to the offer, but these will only increase your salary in the first year.

There are many other things you can negotiate, depending on your position level, the industry, and the type of company. These may include the following:

- Job title
- Remote work
- Flexible schedule
- Performance evaluation date
- Time off
- Professional development funding
- Company equity
- Start date

- Tuition reimbursement
- Cell phone
- Office space
- Equipment and other office supplies
- Project assignments
- Certification and license fees
- Professional association membership fees

Use your best judgment and pick and choose the most important areas to negotiate given your situation and field. And don't get carried away and come across as greedy and unprofessional. If you do, you will lose respect quickly, and you will reduce your negotiating power.

Open and close all your negotiation sessions by thanking the hiring manager for the opportunity. Show your enthusiasm and make sure you receive a revised offer letter that incorporates any changes to the original offer, including anything out of the norm (e.g., a six-month review, increased relocation allowance, remote work, or a signing bonus). Having everything in writing is important, especially if the hiring manager leaves the company prior to your start date.

Accepting the Offer

Take time to think about the job offer and get all your questions answered before you decide to accept or decline. How you handle this stage of the process will say a lot about you and will set the stage for how the employer will view you down the line.

If you ask for four days to make a decision about the offer and then, a day later, decide you want to accept the offer, contact the employer and say you don't need to wait any longer: "I am very excited about the opportunity, and I don't need three more days to decide. I would like to accept the offer now." As long as you have given yourself a day or two to see if you have any questions and resolve any concerns, accept the offer and don't keep the employer waiting.

Hiring managers will appreciate you letting them know as quickly as possible and not leaving your decision to the last minute. At this point, the hiring manager wants you and is anxious to hear about your decision. Accepting the offer early makes the manager feel good and eliminates any concerns about losing you. By accepting the offer sooner rather than later, you also communicate your excitement for the position and the company and begin everything in a positive manner.

Setting the Stage for Your New Job

Your professional, customer service, and above-and-beyond approach doesn't stop once you accept the offer. Now is the time to show the employer you will carry your success mindset right into your new position. Ask the employer what you can do in advance of your start date to get up to speed on the position so you can have an immediate impact. The hiring manager will probably not give you a list or a very long list, but it will show the manager you care about doing a great job from day one. And, if the manager does provide you with some tasks, the tasks will help you succeed and advance in the position.

Always look for ways to show the hiring manager you are willing to go one step beyond everyone else. The halo effect can work just as well at the start of your job as it did at the start of the hiring process. If you impress someone at the very beginning, that person will often continue to be impressed with you over the long haul. Your job is to impress early and often and make your ideal job search a slam dunk while setting yourself up well for a successful long-term career.

Making Your Entire Job Search a Slam Dunk

The Slam Dunk step is what your job search is all about. Your goal is to make each stage of the job search process a slam dunk to moving on to the next stage and ultimately landing and accepting the job offer.

How can you break the script, inspire employers, be remarkable, and land your ideal job? Fortunately for you, this step is missing from most people's job searches, so you will stand out if you complete it.

As you move through the process, pick and choose when you will implement Slam Dunk tactics, and always find a way to stand out during the interview stage of

> "The time your game is most vulnerable is when you're ahead; never let up."
>
> —Rod Laver

the process. You don't need to do anything crazy or gimmicky. Often, all you need to do is apply the Slam Dunk Guiding Principles set forth in the Success Mindset step.

Doing the basics brilliantly across the board may be enough to close the deal in the end, but you don't want to leave anything to chance. Don't assume that being competitive throughout the process is enough to land your ideal job. As Hall of Fame tennis player Rod Laver said, "The time your game is most vulnerable is when you're ahead; never let up."[3] Go beyond competitive, break the script, implement Slam Dunk tactics, stretch higher, and make sure your ideal job search is a slam dunk.

Chapter 18

A SLAM DUNK CAREER

You get whatever accomplishment you are willing to declare.[1]

—GEORGIA O'KEEFFE

Everything presented in this book has been put in place to help you land your ideal job, transition successfully into the workplace, and shine within your job and career. What good is landing your ideal job only to find that you don't have the skills to perform well in the job? Your job search is really about your career—it's about making a smooth transition into a long and successful career where you can advance along your chosen career path and have a significant impact on the world. How well you transition will depend on what you learn along the way and how well you adjust.

An important goal during the job search process and during each career transition is to move closer to who you want to be. Take advantage of your job search to become not only a more appealing job candidate but also a better future employee and a better person.

Everything you do during your job search will feed into your new position and all your future positions. When you look back on your job search, you will want to answer yes to all of the following questions: During my job search, did I

- Identify the value that all my previous jobs and experiences bring to my new job and career?
- Strive to get better during my job search—better as a person, job candidate, and future employee?

- Expand my relationship team and develop deeper relationships?
- Develop my soft skills even further and overcome any critical weaknesses?
- Learn more about my industry and field?
- Become more aware of my strengths, weaknesses, likes, and dislikes?
- Put a solid job search foundation in place to help me throughout my career?
- Develop a success mindset (the Slam Dunk Guiding Principles) with the expectation that I will begin my new job with this same mindset?

Don't ever let a search go by without taking advantage of the process to advance your skills, learn more about yourself and your field, and expand your relationship team. Cherish every job search and always understand its real purpose and value.

As you begin to take the steps outlined in this book and head toward your desired destination, keep the following job search and career tips in mind:

1. **Continue to learn.**

   Find where your gaps are and strive to become better at what you do—better at managing projects, leading people, providing extraordinary customer service, solving complex problems, communicating, getting work done, and helping people. Capitalize on your strengths but always look to improve essential soft skills, including your character and attitude.

2. **Always be the most prepared person in the room.**

   As Super Bowl winning quarterback Russell Wilson said, "The separation is in the preparation."[2]

3. **Put yourself in the employer's or client's shoes and view the world from the other side.**

   Seeing the world from another person's perspective will help you considerably during the job search process and throughout your career, shifting the focus off yourself and making you more compassionate and customer service-oriented.

4. **Find out what is important to the customer (the employer).**

   Ask employers what they need and then do whatever you can to show them you can address their needs better than anyone else. If you don't ask or clarify, you may not know for sure what they want. Show employers how you can add value and generate results that they can't get unless they hire you.

5. **Show you function at a high level even during difficult and challenging times.**

   How you handle stressful and challenging situations during the job search process and in the workplace will show your true character. Follow up with a positive message even when you are turned down for a job, a project, or an award. And always be professional with coworkers, supervisors, and clients.

6. **Tactfully promote yourself.**

   When you get some form of recognition or reach a milestone, update your LinkedIn profile and résumé, modify your professional career website, thank people who helped you along the way, and look for ways to promote yourself in local newspapers, alumni newsletters, local business journals, social media sites, and through personal press releases. Take advantage of the avenues that exist to help you advance your career. Remember, credentials aren't enough. In today's market, you need to show your work and promote yourself.

7. **Understand that everything is connected.**

   When you excel in your job and people know where you went to school, your alma mater's reputation elevates, more students want to attend your school, more employers want to hire graduates from your program, and the value of your degree rises. Also, when you do good work, your company's reputation and credibility advance, your company sells more products or services (helps more customers), and your employer increases your level of responsibility so you can have an even greater impact. Understand the bigger picture and continue to present yourself in a professional manner in every situation. Doing quality work is not just about receiving a paycheck.

8. **Treat others how you would want to be treated.**

    Respect all people and treat everyone fairly and nicely. There is no room for anything less. We all want the same thing: to be accepted for who we are, to excel in life, and to make a difference in the world. The more you can help others get what they want and succeed, the better the world will be—and the more you will excel in your job and get what you want.

9. **Realize that everything great and worthwhile takes effort and some pain.**

    You have probably heard the expression, "It takes 20 years to become an overnight success."[3] Getting to where you want to go may take time. But as long as you are on a path that excites you and you understand that everything you do adds value and gets you closer to who you want to be and what you want to do, you will enjoy the journey and cherish everything along the way. Value all the twists and turns and ups and downs as you work toward realizing your career vision. Each job you hold will change how you think and will provide you with much more value than you ever imagined. You will often find that the most challenging and undervalued situations are the experiences that allow you to grow and advance the most.

10. **Take ownership of everything you do.**

    Boredom and frustration often stem from a lack of creativity and ownership. Treat all your jobs like you own them, and then look for ways to excel in each. It doesn't matter if you are working in your ideal job or a backup job. Find a way to be engaged and inspired. Get as much out of the job as possible, use your creativity to turn your work into something valuable for you and the employer, and know that the experience will come into play down the line in some important way.

11. Understand the importance of having a meaningful career vision in place.

As you embark on your career journey, keep in mind the paraphrased story of the three stonecutters: As three stonecutters in eastern France were working hard at a rock quarry, a visitor asked them what they were doing. Looking exhausted and grumpy, the first said he was cutting the thick stone into a block. The second one, also tired but a little happier, said she was helping build a wall. The third stonecutter, looking energetic and inspired, enthusiastically stood up and said, "I am part of a talented team that is building the largest and most magnificent cathedral in Europe."[4]

In your case, your career vision is the magnificent cathedral—your career masterpiece. You have a purpose and a motivating destination, and all the jobs and activities along the way are the stepping stones that have been put in place to get you to where you are meant to be. There are no straight lines in nature—imperfection leads to perfection. Your path will be unlike any other, and everything along the way will make you unique, special, and invaluable.

Enjoy the Journey

As you move through your career, continue to refine your career vision. Understand that there are no wrong paths as long as you learn something valuable about yourself and uncover the clues that point you toward what you ultimately want to do. Each job you take will more closely reflect who you are as you learn more about yourself and the world around you. The more excited you are about your destination and the path you are on, the more motivated you will be during your job search, and the happier you will be throughout your career.

Continue on the path toward your vision, and each time you need to move from one job to another, use the 6-Step Slam Dunk Job Search Process to help you reach your next goal. You will find the process works well in all types of job markets and with all kinds of jobs. When you combine the right process with the right mindset and tactics, you will often get the results you desire.

If you are true to yourself and you follow the 6-Step Slam Dunk Job Search Process, you will eventually end up reaching your desired destination. Some paths will be short and some long. But no matter what happens, one thing is for sure: Your career path will be unlike any other. And that is good because your unique journey will allow you to bring something different to the world that no one else will bring.

In the end, we only regret the trips we didn't take. Create a vision of what you want, take action toward your vision, trust the process, enjoy your unique journey, wow people along the way, and go out and make each ideal job search a Slam Dunk! Everything you want is available to you now or in the future.

Appendix

RÉSUMÉ AND COVER LETTER DESIGN GUIDELINES

As you read in chapter 7, it is essential to make your résumé and cover letter change-friendly, reader-friendly, and employer-focused. This appendix provides more detailed guidelines as well as additional information about how to design and format these documents, what to include, and how to word content effectively.

Although the guidelines will help you develop impressive marketing documents, you have permission to veer away from the guidelines if you have a better way to do something. Use your best judgment to address each employer's needs and desires effectively.

The guidelines below assume a familiarity with the standard components of résumés and cover letters. If you are unfamiliar with the basics, you might want to skip ahead and look at the examples of an abbreviated résumé and a formal cover letter before continuing with the specific guidelines. Additionally, if you are pursuing federal government positions, you should refer to USAJOBS for comprehensive federal resume content and format guidelines.

Change-Friendly Résumé and Cover Letter

To help you keep your résumé and cover letter change-friendly, use the following guidelines unless you are in a creative field where you may need to add more design elements:

- Use Microsoft Word without headers or footers as your go-to word processing program for designing your documents.
- Use a template only if it allows you to adjust and move content and sections around to market yourself better.
- Design your résumé and cover letter so you can add content without having to make significant design modifications (minimal columns, boxes, tables, vertical lines, fancy logos, shading, and images). Some creativity is fine, but don't get carried away with elaborate design elements unless your field demands it.
- Keep the font and font size the same throughout (except for headings).
- Align text to the left throughout your documents.

Reader-Friendly Résumé

Make it easy for the employer to find the information that is most valuable to them—and therefore to you. Here are some guidelines to help make your résumé reader-friendly:

- Incorporate plenty of white space (margins no less than 0.9 inches on the sides and 0.5 inches on the top and bottom).
- Place the most relevant information toward the top of your résumé.
- Keep the résumé simple. Avoid too much italicizing, bolding, and underlining, and refrain from using different fonts and font sizes.
- Exhibit consistency across the entire résumé and within each section.
- List all your experience in reverse chronological order.
- Use an easy-to-read font and font size. Use 10- to 12-point font, depending on the font style. Consider using Calibri, Arial, Helvetica, Cambria, Garamond, or Verdana for a professional and clean look.
- Create a well-balanced structure: shorter top section, more extended middle section, and a shorter bottom section.
- Develop a visually appealing and engaging look by creating nuggets of readable information (not too bulky). Have plenty of white space between sections, and in most cases, have two to six bullets under each job within the Experience section.

To make your résumé even more reader-friendly, ask yourself, have I

- Included accurate contact information at the top?

- Used my common name at the top of the résumé and not a formal résumé name (e.g., Will Cartwright versus William Grant Cartwright)? A common name can make you appear more approachable and personable, but it's important to consider your audience and brand before making this decision. For example, you might find that you can only get a website domain with your full name. In this case, you will probably develop your brand around your formal name and use it in your marketing documents and on your promotional platforms.
- Listed the city and state where I reside so readers don't need to uncover this information on their own? For privacy and security reasons, exclude your full address.
- Added relevant credentials or certifications (CPA, PE, PhD, RN, PHR, etc.) at the top next to my name so readers can find them quickly?
- Incorporated my LinkedIn and professional career website addresses (or hyperlinks) in the contact information section?
- Used specific headings to grab the reader's attention quickly (Engineering Experience, Marketing Experience, Leadership Experience, Media and Video Project Experience, etc.)?
- Made the bullets within the Experience section one to two lines each so they are easy to scan?
- Covered all significant employment gaps in an Additional Experience section or somewhere else on my résumé?
- Provided dates in the Experience section with both month and year listed? A résumé that excludes months can be a sign that the applicant is hiding gaps or trying to appear more experienced. Listing 2021 to 2022 for the length of employment with a company could mean you worked two full years, two days, or anything in between. Listing only the year is not helpful for hiring managers and recruiters. Your goal is to make their jobs easier.
- Added descriptive words to the job titles so employers can immediately see the link between each job I've had and the position for which I'm applying? For example, change "Project Manager" to "Web Design Project Manager" or "Intern" to "Web Content Intern." Make sure you get permission from the company to change an official job title. If you can't get approval, you can use a different tactic: Project Manager (Web Design) or Intern (Web Content).

- Used subheadings in the Skills section to allow the reader to see a list of pertinent skills quickly and easily (e.g., Computer, Project Management, Leadership, and Language)?
- Shared activities that cover employment gaps and generate interest?

You will need to balance some of these strategies with making your résumé ATS-friendly, especially if you are pursuing opportunities with companies that typically use an applicant tracking system (ATS). For example, some recruitment software favors standardized elements, including one-inch margins on all sides, complete dates for each job (e.g., 08/2021–10/2023 or August 2021–October 2023), and "Experience" headings (Professional Experience, Project Experience, Leadership Experience, etc.).[1]

An ATS can be beneficial because it forces you to keep your documents simple, clean, professional, and consistent. Moreover, it serves as a reminder of why it's important to ensure your documents also reach a real person—the hiring manager.

Since recruitment software is rapidly evolving, design your résumé to address employers' needs first and then run the résumé through an ATS online résumé reviewer to ensure everything will translate well. And, unless the company asks for a PDF, submit your documents in Microsoft Word if you know the company uses an ATS. Some applicant tracking systems have difficulty reading certain types of PDFs. To cover all your bases, send both a Word document and a PDF. The PDF will work best for mobile viewing, while the Word document will work well for the ATS. Do whatever you can to market yourself effectively and make the hiring manager's and recruiter's jobs easier.

Reader-Friendly Cover Letter

Your cover letter is often the first document an employer sees, so it is essential to make a good first impression. Here are some guidelines to help make your cover letter reader-friendly:

- Create the same look as your résumé (same font, margins, and top heading) to ensure consistency across all your marketing materials.
- Develop a visually appealing and engaging document: plenty of white space and well organized.
- Run your cover letter through a digital writing assistance tool like Grammarly or QuillBot to ensure it is well written, and then make sure each paragraph transitions effectively to the next.

- Check the date, job title, and company name to confirm they are accurate for each job you pursue.
- Address the letter to the hiring manager (specific name and correct spelling).
- Keep paragraphs between three and seven lines.
- Use the same font throughout with minimal bolding, italics, and underlining.
- Create a well-balanced letter with similar-sized paragraphs or a paragraph-bullet combination format (more on this below).
- Align the text to the left, including the date and signature.

To make your cover letter even more reader-friendly, ask yourself, have I

- Come up with an engaging, memorable, and relevant opening line (e.g., "Why is a small-town Kansas designer interested in and qualified for an upscale interior design position in New York City?" or "I am a coding fanatic.")?
- Included a referral or a connection at the start?
- Grabbed attention or expressed interest in the job and the company through relevant projects completed, articles read, conversations with key people, or something else that conveys my genuine passion, especially if I don't have a referral, strong connection, or memorable opening?
- Included bullets in the middle to grab the reader's eye and communicate relevant credentials quickly?
- Added some hooks (numbers, percentages, awards, company names, etc.) to bring my accomplishments to life and add variety and intrigue to the letter?
- Ended the cover letter with something interesting and memorable that makes mine different from the other hundreds of cover letters employers receive for each position (e.g., "I have spent time researching Northbrook's competitors. In addition to discussing my qualifications, I would be happy to share some ideas I have for enhancing Northbrook's current marketing campaign.")?

Employer-Focused Résumé

Don't make the mistake of thinking that your résumé is all about you. If you want to impress employers and grab their attention, reset your thinking and make your résumé about connecting with employers. There are many ways to make your résumé employer-focused:

- Add one or two value statements to the top of your résumé that directly relate to the position requirements in the form of a unique value proposition tagline or Summary of Qualifications section (more on each of these below).

- Show alignment with the company's needs and culture; for example, if the employer values a commitment to diversity, equity, and inclusion (DEI) or leadership skills, showcase relevant affiliations or roles on your resume (e.g., President of the Latinx Student Association).

- Craft effective job description bullets that show the results of your work and start with descriptive and relevant action verbs. Use the following formula: Action Verb + Numbers = Outcome (e.g., "Organized and promoted an Invitational Games charity event for 1,200 employees that raised $100,000+ and generated employee goodwill."). Or you can incorporate more of the "how" in your work: Action You Took + Methods You Used + Numbers = Outcome (e.g., "Used the 6-Step Slam Dunk Job Search Process to place 100 percent of job seekers in rewarding positions within a 45-day average; exceeded prior-year placement statistics by 28 percent.").

- Scatter key terminology (buzzwords from the job announcement) strategically throughout the résumé.

- Use some Curiosity Statements with intriguing and relevant words (unique, innovative, cutting-edge, state-of-the-art, etc.) to generate interest (e.g., "Created an innovative recruitment strategy that attracted top candidates and resulted in a 92 percent three-year retention rate.").

- Build some comparisons into your bullets to show you go beyond others (e.g., "Closed 15 more claims each month than the other six adjusters.").

- Include company names and key acronyms within your bullets (e.g., "Worked on 15 Life Cycle Assessment (LCA) consulting projects, including projects with Northrop Enterprises and Marin Cloud Services Inc.").

- List skills that align well with the position requirements and add specific subheadings for each (e.g., Computer, Communication, Language, and Data Analysis).

- Add relevant certifications.

- Show commitment to the field by listing professional association memberships and leadership roles within each.

- Bring yourself to life by sharing some unique or impressive activities.

Length

Either a one- or a two-page résumé is fine as long as you base the length on what is appropriate for your background and each employer. For example, if you have an option on what length to use (given the employer and industry) and you have very diverse and scattered work experience, you may want to condense your most relevant credentials into a one-page résumé to show more focus. On the other hand, if you have a lot of relevant experience, training, and skills, a two-page résumé may work best to showcase your depth of experience and expertise.

If you are pursuing opportunities in fast-paced or entrepreneurial organizations, a one-page résumé may be more appropriate. Consulting firms and corporations also often value people who can produce an impressive one-page marketing document. In contrast, if you want to land a position within a government agency or an academic setting, a two-page (or sometimes longer) résumé would work best. The more you know what employers want and your field requires, the more you can meet or exceed expectations.

If nothing points you toward a particular length, focus on the employer's needs, make your résumé visually appealing, guide the reader where they want to go, and keep your résumé to no more than two pages.

Structure

The structure of your résumé will also depend on your background and audience. When it comes to résumé design, in most cases, form follows function.

If you are a recent college graduate with less experience, you may use a traditional one-page résumé format with the following sections: Education, Experience, Additional Experience, and Skills, Affiliations, and Activities (the last three all in one section). The Education section will often be placed at or near the top of the résumé and will provide much of the selling power, particularly if it adds considerable value and frames your focus.

If the Education section is strong but doesn't frame your focus well, a unique value proposition tagline (e.g., "Innovative interior designer with a reputation for exceeding client expectations.") can precede the Education section to get employers viewing you the right way as they start to move down your résumé. If the Education section doesn't effectively market your qualifications because you have stronger qualifications in other areas, a Summary of Qualifications section (three to six key qualifications with no more than seven lines total) can precede your Education section to pull everything together and market your credentials effectively from the start. With a one-page résumé, this section will need to be concise (three to four hard-hitting bullets).

Some students will graduate with a full suite of technical skills. If you are one of these students, and the skills you acquired are relevant to your career, incorporate them into the Education section or move the Skills section toward the top of your résumé (right below the Education section).

If you are a more experienced job seeker with a two-page résumé, you will include a Summary of Qualifications section at the top of page one to package all key credentials and accomplishments in one place at the start. A tagline could precede the Summary of Qualifications section, depending on how everything looks and what makes sense for the job. You will then add your Experience section and place your Education section closer to the bottom. You could include a Skills section toward the top (below your Summary of Qualifications section) if it helps you stand out more or move it to the bottom as an effective close.

Whether you are a recent graduate or an experienced professional, continue to adjust your résumé to market your credentials in the best way possible. As mentioned before, form should follow function.

At every stage of the job search process, consider your background and audience before developing a strategy for how you will package your credentials and promote yourself. And remember that you have permission to break the rules if you have inside information that points you in a different direction. Your focus should be on employers' needs, and you should address their needs even if it means breaking away from the norm. Think about what adds the most value, and then act like an artist and move information and sections around to present yourself in the most convincing way.

Value Statements

Use value statements to guarantee your résumé is employer-focused. To tap into employers' emotions and help them visualize you in the position from the very start, use one or both of the following tactics at the start of your résumé (You can find an example of each value statement in the sample resume at the end of this section.):

1. **Unique Value Proposition (UVP) Tagline**

   Example: "Experienced event planner with a reputation for creating memorable events at half the cost."

   Here is a simple formula for developing unique value proposition taglines:

   Professional _____ with a reputation for _____.

   Experienced _____ known for _____.

   Innovative _____ skilled at _____.

   Accomplished _____ with experience in _____.

   Creative _____ with expertise in _____.

   Resourceful _____ with a proven ability to _____.

   Skilled _____ with a unique ability to _____.

   You can mix and match the wording to craft the most relevant UVP tagline. Here is another example of a tagline using this formula: "Accomplished Michelin Star chef known for creative and award-winning French cuisine." You can also use the UVP tagline as the branding statement for your promotional platforms and the career value statement for your Career Profile. They are interchangeable, and the formula works well for developing any of them.

2. **Summary of Qualifications Section**

   List your most relevant and impressive qualifications using bullet points. Keep the list between three and six bullets and no more than seven lines total. Your goal is to get the employer to want to find out more about each of these qualifications within other areas of your résumé.

Whether you use one or both of these (or neither) will depend on your background, where you are in your career, how you design your résumé, what content you have available, and what adds the most value.

Here is an example of an abbreviated (only one previous job included) resume with both value statements exhibited (Please note that most one-page resumes will eliminate the Summary of Qualifications section or have fewer bullets.):

EMILIA SANCHEZ

San Diego, California
esanchez@example.com | (619) 555-1234
professionalcareerwebsite.com | LinkedIn Profile (hyperlinked)

Experienced event planner with a reputation for creating memorable events at half the cost.

SUMMARY OF QUALIFICATIONS

- More than 5 years of experience designing, organizing, and managing small and large corporate events
- Master's degree in Hospitality Management (expected May 20XX) and bachelor's degree in Communication
- Expertise in event management software, contract negotiations, social media, client relations, and crisis management
- Coordinated 30+ events each year while consistently maintaining a 90% average satisfaction rating
- Known for producing state-of-the-art events that appeal to the 5 senses and make people feel special
- Strong interest in the apparel industry combined with advanced textile knowledge

EDUCATION

Master of Science in Hospitality Management, 4.0 GPA (expected May 20XX)

University of Northbrook, San Diego, California

  Awards: Graduate Student of the Year Award

  Leadership: Vice President of the Event Planning Association

  Highlighted Coursework: Hospitality Management and Guest Services, Financial Management, Human Resources, Event Production, Sustainability, Legal and Regulatory Aspects, Food Services, Vendor Negotiations

Bachelor of Arts in Communication with a Minor in Art Studio, 3.79 GPA (May 20XX)

Weston East College, Marin, California

  Honors: *magna cum laude,* College Honors Program

  Leadership: Head Team Captain Coordinator for Relay For Life, Special Olympics Coach

  Highlighted Coursework: Mass Communication, Public Speaking, Media Writing, Photojournalism, Principles of Public Relations, Storyboarding, Website Design, Strategic Marketing, Art and Design, Digital Photography

CORPORATE EVENT PLANNING EXPERIENCE

Senior Event Planner – Worth Innovation, Eatonville, CA (6/XX–7/XX)

- Orchestrated 30+ board meetings, sales and charity events, and conferences annually for 25 to 2500 people
- Created, organized, coordinated, and promoted an Invitational Games charity event for 1,200 employees, raising $100,000+ and generating employee goodwill
- Spearheaded a professional conference for 750 attendees at a major hotel; came in under budget by 28%, with 97% of participants rating the event as "Excellent"
- Designed decorations for limited-budget events using all-natural materials; received the following one-word comments: superb, stunning, special, memorable, amazing, incredible, and gorgeous
- Used social media (Facebook, Instagram, X, LinkedIn) to promote events to 10,000+ followers, increasing average registration by more than 20%

SKILLS, AFFILIATIONS, AND ACTIVITIES

Computer: Event Software (Trello, Eventbrite), Customer Relationship Management Tools (Salesforce, Insightly), Microsoft Office (Excel, Word, PowerPoint), Social Media (X, Facebook, Instagram, LinkedIn)
Writing: Designed marketing materials in Canva and Infogram; edited a 12-page monthly newsletter for 3 years
Event Planning: Client/VIP Relations, Budgeting, Crisis Management, Food Preparation, Project Management
Affiliations: National Association for Catering and Events, San Diego Arts Initiative Board
Activities: Hiked the entire 2,650-mile Pacific Crest Trail solo; competed in golf tournaments since the age of 10

Some of the sections in the résumé example might be moved, minimized, or changed depending on a job seeker's situation and audience. A few sections (Summary of Qualifications, Education, and Skills, Affiliations, and Activities) could be shortened, depending on your background, audience, and overall situation. They were left a little longer in this example to provide you with additional content to consider.

Job seekers with more experience and expertise will remove the coursework from their résumés and move the Education section toward the bottom. Know your audience, and then look at your résumé through the hiring manager's eyes to present yourself in the most effective way for each employer. Continue to think like a salesperson and act like an artist throughout the entire job search process.

Employer-Focused Cover Letter

A cover letter is an introduction to your résumé and your most relevant credentials. Your cover letter could be the first document hiring managers will read, so it must grab attention quickly and show managers why they should look at your résumé and consider you for the available position. For a hiring manager to be interested in you, your cover letter must focus on the position, department, and company needs. In other words, your cover letter must be employer-focused, not a generic letter that is written for any company or position.

Length

Some career coaches tell job seekers to write short (half page) cover letters, while other coaches recommend longer (one full page) letters. And you will see everything in between. Except in academic settings, most cover letters should not exceed one page, but within that guideline, the ideal length for a cover letter depends on your audience (field, sector, company, and position).

Unless you have inside information that points you in a different direction, send a one-page combination "paragraph-bullet" cover letter (explained below) through the formal online application portal and then send a shorter "email" cover letter of no more than 225 words directly to the hiring manager (see the Relationship Team step for examples). This two-pronged approach works well for most industries, companies, and positions, and it doesn't rely on one format (short or long) for all job searches. Additionally, by getting your materials in front of the hiring manager, you avoid relying entirely on human resources personnel or recruitment software to get you in the door.

Structure

Strong writers might use three- to seven-line paragraphs throughout their cover letters to tell convincing stories and engage readers. Unfortunately, writing doesn't come naturally for many people, and writing traditional one-page cover letters during the job search process is not something most job seekers feel comfortable doing.

Use a combination paragraph-bullet cover letter format to help communicate your value more effectively and make it easier to write your cover letters. This format accomplishes two goals: 1) helps job seekers feel comfortable writing and modifying effective cover letters, and 2) presents employers with easy-to-read and engaging documents that provide them with everything they need to know at a quick glance. A paragraph-bullet format includes the following:

1. An engaging opening paragraph that grabs attention, expresses interest, and lays the foundation for the rest of the letter.
2. A paragraph (or two) that tells a story, highlights accomplishments, and describes your most relevant core credentials.
3. A bullet section that grabs attention and highlights specific qualifications with hooks (e.g., numbers, company names, computer programs, and key skills).
4. A second-to-last paragraph that pulls in some soft skills or special qualities.
5. An engaging closing paragraph that shows passion and fit.

The goal of your cover letter is to engage the reader and get them to want to know more about you. While the Relationship Team step provided you with shorter "email" cover letter examples, the following section will provide you with an approach you can take to design a more traditional one-page cover letter that is sent to human resources through an online application portal. You can also include the traditional cover letter as an attachment when you send a shorter email cover letter directly to the hiring manager.

With your Career Profile content already in place, you can now use the SD Triangle Offense framework (interest, core credentials, uniqueness, and fit) to help you design and write a traditional cover letter that is employer-focused. The following sections explain how to structure your cover letter using the SD Triangle Offense and a paragraph-bullet format.

Opening Paragraph (Interest)

Show interest in the organization and position through a strong opening line or story, and then lay the foundation (a one-sentence foundational statement) for why the employer should be interested in you. To grab attention, always open with an interesting story, a referral, a connection to the organization, praise for the company, key qualifications, or passion for the field or the company.

Example

While living and working in the Netherlands, I was impressed with the corporate movement toward increasing renewable energy use to mitigate carbon emissions, reduce costs, and limit future risk. With professional experience and advanced coursework in energy efficiency, business, and environmental communication, I am interested in bringing the same Dutch spirit I learned abroad to US corporations as an Energy Efficiency Consultant at Greenridge Consulting.

Example

Helping improve energy efficiency within corporations is my passion and expertise. With more than six years of experience in the energy sector, a master's degree in energy management, and a certificate in energy efficiency, I am confident I can make a strong contribution to the Energy Efficiency Consultant position within your department at Greenridge Consulting.

Second and Third Paragraph (Core Credentials)

In the second and third paragraphs (use one or two paragraphs here, depending on your qualifications), support your foundational statement by describing how your most relevant credentials align with the core job requirements. You will also weave in relevant examples, specifics, or stories about your accomplishments.

Example

With experience in environmental research, consulting, and reporting, I am well versed in helping corporations understand and reduce their carbon footprint. At Greenleaf Performance Group, I collaborated with 12 entertainment companies to reduce waste and increase efficiency in offices and on sets. I also worked on the 60,000-person Global Reach Festival, where I helped ease the event's carbon footprint by 4,169 tons and developed a comprehensive sustainability report.

I have a proven record of exceeding client expectations by effectively managing teams and working closely with stakeholders, from business executives and public officials to concerned community members. I also have extensive training in strategic environmental communication, which will allow me to analyze the scientific and financial implications of a project and communicate them effectively.

Bullet Section (Specific Core Credentials)

Within the bullet section, highlight three to six hard-hitting skills directly related to the position requirements. Show you have the specific skills to do the job and do it well.

Example

Please consider some additional qualifications I would bring to the Energy Efficiency Consultant position:

- **Advanced Education**—Completed graduate degree in energy sustainability from Eastern Cascade University with a specialization in strategic environmental communication.
- **Energy and Climate Expertise**—Conducted cost-benefit analyses and project valuations, both environmental and financial, for a variety of energy alternatives. Completed courses in Energy and Technology, Energy and Resource Productivity, and Life Cycle Assessment (LCA).
- **Project Management**—Led a 3-person sustainability team and consulted with television executives to secure representation for 15 eco-friendly brands.

Directed a 4-person team responsible for 1,100+ Relay For Life participants, raising $150,000+ for cancer research.

- **Business and Financial Modeling Certificate, Wharton Executive Education**—Completed courses in Quantitative Modeling, Spreadsheets and Models, Modeling Risk and Realities, and Decision Making and Scenarios.
- **Environmental Standards**—Trained in CEQA/NEPA regulations and greenhouse gas (GHG) accounting and reporting standards. Received LEED Green Associate certification.

Employers don't have much time to review documents, so you will benefit considerably by adding bullets to your cover letter to highlight key qualifications. Each bullet needs to add considerable value for the employer and the position. If you feel you have covered enough of your key credentials in other areas of the cover letter, you can use the bulleted section to highlight relevant and significant accomplishments. If done right, a bulleted section jumps out, is easy to read, and adds value quickly.

Second-to-Last Paragraph (Uniqueness)

As you move into the second-to-last paragraph, include something that is unique. What is special and memorable about you? This could include soft skills, a testimonial, an extracurricular activity, or an experience that sets you apart. If you have focused on technical skills in other areas, you may want to highlight nontechnical skills here. On the other hand, if you have focused on nontechnical skills in other areas, use this paragraph to touch on your technical skills. Employers often like well-rounded employees who can step in and do a quality job with any task (technical or nontechnical).

Example

Beyond my technical skills, my supervisors have always commented on my resourcefulness and self-motivation. I have a reputation for overcoming obstacles and constraints to get projects done on time, and I would bring this same drive and creativity to the energy division at Greenridge Consulting. Additionally, with my three years of experience playing on a university soccer team, I have developed strong teamwork and leadership skills—two skills I know are important to the consulting position.

Last Paragraph (Fit)

Close with a statement that shows fit (and passion):

> With my technical credentials and nontechnical skills, I am excited to
> hit the ground running and help corporations mitigate environmental
> impacts and improve their bottom line. I would welcome the oppor-
> tunity to meet with you to share the contributions I could make as an
> Energy Efficiency Consultant in your division [or, I would welcome the
> opportunity to share how I could help you and your team reach your
> goals]. I look forward to hearing from you.

Keep your cover letter to one page with plenty of white space, and keep most of your
paragraphs between three and seven lines. The cover letter example that follows is
a one-pager that pulls from the content presented above. Some content was excluded
from the example and modified to make the cover letter more reader-friendly (visually
appealing). More content was included above to provide you with additional material
to explore. Always adjust the length of your documents to fit your audience and field.

Remember, you are the artist, and you can design your cover letter in whatever
way helps you effectively market your qualifications for each position. For example, you
could have three shorter paragraphs at the top (above the bullets) rather than two, or you
could have one paragraph at the bottom (below the bullets) rather than two. Additionally, you could include three, four, five, or even six bullets, depending on the length of
the bullets and the significance of the content. Just make sure your cover letter is visually
appealing and balanced. No matter what you do, know your audience, and make certain
your documents are change-friendly, reader-friendly, and employer-focused.

The SD Triangle Offense cover letter structure can work just as well for
executive-level positions as it does for internship or fellowship opportunities. Get
the content down on paper, and then use the SD Triangle Offense structure to form
a compelling letter that incorporates all the core elements needed to advance you
through the process. And whenever you pursue a posted position, send a formal cover
letter (described here) through the online application portal and a shorter "email"
cover letter message (described in chapter 12) directly to the hiring manager.

JORDAN DAVIS

Seattle, Washington

jdavis@example.com | (206) 555-1234

professionalcareerwebsite.com | LinkedIn Profile (hyperlinked)

April 28, 20XX

Sally Mackay

Director

Greenridge Consulting

Seattle, Washington

Dear Sally:

While living and working in the Netherlands, I was impressed with the corporate movement toward increasing renewable energy use to mitigate carbon emissions, reduce costs, and limit future risk. With professional experience and graduate-level coursework in energy efficiency, business, and environmental communication, I am interested in bringing the same Dutch spirit to Greenridge Consulting as an Energy Efficiency Consultant.

I am well versed in helping corporations understand and reduce their carbon footprint. At Greenleaf Performance Group, I collaborated with 12 entertainment companies to reduce waste and increase efficiency in offices and on sets. I also worked on the 60,000-person Global Reach Festival, where I helped ease the event's carbon footprint by 4,169 tons and developed a comprehensive sustainability report. Additionally, I have a proven record of exceeding client expectations by effectively managing teams and working closely with stakeholders. And with extensive training in strategic environmental communication, I can analyze a project's scientific and financial implications and communicate them effectively.

Please consider some additional qualifications I would bring to the Energy Efficiency Consultant position:

- **Advanced Education**—Completed graduate degree in energy sustainability from Eastern Cascade University with a specialization in strategic environmental communication.
- **Energy and Climate Expertise**—Conducted cost-benefit analyses and project valuations, both environmental and financial, for various energy alternatives. Completed courses in Energy and Technology, Energy and Resource Productivity, and Life Cycle Assessment (LCA).
- **Project Management**—Led a 3-person sustainability team and consulted with television executives to secure representation for 15 eco-friendly brands. Directed a 4-person team responsible for 1,100+ Relay For Life participants, raising $150,000+ for cancer research.
- **Business and Financial Modeling Certificate, Wharton Executive Education**—Completed courses in Quantitative Modeling, Spreadsheets and Models, and Modeling Risk and Realities.

Beyond my technical skills, my supervisors have always commented on my resourcefulness and self-motivation. I have a reputation for overcoming obstacles and constraints to get projects done on time, and I would bring this same drive and creativity to the energy division at Greenridge Consulting.

I am excited to hit the ground running and help corporations mitigate environmental impacts and improve their bottom line. I would welcome the opportunity to meet with you to share the contributions I could make as an Energy Efficiency Consultant in your division. Thank you.

Sincerely,

Jordan Davis

Attachment: Résumé

Employer-Focused Tools

As you develop employer-focused documents, consider using chatbots (e.g., ChatGPT) to help you through the process. Chatbots are highly efficient tools powered by artificial intelligence (AI) that use natural language processing to answer questions and assist with routine tasks. For instance, chatbots can help you brainstorm ideas, create a list of target organizations, pinpoint keywords in job announcements, and even uncover interview questions for specific roles (e.g., "What are the most common behavioral interview questions for a data analyst position?"). They can also help you determine a company's potential challenges, identify your most important selling points (by comparing a job posting to your résumé), and proofread your documents.

While chatbots can be invaluable during your job search, it's important to remember that they are not perfect. As a result, always exercise caution and common sense when using any automated or AI-related platform. You should also educate yourself on the ethical concerns of using AI-generated content. Additionally, make sure you avoid using these tools to write documents and messages for you, especially since employers can often determine if a chatbot generated your cover letter, résumé, or email message.

Use chatbots to generate ideas, extract keywords, compare documents, provide examples, answer questions, check your work, and access information quickly. Seek assistance, but then write your messages and documents in your own words and voice to ensure they appear genuine and sincere.

Quality Control

As mentioned in chapter 7, don't forget to use the Antique Store Editing Approach and other tools like Grammarly, QuillBot, and ChatGPT to check your work. Everything needs to be done at a high level, and you must do whatever you can to deliver a quality product to the employer.

Acknowledgments

I didn't get to where I am on my own. Many people have played a significant role in allowing me to make a difference in other people's lives, and many people have played a key role in helping me make this book a success. I have numerous talented and generous people to thank.

First, dear reader, thank you for investing your time with me. I know there are many other things you could be doing with your time, so I never take for granted your decision to purchase and read my book. This book was written for you. It was written to help you get from where you are to where you want to be. Thank you for believing in me and allowing me to guide you toward your desired destination.

I would also like to thank all the job seekers who trusted me through the years. You have been my inspiration and have made my job so rewarding. You followed the process, took action, and ultimately got to where you wanted to go. Thank you for staying true to yourself and making the world a better place through your unique talents and passions. You are making a difference every day.

I am forever grateful to my immediate family for supporting me through the book-writing process. I appreciate your willingness to allow me to allocate so much time to help serve others and express my passion and creativity. At times, it seemed like this book was a 24/7 endeavor. Often, my best work was completed during vacations and on trips when I had time to think and reflect on what would help job seekers the most. Caryn, Emi, and Will: Thank you for giving me the time, flexibility, support, and guidance throughout the process. You mean the world to me.

An immense thank you to my parents, Gay and David Parker, and my grandparents, Adele and Joseph Horton, for all their guidance and support. I cannot begin to articulate the extent of your impact on my career and life. Thank you for setting me on the right path and making the journey memorable and remarkable.

A very special thank you to my daughter, Emi, for reading the manuscript numerous times and offering constructive feedback. You provided a different perspective and had me view the manuscript in a new light, making the book so much more relevant for all readers. Thank you for your excellent feedback.

A huge thank you goes to a prior colleague and close friend, bj Danetra, for providing me with both encouragement and direction. You were there every time I came to a fork in the road and needed feedback or input. Your advice always got me back on track. Thank you for your friendship, support, and guidance.

I owe an enormous debt of gratitude to all the talented people who gave me detailed and constructive feedback during the editing and design phases. A heartfelt thank you to Mara Eller for helping me bring the book across the finish line. You are an extraordinary editor, and this book is much better because of your terrific work. I appreciate all your creativity, patience, expertise, and enthusiasm. Thank you for caring so much about me and my manuscript. You made the editing process a slam dunk, and you were a joy to work with throughout the entire process.

I am very thankful I was able to work with Brian Baker during both the editing and publishing stages. Brian always went the extra mile to help me through the process. Thank you for answering all my questions and sharing your expertise. You were incredible to work with, and I appreciate all your help.

I would also like to express my appreciation to Jordan Faires, Sharon Goldinger, Tia Kordell, Kelly Lydick, Claire Madden, and Heather Pendley for their adept feedback and edits. Your suggestions were right on target, and they made the book much better. Thank you for sharing your time and perspective with me.

I was very fortunate to have one of my editors refer me to George Stevens for the book's design. I couldn't have asked for a better person to collaborate with on the interior look. Thank you, George. You did a fantastic job. You took the time to understand me, my brand, and my clients' needs, and you added your creativity to bring the book to life. Thank you for your calm demeanor, excellent communication, and expert design skills. I thoroughly enjoyed working with you.

I was also fortunate to find a talented book cover designer. A huge thank you goes out to Miladinka Milic for creating a stunning cover and turning my vision into reality. You were always so accessible and responsive. Thank you for your help and patience.

I am also very grateful I had a group of generous people I could immediately turn to for information, referrals, ideas, examples, stories, testimonials, illustrations, general feedback, and support. A big thank you goes out to Dr. David Abramis, Ian Adam, Dr. Satie Airamé, Dr. Sarah Anderson, Amanda Asquith-Caya, Gina Auriemma, James Badham, Fahmida Bangert, Becca Barnett, Owen Barrett, Lindsay Bass, Andrew Bilich, Kristi Birney, Dr. Jonah Busch, Lisa Campbell, Marc Campopiano, Alandra Michelle Chavarria, Hazel Clegg, Tim Cohen, Ann Haldeman Coppe, Katherine Coppe, Dr. Laurie Counihan-Childs, Yasmin Cronin, Joy Culley, Ariel Curry, Mark D'Antoni, Lacrissa Davis, Sage Davis, Jaime Dietenhofer, Jennifer DuBuisson, Tyson Eckerle, Doug Ellis, Michael Esquivel, Becky Flansburg, Chris Fletcher, Dr. Elissa Foster, Emma Friedl, Kim Fugate, Dr. Steve Gaines, Casey Garrett, Onella Gayraud, Michelle Graff, Dean Graziosi, Bob Haldeman, Jo Haldeman, Susan Haldeman, Ann Hayden, J.J. Hebert, Bryan Henson, Brad Hill, Caroline Holmes, Milly Horton, Monica Illes, Dana Jennings, Eleanor Johnstone, Adam Jorge, John Jostes, Lexi Journey, Stacy Katz, Dr. Bruce Kendall, Marilyn Keys, Kellen Klein, Kate Kokosinski, Matt Koller, Anjana Krishnan, Jess LaGreca, Julia Coke Lampe, Josh Levine, Briny Litchfield, Dr. Don Lubach, Aliana Lungo-Sharpiro, Janell Madison, Brooke Malik, Daisy Martinez, Jill Matteson, Louisa McGuirk, Joaquin Meckler-Pacheco, Anne Middleton, Steve Miley, Michael Millstein, Chris Minton, Lillian Mirviss, Lena Moffitt, Kavitha Nambiar, Derek Nguyen, John Onderdonk, Matt Panopio, Dr. Amy Parker, Brie Parker, Caryn Parker, Chris Parker, Cody Parker, Joe Parker, Lori Parker, Will Parker, Jason Peery, Beth Pitton-August, Ruben Sanchez Ramirez, Dr. Jill Richardson, Dr. Kristen Robinson, Tom Rogowski, Laura Lea Rubino, Dr. Bess Ruff, Jessica Sager, Miya Scheble, Dr. Phil Selinsky, Jota Shohtoku, Sabrina Skelly, Erica Slowik, Krista Soukup, Molly Steen, Caitlin Swalec, Dawnielle Tellez, Alisan Theodossiou, Brian Tracy, Allison Turner, Dr. Lotus Vermeer, Harry Vickers, Elise Wall, Rebecca Webb, Erin Williamson, Patti Winans, and Eric Zimmerman. Thank you for all your assistance and support.

In addition to expressing my gratitude to everyone who helped me, I must recognize the significant role my dog, Milo, played in getting me through the late-night hours of writing and refining my manuscript. He kept me calm and focused, and I am very thankful to have had him by my side throughout this incredible journey.

The path I have taken to get to where I am is unique. My path started in the alfalfa fields and packing sheds in Palisade, Colorado, worked its way through the retail industry and into the retail buying offices in downtown Los Angeles, meandered through a variety of organizational development consulting engagements, made a turn into human resources, and then moved on to career development. Many people helped me along the way, and each job got me one step closer to what I was meant to be and do. And, most importantly, each experience has played a key role in allowing me to bring something unique to my clients that no one else can bring.

> *When you want something, all the universe*
> *conspires in helping you to achieve it.*[1]

—**PAULO COELHO**

Notes

Introduction

1. Flavia Medrut, "25 Michael Jordan Quotes That Are Ingredients for Guaranteed Success," Goalcast, February 11, 2020, https://www.goalcast.com/2020/02/11/michael-jordan-quotes/.

Step 1: Career Design

1. Asad Meah, "38 Inspirational Quotes on Vision," Awaken The Greatness Within, March 15, 2017, https://www.awakenthegreatnesswithin.com/38-inspirational-quotes-on-vision/.

Chapter 1

1. Lewis Carroll, *Alice's Adventures in Wonderland* (London: Macmillan and Co., 1865), 71-72.
2. Anonymous, in-person advising session by author, June 4, 2014.
3. Dean Graziosi, *Millionaire Success Habits* (Phoenix: Growth Publishing, 2017), 34.
4. Peter Burns, "7 Viktor Frankl Quotes to Motivate You to Find Your Purpose," Medium, April 7, 2020, https://medium.com/mind-cafe/7-viktor-frankl-quotes-to-motivate-you-to-find-your-purpose-2ece0c64f1d8.
5. Andre Cronje, "Discover Your Why, Seven Levels Deep," Digital Bloggers, August 24, 2017, https://digitalbloggers.com/business/Discover-Your-Why-Seven-Levels-Deep.
6. Maryam Mohsin, "10 Small Business Statistics Every Future Entrepreneur Should Know in 2021," Oberlo, December 2, 2020, https://www.oberlo.com/blog/small-business-statistics.

7. Alyssa Yeo, "The Story of Two Wolves," Urban Balance, February 24, 2016, https://urbanbalance.com/the-story-of-two-wolves/.

Step 2: Success Mindset

1. "13 of the Best Life Lessons from Marianne Williamson," Oprah. com, accessed August 12, 2021, https://www.oprah.com/quote-lis t/13-of-the-best-life-lessons-from-marianne-williamson.

2. Matt Bonesteel, "Little Kid Asks Good Questions at NCAA Tournament News Conference, Impressing South Carolina Coach," *The Washington Post*, March 26, 2017, https://www.washingtonpost.com/news/early-lead/wp/2017/03/25/ little-kid-asks-good-question-at-ncaa-tournament-press-conferenc e-reporter-gets-upset/.

Chapter 2

1. Gina Belli, "At Least 70% of Jobs Are Not Even Listed—Here's How to Up Your Chances of Getting a Great New Gig," Insider, April 10, 2017, https://www.businessinsider.com/at-least-70-of-jobs-are-not-even-listed -heres-how-to-up-your-chances-of-getting-a-great-new-gig-2017-4.

2. Peter Economy, "This Is the Way You Need to Write Down Your Goals for Faster Success," *Inc.*, February 28, 2018, https://www.inc.com/peter-economy/ this-is-way-you-need-to-write-down-your-goals-for-faster-success.html.

3. Jim Rohn, *The Treasury of Quotes* (Irving: Jim Rohn International, 1994), 91.

4. Lancey Morris, "The 5 Things I Learned Seeing Jack Daly Live," The Growth Faculty, July 26, 2019, https://www.thegrowthfaculty.com/blog/5ThingsILea rnedSeeingJackDalyLive.

Chapter 3

1. Brian Tracy, *Motivation* (New York: American Management Association, 2013), 14.

2. Anonymous, in-person advising session by author, September 16, 2012.

3. Ed Stone, "My Survival Guide in the Business World," Stone Communications, accessed July 23, 2019; site inactive on July 6, 2022, http://www.edstone. net/vandy-info/six-a-s-for-survival.

4. Andy Warhol, quoted by Flavia Medrut in "16 Andy Warhol Quotes to Help You Find Value in Every Moment of Your Life," Goalcast, accessed July 28, 2020, https://www.goalcast.com/2018/08/10/andy-warhol-quotes/.

5. "The Soft Skills Stats You Need to Know," Coursera Blog, August 16, 2017, https://blog.coursera.org/soft-skills-stats-need-know.

6. Ibid.

7. Ibid.

8. Anonymous, in-person interview with a hiring manager by author, March 26, 2016.

9. Steve Krug, *Don't Make Me Think* (San Francisco: New Riders Publishing, 2006), 11.

10. Eleanor Baldwin, *300 New Ways to Get a Better Job* (Holbrook: Bob Adams, Inc., 1991), 262.

11. Anthony Iannarino, *The Only Sales Guide You Will Ever Need* (New York: Portfolio/Penguin, 2016), 3.

12. Anonymous, in-person advising session with PhD graduate by author, April 24, 1998.

13. Anonymous, in-person advising session with a job seeker by author, March 16, 2018.

14. Anonymous, in-person interview with job seeker by author, July 8, 2000.

15. Seth Godin, *Purple Cow* (New York: Portfolio, 2003), 3.

Step 3: Market Ready

1. Asad Meah, "35 Inspirational Quotes on Preparation," Awaken The Greatness Within, April 1, 2018, https://www.awakenthegreatnesswithin.com/35-inspirational-quotes-on-preparation/.

2. Alison & David Price, *The Psychology of Success* (New York: MJF Books, 2011), 109.

Chapter 5

1. "Competitive Positioning," Marketing MO, accessed January 6, 2020, http://www.marketingmo.com/strategic-planning/competitive-positioning/.

Chapter 6

1. Brian Tracy, *Hiring & Firing* (New York: American Management Association, 2016), 45.

Chapter 7

1. Anonymous, in-person advising session with job seeker by author, March 14, 2021.

2. Meredith Lepore, "You Have 7.4 Seconds to Make an Impression: How Recruiters See Your Resume," Ladders, January 30, 2020, https://www.theladders.com/career-advice/you-only-get-6-seconds-of-fame-make-it-count.

3. Victoria Ipri, "Jobseekers: These 5 Tips Will Help You Beat ATS and Get Hired," LinkedIn, November 1, 2018, site inactive on April 14, 2023, https://www.linkedin.com/pulse/jobseekers-5-tips-help-you-beat-ats-get-hired-victoria-ipri-.

4. Regina Borsellino, "Beat the Robots: How to Get Your Resume Past the System and Into Human Hands," The Muse, accessed June 22, 2020, https://www.themuse.com/advice/beat-the-robots-how-to-get-your-resume-past-the-system-into-human-hands.

5. Anonymous, in-person advising session with job seeker by author, January 19, 1996.

6. Joseph F. Bastian, "The Growing Visualization of Our Culture," *DBusiness Magazine*, January 28, 2014, https://www.dbusiness.com/business/the-growing-visualization-of-our-culture/.

7. Noah Parsons, "Do Visuals Really Trump Text?" LivePlan, June 14, 2018, https://www.liveplan.com/blog/scientific-reasons-why-you-should-present-your-data-visually/.

8. Entrepreneur Middle East Staff, "Infographic: Five Scientific Reasons People Are Wired to Respond to Visual Marketing," Entrepreneur Middle East, April 26, 2018, https://www.entrepreneur.com/article/312551.

9. "Should I Send a Thank-You Note After an Interview?" CareerBuilder, accessed April 12, 2023, https://www.careerbuilder.com/advice/are-postinterview-thankyou-notes-still-a-thing.

10. Chris Taylor, "A Career Secret Weapon: Thank-You Notes," *Reuters,* February 19, 2019, https://www.reuters.com/article/us-money-jobs-thankyounotes-idUSKCN1Q81FH.

Chapter 8

1. Lauren Salm, "70% of Employers Are Snooping Candidates' Social Media Profiles," CareerBuilder, June 15, 2017, https://www.careerbuilder.com/advice/social-media-survey-2017.

2. "More Than Half of Employers Have Found Content on Social Media That Caused Them NOT to Hire a Candidate, According to Recent Career-Builder Survey," CareerBuilder, August 9, 2018, http://press.careerbuilder.com/2018-08-09-More-Than-Half-of-Employers-Have-Found-Content-on-Social-Media-That-Caused-Them-NOT-to-Hire-a-Candidate-According-to-Recent-CareerBuilder-Survey.

3. Jonah Berger, *Invisible Influence* (New York: Simon & Shuster Paperbacks, 2016), 10-11.

4. "Eye Tracking Study on How Recruiters See Your LinkedIn Profile," The American Genius, June 5, 2014, https://theamericangenius.com/business-news/eye-tracking-study-recruiters-see-linkedin-profile/.

5. Sean Callahan, "Picture Perfect: Make A Great First Impression with Your LinkedIn Profile Photo," LinkedIn, December 28, 2018, https://www.linkedin.com/business/sales/blog/b2b-sales/picture-perfect--make-a-great-first-impression-with-your-linkedi.

6. Alex Hisaka, "Your LinkedIn Profile: Go Big or Go Home," LinkedIn, July 14, 2014, https://www.linkedin.com/pulse/20140714181548-18278691-your-linkedin-profile-go-big-or-go-home/.

7. Chloe West, "24 Branding Quotes to Inspire You & Build Your Brand Image," Visme, November 13, 2020, https://visme.co/blog/branding-quotes/.

Chapter 9

1. Anonymous, in-person interview with engineer by author, December 18, 2019.

2. Sally Hogshead, *How the World Sees You* (New York: HarperCollins, 2014), 26.

3. Sara Holtz, "Marketing in Less Than 90 Seconds," ClientFocus, accessed October 10, 2019, https://www.clientfocus.net/content/articles-and-resources-Marketing-in-Less-Than-90-Seconds&id=14.

4. Leo Colan, "12 Quotes to Help You Build More Powerful Relationships," *Inc.*, March 30, 2016, https://www.inc.com/lee-colan/12-quotes-to-help-you-build-more-powerful-relationships.html.

Step 4: Relationship Team

1. Brian Buffini, "Change Everything You Know about Marketing with Scott Stratten," The Brian Buffini Show, podcast, April 24, 2018, https://www.thebrianbuffinishow.com/change-everything-you-know-about-marketing-with-scott-stratten-099/.

2. Ronald D. White, "How L.A.'s Halo Top Became America's Bestselling Ice Cream Pint," *Los Angeles Times*, September 15, 2017, https://www.latimes.com/business/la-fi-halo-top-icecream-20170915-story.html.

3. Mike Stafiej, "Employee Referral Statistics You Need to Know for 2020 (Infographic)," LinkedIn, January 13, 2020, https://www.linkedin.com/pulse/employee-referral-statistics-you-need-know-2020-mike-stafiej/?articleId=66gf62177335336961.

4. Anja Zojceska, "Top 50 Hiring and Recruitment Statistics for 2020," TalentLyft, March 9, 2020, https://www.talentlyft.com/en/blog/article/364/top-50-hiring-and-recruitment-statistics-for-2020.

5. Mike Stafiej, "Employee Referral Statistics You Need to Know for 2020 (Infographic)," Medium, January 12, 2020, https://medium.com/@mike-stafiej/employee-referral-statistics-you-need-to-know-for-2020-infographic-19cc720380f2.

6. Gina Belli, "At Least 70% of Jobs Are Not Even Listed—Here's How to Up Your Chances of Getting a Great New Gig," Insider, April 10, 2017, https://www.businessinsider.com/at-least-70-of-jobs-are-not-even-listed-heres-how-to-up-your-chances-of-getting-a-great-new-gig-2017-4.

Chapter 10

1. Jack Flynn, "25+ Important Networking Statistics [2022]: The Power of Connections in the Workplace," Zippia, September 25, 2022, https://www.zippia.com/advice/networking-statistics/.
2. Anonymous, in-person interview by author, July 16, 2008.
3. Anonymous, phone interview by author, February 12, 2020.
4. Anonymous, in-person interview by author, January 18, 2016.
5. Andrew Gelman, "The Average American Knows How Many People?" *The New York Times*, February 18, 2013, https://www.nytimes.com/2013/02/19/science/the-average-american-knows-how-many-people.html.

Chapter 11

1. Anonymous, in-person interview by author, September 9, 2016.
2. Nathan A. Perez and Marcia Ballinger, PhD, *The 20-Minute Networking Meeting* (Tampa: Career Innovations Press, 2015), 7.
3. Dustin Smith, "Nonverbal Communication: How Body Language & Nonverbal Cues Are Key," Lifesize, February 18, 2020, https://www.lifesize.com/en/video-conferencing-blog/speaking-without-words.
4. Nathan A. Perez and Marcia Ballinger, PhD, *The 20-Minute Networking Meeting*, 7.
5. Richard H. Smith, PhD, "The Best Time to Plant a Tree Was 20 Years Ago, No Matter," *Psychology Today*, April 14, 2015, https://www.psychologytoday.com/us/blog/joy-and-pain/201504/the-best-time-plant-tree-was-20-years-ago-no-matter.

Chapter 12

1. "2019 Recruiting Benchmark Report," Jobvite, 2019, https://www.jobvite.com/wp-content/uploads/2019/03/2019-Recruiting-Benchmark-Report.pdf.
2. Anonymous, in-person interview by author, March 26, 2018.

Step 5: Competitive Commitment

1. Dr. Jennie Ward, "What Makes You a Champion at Life?" Ward & Associates Psychological Services, September 21, 2018, http://www.wardaps.com/what-makes-you-a-champion-at-life/.

Chapter 13

1. Phil Mutz, "When A Young Man Turns to God for Money, He Gets the PERFECT Response," LittleThings, November 4, 2019, https://www.littlethings.com/god-lottery-ticket/.
2. Dr. John Sullivan, "Rejecting Resumes with Spelling Errors: A Silly and Costly Hiring Mistake," ERE Media, February 11, 2020, https://drjohnsullivan.com/articles/rejecting-resumes-with-spelling-errors-costly-hiring-mistake/.
3. Anonymous, phone interview by author, February 2, 2012.
4. Anonymous, in-person interview by author, August 23, 2021.
5. Brian Tracy, "Sales Success (The Brian Tracy Success Library)," O'Reilly, https://www.oreilly.com/library/view/sales-success-the/9780814449196/xhtml/chapter01.html.
6. Eleanor Baldwin, *300 New Ways to Get a Better Job* (Holbrook: Bob Adams, Inc., 1991), 262.

Step 6: Slam Dunk

1. *Harper's BAZAAR* Staff, "21 of Maya Angelou's Best Quotes to Inspire," *Harper's BAZAAR*, May 22, 2017, https://www.harpersbazaar.com/culture/features/a9874244/best-maya-angelou-quotes/.

Chapter 14

1. Alison & David Price, *The Psychology of Success* (New York: MJF Books, 2011), 162-163.
2. Harvey Mackay, "Putting the Fun in Fundraising," *The Business Journals*, December 26, 2017, https://www.bizjournals.com/bizjournals/how-to/growth-strategies/2017/12/putting-the-fun-in-fundraising.html.

3. Anna Kula, *The Guide—A Great Palm Springs Magazine*, Desert Publication Inc., September 2019-2020, 18-141, https://digital-palmspringslife.com/guide/2019-september/.

4. Ibid., 20.

5. Ibid., 88.

6. Ibid., 106.

7. Ibid., 128.

8. Vanessa Van Edwards, *Captivate* (New York: Portfolio/Penguin, 2017), 64.

9. Anonymous, in-person advising session by author, January 31, 2021.

10. Anonymous, in-person interview by author, March 27, 2018.

11. Anonymous, in-person interview by author, October 22, 2020.

12. Anonymous, phone interview by author, May 4, 2007.

13. Hanz Zimmer, "Hanz Zimmer Quotes," Goodreads, accessed April 18, 2020, https://www.goodreads.com/author/quotes/83084.Hans_Zimmer.

Chapter 15

1. Jessica Krampe, "John C. Maxwell: Are You Stretching Toward Your Goals or Just Coasting?" *SUCCESS,* November 14, 2014, https://www.success.com/john-c-maxwell-are-you-stretching-toward-your-goals-or-just-coasting/.

2. Sara Blakely, Interview by Darren Hardy, *SUCCESS Talks Collection*, YouTube, January 2016, audio, 5:06, https://www.youtube.com/watch?v=3tyaO6XLaNQ.

3. Norbert Juma, "Arthur Ashe Quotes about Life, Sports, and Success," Everyday Power, May 17, 2021, https://everydaypower.com/arthur-ashe-quotes-2/.

4. Anonymous, in-person advising session by author, April 14, 2020.

5. Laurence McCahill, "You Can't Read the Label When You're Inside the Bottle," Medium, November 29, 2017, https://medium.com/the-happy-startup-school/you-cant-read-the-label-when-you-re-inside-the-bottle-9e1f51439be8.

6. Anonymous, phone interview by author, September 28, 2016.

7. Lauren A. Rivera, "Guess Who Doesn't Fit In at Work," *The New York Times*, May 30, 2015, https://www.nytimes.com/2015/05/31/opinion/sunday/guess-who-doesnt-fit-in-at-work.html.

8. Steve Nash, "Steve Nash Quotes," BrainyQuote, accessed February 6, 2022, https://www.brainyquote.com/authors/steve-nash-quotes.

Chapter 16

1. Peter Harris, "Study: How Quickly Do Interviewers Really Make Decisions?" Workopolis, June 15, 2015, https://careers.workopolis.com/advice/study-how-quickly-do-interviewers-really-make-decisions/#:~:text=Some%20of%20the%20interviewers%20did,after%20five%20minutes%20or%20longer.

2. Serenity Gibbons, "You and Your Business Have 7 Seconds to Make a First Impression: Here's How to Succeed," *Forbes,* June 19, 2018, https://www.forbes.com/sites/serenitygibbons/2018/06/19/you-have-7-seconds-to-make-a-first-impression-heres-how-to-succeed/#359c8c3156c2.

3. Lindsay Lavine, "Why You Should Say Thank You More Often," *Fast Company*, December 17, 2014, https://www.fastcompany.com/3039910/why-you-should-say-thank-you-more-often.

4. Harvey Mackay, "Your Business Depends on Your Personal Touch," *Des Moines Register*, September 29, 2017, https://www.desmoinesregister.com/story/money/business/2017/09/29/arvey-mackay-your-business-depends-your-personal-touch/716808001/.

5. Vanessa Van Edwards, *Captivate* (New York: Portfolio/Penguin, 2017), 42.

6. Amy Vetter, "Maintain Eye Contact 70 Percent of the Time—and Other Key Tips to Become a Better Listener," *Inc.,* April 25, 2018, https://www.inc.com/amy-vetter/maintain-eye-contact-70-percent-of-time-and-other-key-tips-to-become-a-better-listener.html.

7. Daniel Goleman, "A Feel-Good Theory: A Smile Affects Mood," *The New York Times*, July 18, 1989, https://www.nytimes.com/1989/07/18/science/a-feel-good-theory-a-smile-affects-mood.html.

8. Tim Cohen, in-person interview by author, November 3, 2015.

9. Jon Michail, "Strong Nonverbal Skills Matter Now More Than Ever in This 'New Normal,'" *Forbes*, August 24, 2020, https://www.forbes.com/sites/forbescoachescouncil/2020/08/24/strong-nonverbal-skills-matter-now-more-than-ever-in-this-new-normal/?sh=484c9fa65c61.

10. Dustin Smith, "Nonverbal Communication: How Body Language & Nonverbal Cues Are Key," Lifesize, February 18, 2020, https://www.lifesize.com/en/video-conferencing-blog/speaking-without-words.

11. Nicholas Boothman, *Convince Them in 90 Seconds or Less* (New York: Workman Publishing, 2010), 174-175.

12. Jonah Berger, *Invisible Influence* (New York: Simon & Schuster, 2016), 40.

13. Tony Robbins, "The Magic of Rapport Presentation," YouTube, December 2, 2017, video inactive on April 14, 2023, https://www.youtube.com/watch?v=wnLYXalpZcM.

14. Lancey Morris, "The 5 Things I Learned Seeing Jack Daly Live," The Growth Faculty, July 26, 2019, https://www.thegrowthfaculty.com/blog/5ThingsILearnedSeeingJackDalyLive.

15. Ibid.

16. Aditya Shukla, "Why Fun, Curiosity & Engagement Improves Learning: Mood, Senses, Neurons, Arousal, Cognition," *Cognition Today*, August 23, 2020, https://cognitiontoday.com/why-fun-improves-learning-mood-senses-neurons-arousal-cognition/#:~:text=Having%20fun%20and%20being%20excited,which%20improve%20learning%20and%20memory.

17. Chip Heath and Dan Heath, *Made to Stick* (New York: Random House, 2008), 242-243.

18. Rob Biesenbach, *Unleash the Power of Storytelling* (Evanston, Eastlawn Media, 2018), 11.

19. Joseph F. Bastian, "The Growing Visualization of Our Culture," *DBusiness Magazine*, January 28, 2014, https://www.dbusiness.com/business/the-growing-visualization-of-our-culture/.

20. Claire Arnold, "How to Get a Job LIVE!" Glassdoor panel podcast interview, YouTube, video, 58:45, https://www.youtube.com/embed/bQE_RSoNsyg?start=8&autoplay=1&showinfo=0.

21. Anonymous, phone advising session by author, May 3, 2017.

Chapter 17

1. Jenna Goudreau, "Not Negotiating Your Salary Could Cost $1 Million Over Time," Insider, September 23, 2013, https://www.businessinsider.com/not-negotiating-costs-workers-1-million-2013-9.

2. Robin Madell, "What to Say When Negotiating Salary in a Job Offer," *U.S News & World Report*, February 12, 2021, https://money.usnews.com/money/blogs/outside-voices-careers/articles/the-exact-words-to-use-when-negotiating-salary-in-a-job-offer.

3. Peter Economy, "20 Brilliant Quotes on Competition From Highly Successful Business Leaders," *Inc.,* July 4, 2018, https://www.inc.com/peter-economy/20-brilliant-quotes-on-competition-from-highly-succe ssful-business-leaders.html.

Chapter 18

1. Georgia O'Keeffe, "Georgia O'Keeffe Quotes," georgiaokeeffe.net, accessed April 4, 2022, https://www.georgiaokeeffe.org/quotes/.

2. Matt Lower, "'The Separation is in the Preparation' – 5 Tips to be Successful like Seattle Seahawks Quarterback Russell Wilson," CoachUp Nation, January 29, 2014, https://www.coachup.com/nation/articles/the-separation-is-in-the-preparation-5-steps-to-be-successful-like-seattle-seahawks-quarterback-russell-wilson

3. Eddie Cantor, "Overnight Success Quotes," AzQuotes, accessed June 12, 2019, https://www.azquotes.com/quotes/topics/overnight-success.html.

4. Clara Piano, "The Story of the Three Stonecutters," LinkedIn, July 27, 2015, https://www.linkedin.com/pulse/story-three-stonecutters-clara-jace/.

Appendix

1. Lea C, "Dos and Don'ts for Applicant Tracking Systems," Career-Higher, September 6, 2022, https://www.careerhigher.co/career-advice/dos-and-donts-for-applicant-tracking-systems-124498/

Acknowledgments

1. Paulo Coelho, "Paulo Coelho Quotes," BrainyQuote, accessed August 28, 2021, https://www.brainyquote.com/quotes/paulo_coelho_406635.

Index

N

About the Author

David Parker is the executive director of career development and alumni relations at the Bren School of Environmental Science & Management—University of California, Santa Barbara. He developed the Bren School career development program more than 25 years ago. Under his leadership and with the help of a talented team, the program has become one of the leading university placement programs in environmental science and management. David has devoted his entire career to helping people realize their career aspirations and reach their highest potential.

Through his experience as a recruiter at a Fortune 50 company, David developed a highly successful job search process that has helped thousands of job seekers land rewarding jobs in both weak and strong markets. Job seekers have used his process to secure positions in more than 65 different industries, on seven continents, and in hundreds of fields and companies, including positions with AARP, AECOM, Amazon, Apple, CBS, Conservation International, Deloitte, Gap Inc., Google, KPMG, LEGO Group, Levi Strauss & Co., Lockheed Martin, Lyft, Microsoft, Nike, NOAA, Nordstrom, Northrop Grumman, Patagonia, PwC, REI, Salesforce, Tesla, The Nature Conservancy, The Walt Disney Company, Toyota, UCLA, United Nations, US Environmental Protection Agency, US Forest Service, Walmart, Waste Management, World Wildlife Fund, World Resources Institute, and many other organizations.

David holds a BA in economics from the University of California, Santa Barbara, an MBA from California State University, Long Beach, and an MS in counseling from California Lutheran University. He has more than 30 years of experience in human resources and career development, including work as a career director, employment supervisor, corporate trainer, career coach, college recruiter, organizational development consultant, and an at-promise student mentor. David lives in Southern California with his wife, two children, and his trusty sidekick dog, Milo. Visit slamdunkjobsearch.com to learn more.

Connect with the Author

Thank you so much for allowing me to assist you with your job search. Please let me know how the 6-Step Slam Dunk Job Search Process has helped you reach your career goals. You can email me at david@slamdunkjobsearch.com or connect with me through the slamdunkjobsearch.com website.

If you have stories about Slam Dunk tactics you or others have used during the job search process that you believe belong in future Slam Dunk Job Search books, please send them my way. I am working on other books, and I would love to consider including your stories and tactics. If I include them, I will make sure you are credited for your contributions.

Please also feel free to scan the QR code on the right to visit slamdunkjobsearch.com for complimentary tips on how to identify hiring managers and locate their email addresses. I have provided this important resource so you can become an insider by getting yourself and your marketing documents in front of hiring managers.

Thank you again for reading my book. I hope you have enjoyed following the 6-Step Slam Dunk Job Search Process as much as I have enjoyed sharing it with you.

With much appreciation,

David Allen Parker Jr.

Made in the USA
Columbia, SC
09 March 2024

32364438R00204